Byron and the
Limits of Fiction

LIVERPOOL ENGLISH TEXTS AND STUDIES

General editor: PHILIP EDWARDS

Titles available in this Series

The Poems of Joseph Hall
Bishop of Exeter and Norwich. Edited by ARNOLD DAVENPORT

Poems by Nicholas Breton
Edited by JEAN ROBERTSON

John Keats: A Reassessment
Edited by KENNETH MUIR

Life and Letters of Sir Thomas Wyatt
By KENNETH MUIR

Collected Poems of Sir Thomas Wyatt
Edited by KENNETH MUIR and PATRICIA THOMSON

The Poetry of Sir Philip Sidney
By J. G. NICHOLS

Yeats and Anglo-Irish Literature
Critical Essays by PETER URE. Edited by C. J. RAWSON

Elizabethan and Jacobean Drama
Critical Essays by PETER URE. Edited by J. C. MAXWELL

Literature of the Romantic Period, 1750–1850
Edited by R. T. DAVIES and B. G. BEATTY

The Singularity of Shakespeare and Other Essays
By KENNETH MUIR

Shakespeare's Chaucer: A Study in Literary Origins
By ANN THOMPSON

Dramatic Identities and Cultural Tradition:
Studies in Shakespeare and his Contemporaries
Critical Essays by G. K. HUNTER

The Pilgrim's Progress: Critical and Historical Views
Edited by VINCENT NEWEY

Essays on Shelley
Edited by MIRIAM ALLOTT

Cowper's Poetry: A Critical Study and Reassessment
By VINCENT NEWEY

Memory and Writing From Wordsworth to Lawrence
By PHILIP DAVIS

Byron and the Limits of Fiction
Edited by BERNARD BEATTY and VINCENT NEWEY

Byron and the Limits of Fiction

EDITED BY

BERNARD BEATTY

AND

VINCENT NEWEY

Senior Lecturers in English Literature
in the University of Liverpool

LIVERPOOL UNIVERSITY PRESS

Published by
LIVERPOOL UNIVERSITY PRESS
PO Box 147, Liverpool L69 3BX

ISBN 0 85323 026 9

First published 1988

British Library Cataloguing-in-Publication Data

Byron and the limits of fiction. —
(Liverpool English texts and studies; v.22)
1. Poetry in English. Byron, George Gordon
Byron, Baron, 1788–1824. Critical studies
I. Beatty, Bernard   II. Newey, Vincent
821.1′7
ISBN 0–85323–026–9

Text set in Linotron 202 Baskerville by
Wilmaset, Birkenhead, Merseyside
Printed and bound in Great Britain by
Oxford University Press Printing House, Oxford

Contents

Preface

The Liverpool English Texts and Studies series has over the years presented a number of studies of the major Romantics—Keats (1958), Literature of the Romantic Period (1976), Shelley (1980). The present volume differs from its predecessors in two respects. The collection is prompted by the bicentenary of Byron's birth in 1788, which is, properly, the occasion for a number of scholarly and popular events. We can say that 'Among thy mightier offerings' here are ours. Secondly, unlike others in the series, this volume has a distinct theme: Byron and the Limits of Fiction. The reader will soon discover that it is Byron's poetry rather than a theoretical perspective which is our primary and sustained object of attention, but the title does more than provide a common reference point.

In the years following the appearance in 1957 of the Variorum edition of *Don Juan* and Leslie Marchand's acclaimed biography of the poet, a spate of critical books appeared (by Ridenour, Gleckner, Cooke, McGann, Joseph, Blackstone, Kernan, Wilkie and others) which, though differing in their particular final emphases, presented a recognizably similar view of Byron that has become the starting point for all serious readers of the poet. Their approaches, inextricably bound up with coeval critical vocabularies and undeniably impressive, transformed Byron studies but, for a variety of reasons, did not markedly affect the familiar habits of reading and interpretation established by earlier consensus in Romantic studies and general opinion. A tale like *The Island*, for example, remains unattended to by readers at large despite the almost universal opinion of recent critics that it is a great poem.

More recently, we have seen, with pleasure and with awe, the successful completion—or nearly so—of the editorial

labours of Professors Marchand and McGann, to whom the
world of Romantic scholarship will be permanently indebted.
We will soon have a new complete text of the poems and
already have the complete letters and journals. At the same
time, the entire critical perspective has been transformed by
the meteoric rise of ideologically explicit and reader-orientated
theories of literature which in their turn have provoked, even in
the unenamoured, an extreme self-consciousness with relation
to texts and their real or putative authors.

It is time, we think, to have another look at Byron's poetry.
For Byron's work both insists upon and ridicules, celebrates
and devalues, its own status as fiction. Byron too, pilgrim of
eternity, seeks out and relishes, far more than his Romantic
contemporaries, the limits inherent in writing whilst using
them to dramatize the clash between limitless energies and
bounded existences.

Contributors to this volume (all of them academics from
Cambridge, Glasgow, Keele, or Liverpool universities) were
invited to use the title of the book to examine major aspects of
Byron's work. We tried to ensure that a considerable range of
Byron's poetry was discussed but did not wish to insist on a
schematic coverage. In the event, the poems foregrounded—
Don Juan, of course, but also the *Tales*, *Childe Harold*, and the
Dramas—tell us something important about current taste. We
have grouped essays together where their references converge
and, apart from those essays whose range of reference prevents
it, we have matched Byron's chronological sequence with our
series.

The editors, in preparing the volume, were struck by the
freshness which contributors so readily located in Byron's
poetry. Perhaps that is no bad thing to mark the anniversary of
a poet born 'when George the Third was King'. Less predict-
able was the apparent consonance between what strikes the
reader now and what, in less articulated form, characterized
the most percipient of Byron's contemporaries. The essays
collected here usually see Byron as an original narratologist, a
thinker (moral, philosophical, religious) of considerable force,
a poet of almost unbelievable immediacy who blurs and yet
disentangles the realms of fictional and historical life. But then
this is how Sir Walter Scott saw Byron too. It is a comfort if,

however disingenuously, we can claim Scott's authority that we may be somewhere on the right track in these essays before committing them to the opinion of those in 1988 and subsequent years.

B.B.
V.N.

Liverpool
December 1987

Acknowledgements

We would like to thank Professor J. F. Norbury and the Academic Committee of Liverpool University for their unstinting support, Professor Philip Edwards for his informed advice, Robin Bloxsidge and Colin Rogers of Liverpool University Press for their courtesy and acumen, and Catherine Rees and Elizabeth Birrell for their patience and accomplishment in turning indecipherable manuscripts via innumerable revisions into lucid copy.

Note

Quotations from Byron's poetry are taken from the first four volumes of Jerome J. McGann's *Lord Byron: The Complete Poetical Works* (Oxford, 1980–). Poems not available in this edition at the time of preparation are taken from *The Poetical Works of Lord Byron*, ed. E. H. Coleridge, 7 vols (London, 1898–1904). All quotations from *Don Juan* are taken from *Byron's Don Juan: A Variorum Edition*, ed. T. G. Steffan and W. W. Pratt (Austin, 1957). All quotations from Byron's letters and journals are taken from *Byron's Letters and Journals*, ed. Leslie A. Marchand, 12 vols (London, 1973–82). The source for all other references is given in the notes.

Fiction's Limit and Eden's Door

BERNARD BEATTY

Coleridge's Mariner and Byron's Heroes

If we take 'the limits of fiction' as a problem, what kind of problem is it? We could insist that it is a literary problem, perhaps the defining literary problem, but then something seems to be left out. It is not long since that Bunyan was praised for his 'realism' and Keats criticized, as poet and man, for that 'escapism' which, allegedly, he would have overcome had not death overcome him. Who would not smile if these terms and these judgements were now to be advanced? Byron had at least as delicate a literary imagination as any of his contemporaries, but alternately bullied and protected it with something like the coarse affection shown to him by his matter-of-fact, yet slightly dotty, mother. From his mother's family and from his Scottish nurse Byron picked up an eminently rational frame of mind, contradicting passions, and a preoccu-pation with Adam's fall. If, as a poet, his characteristic stance is at the limits of fiction, this is bound up in his mind with the strange patterns of his own life and their relation to the archetypal pattern of the Fall. We could of course substitute 'events' for 'pattern' in both cases and Byron would not smile.

The importance of the Fall in Byron's thought and art has always been recognized.[1] It may seem that there is little point in reiterating its centrality. Twentieth-century interest in the use of myths in literature, however, and the subsequent, but in some ways contrary, concern with fictions and fictionality now begin to place Byron's conviction of the Fall in sharper perspective and help us to understand his own use of, and celebrated aversion from, literary fiction. In this section, I want to develop these ideas by contrasting Byron's practice with that of Coleridge in *The Ancient Mariner*. In subsequent sections, we will examine metamorphoses of the Fall in *Mazeppa*, *The Island* and the final cantos of *Don Juan*.

The Fall postulates the satisfactions of limitation in an enclosed garden, man's rejection of this archetypal home, and preference for the apparent unlimitation of exile, wandering, and homelessness. 'Man' here means genus but also signals typical masculine activity and understanding. Unlimitation in the Fall story is at once taboo, reward, and punishment. So it is throughout Byron's verse and, we may add, throughout his life.

The Byronic hero rather than the poet is at the centre of this concern. Dante, Tasso, and Byron himself may claim attention but do so because their acts of imagining involve their will as much as their fancy. Byron appears to be more interested in the boundaries crossed by the human will than were most of his contemporaries. For them, boundary crossing is usually an emblem of imagination's force and thus can never be finally repudiated. For Byron, boundary crossing remains a form of moral and metaphysical transgression. He is sympathetic to it, sometimes wholly so, but he declares and shows the punishment which is its consequence.

If we take the most obvious example of punished transgression in English Romanticism, Coleridge's *The Ancient Mariner*, it is easy to see why Byron admired the poem. It too appears as a version of the Fall. Coleridge juxtaposes the vocabularies of Christian redemption, forgiveness, love, and unity with Nature, against the inexplicable crime and apparently endless punishment of the Mariner, much as Byron does in *Manfred*. But whereas Byron makes us notice where these vocabularies are taken up or rejected, Coleridge blurs the boundaries between them. The Abbot, for instance, recognizes that Manfred's diagnosis of human life is founded on a sense of sin and thus proffers the intelligibility and force of the Christian cure:

> And the commencement of atonement is
> The sense of its necessity.
>
> (III.i.84–85)

Manfred rejects this as explicitly as it is offered. Coleridge, however, contrives a Mariner who seems to be both fully redeemed and wholly condemned. We may prefer this and think Byron's request, in a different context, that Coleridge 'would explain his Explanation'[2] to be a trifle vulgar. But if we do so our poise probably depends upon taking punishment and redemption as self-cancelling polarities within imagination's other world where we might also find, similarly intense yet neutralized, 'A sunny pleasure-dome with caves of ice'. The imagination is enthralled rather than appalled by such transgressions, for it contemplates patterns rather than bears consequences. The last line of Byron's *Cain* suggests the difference:

> *Adah* Peace be with him!
> *Cain*   But with *me!—[Exeunt.*

The Ancient Mariner's pain is aestheticized and thus, like the Falls of Terni, 'Horribly beautiful'.[3] Cain's fabled pain is unbearable and we recognize it as the foundation of adult life. Coleridge's myth is not a myth, for it does not explain anything. Instead the reader, like the Mariner himself, is mesmerized by the spectacle of past experience as spectacle. Byron's myth functions like its Biblical prototype; it leaves us with the consequences that it has explained. By 'myth' here and in what follows I mean a communally appropriated story that is seen to engender and find repetition in human history. In this way, unlike a fiction, it is never simply its own terminus, nor, despite its openness to interpretation, is that the secret source of its fruitfulness and efficacy. Byron's *Cain* is a myth. Coleridge's *Ancient Mariner* is a fiction.

This distinction is a real one and we keep coming across it when we try to understand Byron and Coleridge together. But we have arrived at it too easily because not all the evidence fits. If we turn momentarily to classical literature's most celebrated myth of punished transgression, the myth of Prometheus, the picture looks a little different because Prometheus is a prototype artist as well as archetypal sufferer.

Prometheus (as mediated by what survives of Aeschylus's trilogy and therefore without the benign consequences which we think he intended) offers us the spectacle of pain. This pain, Carl Kerényi points out, has two elements:

on the one hand Prometheus' suffering, his punishments for taking the standpoint of man, and on the other hand his secret knowledge.[4]

These two elements are signalled in Byron's 'Prometheus' who suffers both 'pity's recompense' and the result of what he can 'foresee' but refuses to 'tell' ('Prometheus', ll.29–30). He is thus a forerunner of Manfred who 'champions human fears' (II.ii.205), has 'this cautious feeling for another's pain' (II.i.80), craves and possesses forbidden knowledge. But he is also a forerunner of Byron's Dante and all other poets:

> For what is poesy but to create
> From overfeeling good or ill; and aim
> At an external life beyond our fate,
> And be the new Prometheus of new men,
> Bestowing fire from heaven, and then, too late,
> Finding the pleasure given repaid with pain,
> And vultures to the heart of the bestower,
> Who having lavished his high gift in vain,
> Lies chain'd to his lone rock by the sea-shore?
> (*The Prophecy of Dante*, IV.11–19)[5]

We find the same insistence on the identity of suffering and creativity throughout Cantos III and IV of *Childe Harold*. Indeed, when Art does not immediately disclose this connection as it does in the Laocoon group, Byron goes out of his way to remind us that the serene dome of St Peter's is 'Christ's mighty shrine above his martyr's tomb!'[6] or, more emphatically still, that the Apollo Belvedere's life of 'beautiful disdain' must somehow proceed from the suffering of its creator:

> And if it be Prometheus stole from Heaven
> The fire which we endure, it was repaid
> By him to whom the energy was given
> Which this poetic marble hath array'd
> With an eternal glory—
> (*Childe Harold*, IV.163)

Byron insists that all Art is like this, indebted to Promethean fire as suffering as well as spark, and that we can therefore always detect the way it 'breathes the flame with which 'twas wrought'.

If then Byron is more concerned with what Kerényi calls 'the moral suffering fundamental to human existence'[7] than, say, Keats and Coleridge, for all their vocabulary of hearts 'high sorrowful and cloyed' and 'sadder and a wiser man', ever manage or mean to be, nevertheless Byron, too, seems to fuse suffering with imagination and thus escapes consequence and limitation on the wings of an obliging fiction. If we alter our perspective, however, we can find a way out of this much as Byron did himself. What happens to this fusion once it is established? In Byron's case it becomes itself an object of attention rather than simply triggering an aesthetic reaction in the reader. This needs explaining. In *The Ancient Mariner*, for example, we can never resolve the puzzle of the poem by the use of any one of the master-languages (religious, moral, psychological, philosophical) that the poem so fulsomely supplies. It is not hard to see why this is so. Coleridge's poem is a projection of his own nightmare of dejection. It proffers a 'One Life' philosophy which he does not really believe, a religious release from the burden of his self which he has never experienced, a psychology whose origin and real character cannot be probed, and a moral which no one will ever carry out as a result of reading the poem. The horror is real enough but its causes and consequences are hidden, subordinated to its overwhelming realization. It is just this very blurring of agony, pastiche, theoretical knowledge, and unhoped hope which makes the poem what it is and not some other thing. But, and it is a very large Byronic 'but', though Coleridge's poem makes something delightful out of these concealed limitations, it does not transcend them. Nor, unlike a myth, does it restore us to the immediacy which its own immediacy has displaced. Coleridge is careful to provoke the expectations of myth without allowing any myth to use, and thereby explain, him. We do not contemplate these problems aesthetically and morally because we do not recognize them as problems in the act of reading the poem. In this way, *The Ancient Mariner*, splendid as it is, always implies far more than it will ever yield.

Far other scene is Byron's field of fiction. Byron's poetry seeks to understand the ground of its own intensities as well as relishing them. It comes to the reader, therefore, as curtailer of the intensities which it stimulates, because it is simultaneously object and agent of attentiveness thus:

> 'Tis to create, and in creating live
> A being more intense, that we endow
> With form our fancy, gaining as we give
> The life we image, even as I do now.
> What am I? Nothing; but not so art thou,
> Soul of my thought! with whom I traverse earth,
> Invisible but gazing, as I glow
> Mix'd with thy spirit, blended with thy birth,
> And feeling still with thee in my crush'd feelings' dearth.
> (*Childe Harold*, III.6)

Would Coleridge have recognized his own earlier enterprise in these terms? Certainly both poets write out of their 'crush'd feelings' dearth', project themselves into wanderer figures that epitomize death-in-life as punishment but offer us the Promethean recompense of 'A being more intense'. In Byron's case, however, the self-conscious, explicit character of this offering refers us beyond itself to 'the moral suffering fundamental to human existence', whereas Coleridge's apparent concern for religious and moral truth conceals the secret burden of aesthetic intensity which is all-sufficient provided that it passes unrecognized.

Perhaps this point needs to be re-stated—there is a sense in which this essay will not get beyond it—because it may appear as too confident a demolition of the moral case for Coleridge's art to which some remain attached, whilst, on the other hand, it may appear to take for granted the superiority of moral over aesthetic concerns which, though obvious to Byron ('in my mind, the highest of all poetry, is ethical poetry'),[8] is scarcely the shared postulate of today's desperate men. In any event, the borderline may be less distinguishable than the territories which it separates. We will need to track the consequences of the Fall carefully.

Adam's Fall is, in the first place for Byron, a story of punishment. Punishment is a limit which the past imposes on the experienced present and imagined future. Death, from one point of view, is the supreme punishment. It is a final limit on present and future imposed by Adam's past which, we must learn through this very claim, is our past also. From another point of view, there is a punishment beyond this, peculiarly interesting to Byron, which though limiting is limitless. The

Fall inaugurates both the familiar boundaries of pain and
death which we suffer from but continue to will and the latent
possibility of endless limitation which may be dreaded but
craved by those who can 'champion human fears'. Such endless
suffering is Manfred's and the Mariner's prerogative:

> I dwell in my despair—
> And live—and live for ever.
>
> (*Manfred*, II.ii.149–50)

It is important here that although Cain, Manfred, Harold
may have always been marked out for their 'silent suffering and
intense', they have, at some point, crossed a threshold. They
have transgressed. Manfred, for instance, acknowledges this in
a searing compound of grammatical and autobiographical
tenses and in-tensity:

> And to be thus, eternally but thus,
> Having been otherwise!
>
> (*Manfred*, I.ii.70–71)

Harold, similarly, finds that suddenly 'Worse than adversity
the Childe befell' (I.4), and the change in Cain from intellec-
tualized to actual desolation, as from a notion of death to the
presence of a dead brother, is the point as well as the
conclusion of the play.

What could terminate and thereby structure this unstruc-
turable pain? We could leave it as it is. *Childe Harold* and *Don
Juan* are inherently unfinished. We could put Art's full stop at
the point where it all begins. *Cain*'s final full stop and '*Exeunt*'
work like this. We could terminate in death, which *Manfred*
very precisely does (and the majority of Byron's stories end in
death), or we could resurrect out of it into marriage, or
something like it, as Torquil, Mazeppa, and Juan manage to
do. These three terminations—Death, Hell, and Marriage—
are staple in Byron's poetry and he loves to joke about their
interchangeability. They are the preferred destinations in
Coleridge's verse too, but no one ever reaches them. Christabel
may well have been destined for marriage in Coleridge's head
but his poem will never consummate it. The wedding guest is
barred from this ending also but he is taken neither to death

nor, quite, to hell, for the Ancient Mariner is an embodiment of blessing as well as curse, wisdom as well as terror. Coleridge directs us instead to repetition of the tale ('could I revive within me / Her symphony and song') or the excuse of fragmentation with its *diabolus ex machina* from Porlock. These are not so much devices of inanition as of obfuscation. Coleridge takes our attention away from the change in the Mariner, punished or redeemed, and redirects us to the change in the wedding-guest and therefore to us as readers. This change is not itself an object of attention; rather it is glossed (an appropriate word for *The Ancient Mariner*) as wisdom ('sadder and wiser man') and morality ('he prayeth best who loveth best'). It cannot be either of these in literal fact but the misdirection placates us into accepting the aesthetic residue as spiritual truth. This 'spiritual' meaning is that suffering intensity is worth having for its own sake because it enlarges the imagination to know itself beyond good and evil. In its present form, beyond Coleridge and Nietzsche, the print-out would be something like this—*The Ancient Mariner*'s indeterminacy of meaning is itself the self-conscious but disguised object of the poem's attention and its deepest meaning. We could apply the same diagnosis to Byron's heroes but not to the poems in which they are placed. If Manfred also knows himself to be beyond good and evil, that is not the perspective of the chamois-hunter or the Abbot, who are put in precisely to demonstrate but also to undermine Manfred's claim. That is not why Coleridge put the hermit in *The Ancient Mariner* or Keats includes the beadsman in *The Eve of St Agnes*. *The Ancient Mariner*'s superiority to what the chamois-hunter and the Abbot represent is unquestioned.

I have rounded on Coleridge here because so much twentieth-century criticism of the Romantic Imagination has relied on Coleridge's authority for allowing religious, moral, and psychological vocabularies to neutralize themselves within a fictional interplay as though something of import was going on. Whatever *The Ancient Mariner* is concerned with (and it becomes less and less decent to ask) we may be sure that it puts to one side anything so vulgarly intractable as punishment. Unlike a myth, it does not function as explanation but tantalizes us with its insolubility which, should we seek further, will only refer us back to its provocatively concealed author.

Grecian Urns have been known to behave in the same teasing (Keats's word) fashion.

In Byron's case, however, the limitation of punishment is disclosed rather than hidden by the shaping of the fiction. Conversely, where such limitation is not encountered, that too becomes part of the explicit design as well as the content. If for instance death, hell and marriage are clearly evident as Byron's end points, we should also insist on the public and recognizable character of the devices which bring us to these terminations. In a sense, as Brian Nellist argues so persuasively elsewhere in this volume, Byron is always a lyric poet whose only purchase, even when he surveys vast tracts of space and history, is the immediacy of the present moment 'where my steps seem echoes strangely loud'.[9] But, just as throughout *Childe Harold* the great communal shapes of history, landscape, and architecture press in upon, offer release from, mediate, and express the charged yet vacant present ('And that one word were Lightning' (III.97)), so throughout Byron's verse the bleeding heart finds and bears its public pageant or makes a Roman holiday. Public trial or imprisonment, so obvious in *Parisina*, the Venetian plays, *The Prisoner of Chillon*, *The Lament of Tasso*, or the 'Ode to Napoleon Buonaparte', fuse grief and pageant in this way. *The Vision of Judgement* is a kind of trial, too, in which George III finally escapes and Southey forever finds public chastisement. We are always interested in the final verdict and Byron never avoids it. Curse is a different but equally explicit form of judgement. Byron allows Dante and Marino Faliero to conclude their utterance in his poetry by a protracted curse. Byron shapes one himself to conclude *English Bards* and structure *The Curse of Minerva*. Most of Byron's fictions offer public guide-lines of this kind and show clearly who finds and who evades punishment.

The explicitness of all this has to do with the coincidence of the outer shape of Byron's fictions with the transgressions of will and heart which they chronicle, but even these inward territories are understood and traced out for us in a manner that belongs as much to 'the moral suffering fundamental to human existence' as to lyric pattern. We can see this when we ask more precisely where Byron's concern with punishment finds it focus. If, unlike Coleridge, Byron really is interested in understanding punishment, that is to say finding its antecedents and consequences, it does not follow that he is convinced of its justice. He is always chary of punishing others, which is why, despite his curses and visions, he decided to withdraw *English Bards* from circulation and, unlike Southey, allows his political foe (George III) into heaven. Those who do suffer punishment within his work are, as often as not, objects of admiration. Imprisonment, for instance, is real enough but unjust in the case of Tasso, Jacopo Foscari, and Bonnivard, much as Byron's sympathies lie with Prometheus and only rarely does he acknowledge his transgression. Public executions (Marino Faliero, Hugo in *Parisina*) endorse the victims rather than the judges. Jacopo Foscari's is the one case, apart from Prometheus himself, of public torture, but we are not directed to Jacopo's physical pain so much as to Doge Foscari's suppressed and wholly interior suffering as he witnesses and supervises it. Jacopo's most intense and ethereal pain is caused by the idea of banishment. Byron is indeed not interested in physical pain as such in comparison with, say, Act I of Shelley's *Prometheus Unbound*. Nor is he ever interested in as plain a fable of punishment as Crabbe's *Peter Grimes*. He is interested in pain as consequential in some sense and, above all, in its recognition and acknowledgement by those who endure it. Why else should Byron's best poem on Napoleon have been released by his abdication and imprisonment? One stanza from 'Ode to Napoleon Buonaparte' tells us instantly and takes us straight to Byron's peculiar territory:

> He who of old would rend the oak,
>   Dreamed not of the rebound;
> Chained by the trunk he vainly broke—
>   Alone—how looked he round?
> Thou, in the sternness of thy strength
> An equal deed hast done at length,
>   And darker fate hast found:
> He fell, the forest-prowlers' prey:
> But thou must eat thy heart away!
>   (stanza 6)

The 'He who' of the exemplum is, of course, Milo, whose hubris in rending the oak with his fist was punished by finding

himself trapped within its 'rebound'. Byron's point is simpler
and larger:

> Alone—how looked he round?

Byron is only concerned with that instantaneous point of
recognition, Cain's 'But with *me!*', where outer look and hidden
pang coalesce for ever in ghastly equipoise as they do in
Michelangelo's great painting of 'the damned before the
Judgement-throne'.[10]

Byron dated that point at which Napoleon has reached the
limit of his fiction. Byron pinpoints his in 'The Dream', but we
may not altogether believe it:

> a moment o'er his face
> A tablet of unutterable thoughts
> Was traced, and then it faded, as it came; . . .
>
> (ll.96–98)

The same point is repeated (ll.149–55) a few lines and years
later. In such passages, Byron engages and embarrasses us by
the reflexive posing of his own private turmoil and by the open
fictionalizing of autobiographical fact. The effect is similar to
but not the same as Hardy's 1912 poems, for Hardy does not
direct us to the stricken and inalienable remorse of his present
experience, as Byron would, but to memory and colloquy with
the dead. Hardy's predicament is separately picked out for us
in a sequence of lyrics, but the pain that interests Byron,
though paralysing, is the force that drives his poems along. It is
in this sense that suffering and fiction unite not only at the
boundaries (as in the stage sets of trial or imprisonment) but at
the centre of Byron's poems. The most interesting case here is
Mazeppa, which, since it is the only one of Byron's poems whose
entire action is synonymous with punishment, may be briefly
considered on its own.

Mazeppa

Mazeppa should help us not only because of the self-consciously
fictional treatment of the natural energies that are its focus but
also because the poem, rarely seen in this way, nevertheless
occupies a pivotal position in Byron's opus. We can see how the

avoidance of punishment begins to oust punishment itself as
Byron's major fictional theme in his non-dramatic poems. This
has extra-fictional resonance since, not much earlier, Byron
turned his great curse in *Childe Harold* (IV.131–37) into a
proclamation of forgiveness that remains edged with threat[11]
but seeks to move 'In hearts all rocky now the late remorse of
love'. That wish remained fiction to the quite otherwise fact so
far as Lady Byron's rocky heart, if not that of Ada and the
reader of the poem, was concerned, but its positioning towards
the end of *Childe Harold* as a counter to its record of the cycle of
destruction that forms human history is part of Byron's moral
strategy as well as of his fictional design. Byron's 'look' at the
end of this pilgrimage can no longer be mistaken for Harold's.
In the case of Mazeppa, however, we do not see Mazeppa's
'look' at all. This brings us close to *The Ancient Mariner*, which
was, it seems probable, in Byron's mind when he wrote the
poem. There are many passages that recall both this and
Christabel.[12] Moreover, the central device of retelling a past tale
of terror to a listener from a different world is common to both.
We are caught up in the intensity and duration of Mazeppa's
sudden punishment but, unlike the Mariner, what happens
next can and does displace what precedes it just as it does
throughout *Don Juan*. Mazeppa is not to be 'eternally but thus'
nor, and perhaps for the same reason, is his pain magnified by
the consciousness of 'Having been otherwise'. For Mazeppa's
punishment is, as everyone observes, a parallel and continua-
tion of the wayward energies that engender it. In Coleridge's
poem, sexuality is latent in the wedding framework, in the
vision of Death in Life and, doubtless, in the ambivalent
watersnakes but, like everything else in *The Ancient Mariner*, it
cannot be greeted for what it is. In *Mazeppa*, the progress from
sexual transgression via emblematic punishment (bound,
naked, to a wild horse) to sexual resurrection ('The sparkle of
her eye I caught, / Even with my first return of thought'
(ll.808–09)) is as explicit as may be. For example, the lovers are
bound by a 'burning chain' (l.240) of 'absorbing fire' (l.243), and
Mazeppa's sudden understanding that Theresa will yield
to him comes 'Even as a flash of lightning there' (l.272).
Exactly the same metaphor is continued into his punishment,
where he is bound to the horse 'as on the lightning's flash'

(1.408). Similarly, the horses encountered by Mazeppa are 'the wild, the free' (1.684) but the girl that later wakes him from his ordeal has 'black eyes so wild and free' (1.812).

This sense of a sustained and identical energy throughout Mazeppa's progress is linked with the life of the poem itself, for the account of Mazeppa's experience comes to us as sharp, exhilarating, and yet dizzy, vague, and unfocussed. At the same time, the whole poem is framed by irony, for Charles XII is the silent, and finally sleeping, recipient of the narrative. As such he is in manifest contrast to the uncontrollable Mazeppa:

> But all men are not born to reign,
> Or o'er their passions, or as you
> Thus o'er themselves and nations too.
>   (ll.287–89)

In another way, however, Charles resembles Mazeppa, for he too inhabits the rainbow of energy inscribed by his will. Here, Mazeppa's folly seems the more attractive of the two. Byron's deliberate confounding of animal energy and comic detachment as the foundation of his tale is a wonderful transformation of his source in Voltaire's life of the Swedish Alexander, which does not envisage Mazeppa telling his own tale to Charles and passes over the ride in a sentence. The composition of the last part of *Mazeppa* (end of September 1818) overlapped with the composition of *Don Juan* Canto I. Manuscripts of both poems were sent off together and the proofs were probably corrected together. It is, undoubtedly, closer in major respects to the mode of *Don Juan* than *Beppo*, for, like *Don Juan*, it depends upon conveying immediacy of life and sceptical detachment simultaneously. Where *The Ancient Mariner* gives us crime, penance, forgiveness, and hell in such a way that none of these can quite be meant, *Mazeppa* gives us both punishment and escape from punishment in a manner that confirms the validity of both. This can only be achieved by the self-conscious use of fictionality (tale-telling in *Mazeppa*, the narrator in *Don Juan*) but any self-conscious fiction is offering itself as an instance of the extra-fictional as well as heightening fictionality. We can see this most clearly in *The Island* and how, once again, it is bound up in Byron's mind with transgression, punishment, and escape, in myth and history.

The Island

Where Mazeppa is both the recipient of punishment and the one who evades it, these roles are quite separate in *The Island*. There is a magnificent section in Canto III which dramatizes this separation. It is worth quoting in full:

> Beside the jutting rock the few appeared,
> Like the last remnant of the red-deer's herd;
> Their eyes were feverish, and their aspect worn,
> But still the hunter's blood was on their horn.
> A little stream came tumbling from the height,
> And straggling into ocean as it might,
> Its bounding chrystal frolicked in the ray,
> And gushed from cliff to crag with saltless spray;
> Close on the wild, wide ocean, yet as pure
> And fresh as Innocence, and more secure,
> Its silver torrent glittered o'er the deep,
> As the shy chamois' eye o'erlooks the steep,
> While far below the vast and sullen swell
> Of ocean's alpine azure rose and fell.
> To this young spring they rushed,—all feelings first
> Absorbed in Passion's and in Nature's thirst,—
> Drank as they do who drink their last, and threw
> Their arms aside to revel in its dew;
> Cooled their scorched throats, and washed the gory stains
> From wounds whose only bandage might be chains;
> Then, when their drought was quenched, looked sadly round,
> As wondering how so many still were found
> Alive and fetterless:—but silent all,
> Each sought his fellow's eyes, as if to call
> On him for language which his lips denied,
> As though their voices with their cause had died.
>
> (III.59–84)

Ruskin paid eloquent tribute to the fidelity of Byron's imagination here.[13] If we cannot but be aware of innumerable sources for the symbolic conventions in play yet someone, Lord Byron, has also had occasion to look closely at a non-fictional stream in order to write like this. It is just this tantalizing juxtaposition of factual and symbolic detail which, here and elsewhere in Byron, is the poetry of the scene, much as, in the previous canto, he recalls how his first sight of the real but fabled landscape of Troy fused with his earliest memories of Scotland so that, amazingly,

> Loch-na-gar with Ida looked o'er Troy . . .
> (II.291)

In this almost operatic set-piece, experienced ('worn'), sick ('feverish'), and animal-like ('red-deer's herd') men rush to a stream of pure and innocent water which, in contrast to their hunted retreat, peeps out shyly on the world like 'the shy chamois'. They attempt to renew themselves and wipe away their 'gory stains'. However, their rush to the stream and the subsequent anxious inspecting of each others' looks ('But with *me*') after their unbaptizing immersion in it reveals their inability to receive what they seek. Contrast this with Byron's account of a more successful dialogue between Man and Nature in Canto II:

> How often we forget all time, when lone,
> Admiring Nature's universal throne,
> Her woods—her wilds—her waters—the intense
> Reply of *hers* to our intelligence!
> (II.382–85)

The 'we' here includes the poet, reader, and extra-textual common humanity, but it is authorized fictionally by Torquil and Neuha's intense silent interrogation of one another and the surrounding landscape in the same section of the poem. This canto is the most obviously fictionalized in the poem. The island is placed in a deliberately mythical setting of song, dance, and festivity where 'from the sepulchre we'll gather flowers' (II.21). The inhabitants of the island, though now introduced into the arts of war, prefer to spend their time simply gazing on Nature, receptive to her 'intense Reply':

> And we will sit in Twilight's face, and see
> The sweet moon glancing through the Tooa tree, . . .
> Or climb the steep, and view the surf . . .
> How beautiful are these! how happy they,
> Who, from the toil and tumult of their lives,
> Steal to look down where nought but Ocean strives!
> (II.9–10, 12, 16–18)

This gazing outwards ('Who thinks of self when gazing on the sky?' (II.393)) is the opposite of the inner interrogation that fixes the dreadful look of Cain and all Byronic heroes. It is here marked on the brow of Fletcher Christian, who, like his ancestor, has tried to return to Paradise and has made and found death there:

> His light-brown locks, so graceful in their flow,
> Now rose like startled vipers o'er his brow.
> Still as a statue, with his lips comprest
> To stifle even the breath within his breast,
> Fast by the rock, all menacing, but mute,
> He stood;
>
> (III.89–94)

But where is the fictional reference here? If we begin with a mythical island, then Christian and his followers seem to be wretched historical outsiders. A Fletcher Christian certainly existed. His failure in the poem to return and stay on the island, his inability to renew his self, wash away 'gory stains' in the 'little stream' and become a gazer as the stream itself is (III.70), seems like Lycius's failure in Keats's poem to stay in the enchanted world of Lamia. But if the oppositions of Keats's poetry can no longer be thought of simply as Dream versus Reality since Keats's 'reality' is as distorted and stylized as his 'dream', this is far more true of Byron's poetry. Keats used myths and even, as in the 'vale of soul-making', experienced the precocious pleasure of watching himself make one up. But Keats never allowed myths to use him. Keats insisted on his absence from his poems ('negative capability') in order to become their rifter ('load every rift with ore'), active in every nook and cranny of them. Byron, on the other hand, projects his self, his imaginings, and his historical/factual recall into verse so that these may appear as what they are and what he believed them to be, versions of archetypal stories, beyond his complete manipulation, which soothe, outrage, baffle, and clarify. In such a continuum, Byronic heroes, historical mutineers, paradisal islands, and South Seas' topography exist as sharply defined and yet interchangeable. We could never find a privileged point of reference which would enable us to read off where the fiction begins and ends. And yet Byron's island, impossible to classify as fiction or fact, bifurcates into its separate staple endings of comic marriage and tragic death whilst insisting that those who mistake fiction for fact (Christian) are punished for it or (Torquil) thrive only in such a fiction as *The Island*.

The commencement of this bifurcation occurs in the long section from Canto III already instanced. The mutineers are set between the oceans' 'vast and sullen swell' and the 'silver torrent' of the little stream. They have a few minutes of conscious pause before two sets of craft are to appear and take them to separate endings and worlds. One (Neuha's) is to rescue Torquil from punishment, the other (H.M. Navy) is to exact punishment from Christian and his two companions. In this space of time, they rush first, as we have seen, to the island's spring of life which offers momentary rather than eternal renewal and then each one of the four is presented in close-up. Torquil, one of the four, has to be presented as part of them. It is from the world of the mutineers that he is rescued and his transition from one world to another must be palpable. Yet he cannot wholly belong to them, for, in that case, Neuha could not reach the self-enclosed interiority of his being. Byron always manages these details with superb instinct and nonchalantly constructs our response. Here is how he does it:

> Some pace further Torquil leaned his head
> Against a bank, and spoke not, but he bled,—
> Not mortally:—his worst wound was within;
> His brow was pale, his blue eyes sunken in,
> And blood-drops, sprinkled o'er his yellow hair,
> Showed that his faintness came not from despair,
> But Nature's ebb.
>
> (III.97–103)

Three elements make up this representation, but their effect is controlled by the sequence in which they are presented. Torquil bleeds. The stream has not removed the 'gory stains' of his mortality and his kinship with Cain. But yet 'his worst wound was within'. There is the clue to a deeper kinship still. Interior pain is the mark of all the mutineers. The bloodstain of his outer wound and the deeper pain within constitute Torquil's credentials as part of the group. But what is the character or cause of this 'worst wound'? We are not told. It could, after all, be separation from Neuha. If Byron was writing about Lara or the Giaour or, more to the purpose, Christian, then this 'worst wound' and its ramifications would be articulated at length. Instead of this, we move instantly to outer description and then to a new element which engineers a neat reversal:

> And blood-drops, sprinkled o'er his yellow hair,
> Showed that his faintness came not from despair,
> But Nature's ebb.

It appears from this that the suggestion of inner pain is only a momentary and ambiguous one. Instead, we are directed to a pain which is simply part of 'Nature's ebb', therefore curable and transient on Nature's island, rather than caused by that deathly fixity of will which the mariners bring to their paradise. The brevity of this description, too, in comparison with the next sixty lines which are devoted to the mental states of Torquil's companions, suggests the comparative simplicity of Torquil's pain. It is in him a temporary diminution of consciousness—'his blue eyes sunken in'—rather than the preternaturally acute consciousness of his companions. It is this awareness which is in sharp contrast to the relaxed 'looks' and gazings of the islanders glimpsed at the beginning of Canto II. All four of these men are positioned at their limit. Their position by the jutting rock and, shortly, by a still more liminal rock which will be 'their latest view of land' (IV.245) epitomizes their consciousness and, by presenting the limits of that consciousness to them, makes them recognize their own mental and moral territory for what it is.

Limits have two characteristics, as we may discover at any frontier post. In one way they maximize the character and status of the territory whose extent and appearance they announce. In another way, they are immediate transition points to unimaginably different territories. Of the four mutineers, three are to die into the limits which, alone, they now signify. One is to cross into a different world. If we stand back a little, we can see that *The Island* begins with Christian's transition, via transgression, from European history misnamed 'the Bounty' to intended paradise but in fact to Hell (as he deems but we should, perhaps, not (I.164; IV.352)). It ends

with Torquil's transition from kinship with his fellow Euro-
peans, marked as Cain's heirs, to kinship with Neuha, Nature,
and the Island. The mutineers cannot metamorphose them-
selves by drinking and bathing in the innocent torrent which
the island permanently offers, but Torquil's plunge into the sea
is a later baptism that functions. He finds himself immediately
resurrected (IV.226) into a different dimension of time and
space. Paradoxically, Torquil transcends limits by submitting
and trusting himself to Neuha. He follows her as much child as
lover. Christian, on the other hand, celebrates his petrification
under the guise and boast of liberty:

> For me, my lot is what I sought; to be,
> In life or death, the fearless and the free.
>
> (III.163–64)

In this he is more clearly presented as mistaken than any of his
dark predecessors, not excluding Cain. Like Lara he is 'A thing
of dark imaginings' (*Lara*, I.317) but we fully understand
Christian, as we do not Lara, and the island itself remains a
place of bright imaginings which he can neither reach nor
destroy. The Corsair is, however mysteriously, the cause of
Medora's death on his island retreat. So, too, is that other
returning pirate, Lambro, who transforms a bright island into
a tomb for himself and his daughter in Canto IV of *Don Juan*.
Christian's status is less assured than these for another reason
also. He is presented as wholly superior to his three com-
panions 'Beside the jutting rock' in an extended image that
could belong to Corsair, Lara, or Giaour:

> But Christian, of a higher order, stood
> Like an extinct volcano in his mood;
> Silent, and sad, and savage,—with the trace
> Of passion reeking from his clouded face;
>
> (III.139–42)

As it happens, we can test and reject this simile for, unlike
the Corsair's companions, who function simply as colourful
film extras, we know exactly what it's like to be Ben Bunting
and Jack Skyscrape and wait a few minutes before death with
Christian. Ben Bunting passes the time by washing, wiping,
and binding Torquil's wound, 'then calmly lit his pipe'

(III.106). He has always lived within the confines of practical life like this. His pipe-smoking is an indication of his relentless metaphysical inattention rather than of relaxation. He is an older version of Johnson in the middle cantos of *Don Juan*, but at once more ridiculous and more deadly. When we first encounter him in Canto II, he is festooned with weapons of all kinds ('our Europe's growth') and, though trouserless ('For even the mildest woods will have their thorn'), he retains his European decency (Neuha and the islanders are, like Mazeppa, naked) by a 'somewhat scanty mat' which 'served for inexpressibles and hat' (II.483). He is a grotesque example of the incongruity which is Christian's pain. He is a practical, charitable man, and a killer. He is Cain's comic, wandering heir, not at peace but accustomed to restlessness and pipe-smoking his way through it. He is a brilliant creation. The fourth mutineer, Jack Skyscrape, cannot hide his restlessness so readily. Byron pinpoints his disturbed occupancy of time:

> The fourth and last of this deserted group
> Walked up and down—at times would stand, then stoop
> To pick a pebble up—then let it drop—
> Then hurry as in haste—then quickly stop—
> Then cast his eyes on his companions—then
> Half whistle half a tune, and pause again—
> And then his former movements would redouble,
> With something between carelessness and trouble.
> This is a long description, but applies
> To scarce five minutes passed before the eyes;
> But yet *what* minutes! Moments like to these
> Rend men's lives into immortalities.
>
> (III.109–20)

Byron's comment on this undistinguished and slightly ridiculous figure aligns him with Manfred who is 'Now furrowed o'er / With wrinkles, plough'd by moments, not by years' (I.ii.71–72) and also with Christian who, though 'still as a statue', nevertheless betrays his agitation by 'a slight beat of the foot' (III.94). Thus Christian's interior and his conscious predicament are virtually identical with those of his vulgar companions. The Abbott and the Chamois-hunter genuinely probe and, to some extent, understand Manfred, but he retains his mystery, superiority, and separate destiny. Christian cannot do this. More complex, more stylish perhaps, than his fellows, he is nevertheless of their kind, which means that we are of his kind too. There is no essential difference between the intolerable boredom and time-filling routines which any reader will recognize in Skyscrape and Bunting, or the inhabitants of Norman Abbey, and the intense ennui which is the foundation of the Byronic hero's claim to superiority.

Hence that remarkable scene where 'the last remnant' of the mutineers rush to the young spring which is 'as pure / And fresh as innocence', bathe their 'gory stains' and cool their 'scorched throats' and then look 'sadly round' is not at all an advertisement for the romance world which it so thrillingly embodies. It is, we might say, a depiction in another mode of where *Don Juan* is written from. The last cantos of *Don Juan* coincide with the writing of *The Island*. Romance worlds and their 'sober sad antitheses'[14] have been the staple ingredients of *Don Juan* but, alongside them at the end of his poem, Byron invokes a different vision and alters the limit of his fiction altogether.

Aurora Raby and Byron's Heroes

The narrator of *Don Juan*, like the mutineers 'Beside the jutting rock', lives in that fully understood space of time and consciousness which knows its immediate proximity to death, can mingle in but not be remade by untainted sources of life, and sees the world directly in front of him with sober clarity as his 'latest view of land' but also as pure illusion. The narrator is both Christian ('aloof a little from the rest') and Everyman who has time to fill and needs distraction from death. He lives at this limit where, terrified, free, defiant, nonchalant, witty, he sets about constructing the unexpected and improvises an auld sang 'with something between carelessness and trouble'. He sits at night ('I sing by night'), thinking aloud and telling stories, poised between the inextinguishable stream and coming death. Torquil is to enter the first, Christian to find the other consummation, but the narrator of *Don Juan* knows them only as Cain knows death before he murders Abel.

Juan, of course, is the narrator's counterpart here as Torquil is Fletcher Christian's. Juan does not have Torquil's once for all resurrection to an unlimited world; rather, Byron presents him as experiencing a series of Mazeppa-like resurrections from apparent end-points. But what in that case happens to the notion of punishment in *Don Juan?*

The original Don Juan story is nothing other than a fable of punishment. Don Juan Tenorio's limitless will, and the repeated pattern of seductions which implements it, is countered by the unambiguous limitation of the Stone Guest's icy hand which summons Juan Tenorio to death and hell, leaving most of the other characters to *exeunt* to the wedding bells Christabel never hears. Byron's *Don Juan* begins by spectacularly reversing this pattern. His Juan seeks resting places with women rather than escape from them, his will is subject to theirs. At the end of the poem, the interruption of Canto XVII implies the narrator's death (what else could stop him talking?), but Juan is left unlimited though drawn to marriage with Aurora.

Similarly, Don Juan Tenorio imposes his will on circumstances, and this shapes the pattern of the original play much as trial or imprisonment shape many of Byron's fictions. Byron's Don Juan, however, never seeks to impose himself on circumstances,[15] and the apparent randomness of his adventures clearly parallels the unpredictable mode of Byron's poem.

This simple pattern and apparent unlimitation is not the whole pattern. Byron's Juan, like Tirso da Molina's, leaves behind him Julia, Haidée, Lambro, drowned sailors, and slaughtered combatants in the siege. All these find limitation, almost punishment. Their immobility is a foil for Juan's invariable renewal, yet, as the poem proceeds, it seems also to threaten and taint that renewal.

We could see the pattern differently. Some readers have wanted to stress Juan's fall from innocence. Byron himself makes the point explicitly[16] and through the symbolic presence of Leila and Aurora. If, as we predict in Canto XIII,[17] Don Juan was to revive the neglected theme of love in the poem by becoming the minion of Lady Adeline, then we would have to regard Juan as incapable of subsequent resurrection. But he does not do so and Aurora Raby, far from being simply a symbolic counterpart to Juan's tainted innocence like Leila, becomes the object of his attention, bearer of new meaning in the poem, and an occasion for a transition to limitlessness as startling and more substantial than that epitomized in Torquil's dive. For Aurora is 'pure / And fresh as innocence' like the little stream on *The Island*, but she knows all that Christian knows.

Byron often tends to separate moral characteristics out into different figures. Obvious examples are Medora and Gulnare in *The Corsair*, Dudù and the Sultana in the harem cantos, or the different ways of loving Venice represented by the two Foscari. In the last cantos of *Don Juan*, Byron's three graces— Fitz-Fulke, Lady Adeline, Aurora Raby—represent his most ambitious attempt to write in this almost allegorical fashion. The sure-footedness with which this markedly abstract schema is rendered satirically and historically concrete whilst activating the buried archetypes of religion, comedy, and romance is dazzling. It has not been sufficiently noted[18] and cannot be too highly praised. But Byron has another way of drawing character. Haidée, for instance, combines several features which Byron could have separated into distinct figures. She is innocent, experienced, orthodox, pagan, rescuer, death-dealer, wife, mistress, mother, daughter, princess, criminal, Nature's bride and, finally, subject of song and object of art. Her presence and importance in the poem is bound up with this multiplicity.

Aurora Raby is named explicitly as Haidée's counterpart in Norman Abbey (XV.58). This confirms what we have already begun to suspect—that Aurora, though a functioning part of an emblematic trio, is herself a synthesis of opposing factors. The pairings that particularly concern us here have to do with fiction, the limitless, and punishment. Aurora is a new way of dealing with these things. She is, in both senses, the furthest limit that Byron's fiction reached, or, as T. S. Eliot described her, 'the most serious character of his invention'.[19] Byron used to be accused of not being serious enough or, kinder but worse, was granted seriousness when talking about politics but not puberty or stomachs. If we have moved on, as we have left behind Bunyan's 'realism' and Keats's 'escapism', we may have lost more than we have gained, for we seem to have lost interest in seriousness altogether. Aurora Raby, deftly intro-

duced and handled as she is, is a very serious fiction indeed and
intended to surprise us into life.

The Island has its seriousness too, but finally separates the
responsibilities of historical and fictional life. It tells us that we
cannot return to Paradise in historical fact because attempting
to do so renews our exclusion from it. The unreachable bias of
our will can only recognize its misdirection in the renewed
expulsion from Eden visited as punishment upon it. Cain is the
first to find this out, Christian is one of his many successors.
On the other hand, we can and must return to Paradise in our
imagination by some inexplicably available shift of mode of
which Torquil's dive is the fictional prototype. It is all
astonishingly explicit and clearly signposted.

Aurora Raby, however, is both 'Radiant and grave'
(XV.14). She is 'Radiant' because of what she is and 'grave'
because of what she knows, just as we may separate Neuha's
being from Fletcher Christian's knowledge, and much as
Manfred sets out in his first speech the complaint of his divisive
diagnosis and divided being:

> Sorrow is knowledge: they who know the most
> Must mourn the deepest o'er the fatal truth,
> The Tree of Knowledge is not that of Life.
>
> (I.i.10–12)

But Aurora has moved on from these familiar oppositions. The
gravity consequent upon her knowledge ('Aurora, who looked
more on books than faces' (XV.85)) has not tainted the
radiance of her being ('Aurora Raby, a young star who shone /
O'er Life' (XV.43)). Indeed it is Byron's capacity to create
unbridgeable antitheses which is the foundation of his miracu-
lous ability to create syntheses that convince profoundly.
Aurora is the most substantial and daring of all these syn-
theses.

In the first place, Aurora's sadness is quite distinct from
Manfred's or Christian's:

> Early in years, and yet more infantine
>   In figure, she had something of sublime
> In eyes which sadly shone, as Seraphs' shine.
>   All Youth—but with an aspect beyond Time:
> Radiant and grave—as pitying Man's decline;

> Mournful—but mournful of another's crime,
> She looked as if she sat by Eden's door,
> And grieved for those who could return no more.
>
> (XV.45)

That is an extraordinary position for anyone to be placed within Byron's poetry or outside it.[20] She sits 'by Eden's door'. She does not herself grieve like Manfred or rail like Cain and Christian at her exclusion from Eden. Nor does she represent, as Neuha does, Imagination's hope of re-entry to a natural paradise. Neuha, mythical, 'naiad of the deep', plucks Torquil from the punishment intrinsic to human history, but Aurora sits and does not intervene, much like the angels in Blake's 'Night'; she sits, knows, and mourns the crime and punishment of those who can return to Paradise no more. Despite this knowledge, she remains 'All Youth', her eyes are 'sublime', and she has an aspect 'beyond Time'. She is thus positioned by the archetypal limit (Eden's shut door) but is in touch with unlimited reality. Juan, who so soon after his expulsion from Haidée's Eden could not 'altogether call the past to mind' (IV.75), moves towards this grave radiance, a fiction so retentive of an actual history, and is then galvanized by the shocks of religious fear (Black Friar) and sudden sexual arousal (blonde Duchess) which are its cruder, concomitant, and almost interchangeable bestowals.

The use of landscape is important here and echoes back the serenity and tragic consciousness that mark the 'infantine' Aurora in more complex ways than Toobonai. Neuha plucks Torquil to an elemental and mythical island which is a version of herself. Aurora dwells as guest within a ruined house. This house is both the focus of Byron's satire on his contemporary world and a great religious ruin despoiled by human history like the ruined edifices of *Childe Harold*. Aurora is receptive to these resonances, the result of 'another's crime', and to the strange interplay between the building and its surrounding landscape. Night, that 'religious concern' for Byron,[21] is the harbinger of this 'strange unearthly sound' (XIII.63). Hence Aurora summons Juan from his instinctive immersion in present pleasure and summons him simultaneously to a real history of waste and the opportunity to transcend it.

It is difficult to find a vocabulary that will enable us to keep

track of all this. The thought in process in Byron's last poems—
The Island, The Deformed Transformed, Heaven and Earth, and the
last cantos of *Don Juan*—is so ambitious in its scope, so
exploratory, relentlessly paradoxical, and yet so openly re-
activating the inherited modes of European thought and value,
that only a critic like the late G. Wilson Knight could sustain
the panache with which to salute and elucidate the mysterious
obviousness of Byron's endeavour.

Aurora's eyes, for example, 'sadly shone, as Seraphs' shine'
(XV.45). That, we may say, is their grave radiance. But let us
pose a daft question. How do seraphs' eyes shine exactly? Not
so daft, as it turns out, for Byron knew the answer. They do not
shine like this:

> in his eye
> There is a fastening attraction which
> Fixes my fluttering eyes on his; my heart
> Beats quick; he awes me, and yet draws me near,
> (*Cain*, I.i.409–12)

This sounds erotic, and in its way it is, for Byron uses the same
image in 'Last Words on Greece' to describe the snake-like
fascination by which Loukas Chalandritsanos charmed him
like some stricken bird 'whose pinion fluttering down / Wafts
unto death the breast it bore so high'. But seduction in both
these cases is primarily a form of temptation to forbidden
knowledge. In the extract from Act 1 of *Cain* above, Adah is
reacting to the shine in Lucifer's eye which she later categorizes
with scholastic precision:

> The seraphs *love most*—Cherubim *know most*—
> And this should be a Cherub—since he loves not.
> (I.i.421–22)

Adah, like Astarte, represents love but most of *Cain* has to do
with the murdering knowledge represented by Lucifer's eye
and Cain's deed. *Heaven and Earth*, that baffling, flawed, but
sublime extravaganza, is a deliberate attempt to move on. *Cain*
treats of Man's (Cain's) intellectual commerce with cherubs
(Lucifer). *Heaven and Earth* dramatizes Woman's equally des-
tructive but love-based commerce with seraphs. Hence we are
close to both Manfred and Aurora. This sounds impossible but

indicates, what is undoubtedly the case, that Aurora Raby, not Fletcher Christian, is the final metamorphosed appearance of the Byronic hero. Let us try to set some of these connections out.

Manfred's 'Sorrow is knowledge' becomes Japhet's 'Alas! What else is Love, not Sorrow?'.[22] *Don Juan*'s subject, in the simplest statement which remains useful, is Love and Knowledge. Normally this means Juan (Love) and the narrator (Knowledge), but at the beginning and end of the poem Juan experiences in himself and then in Aurora the conjunction of the two. The first instance is comic and debunking. The sixteen-year-old Juan, 'Tormented with a wound he could not know' (I.87), imagines that he is enraptured by knowledge:

> He thought about himself . . .
>   . . . and of the many bars
> To perfect knowledge of the boundless skies—
> And then he thought of Donna Julia's eyes.
>   (I.92)

Here puberty ousts philosophy as the hidden spring of Juan's enlargement. In the sixteen-year-old Aurora, however, Juan discovers at the other end of the poem a fusion of seraphic love and cherubic knowledge which, though inextricably mingled with his own sexual drives (XVI.108) in its apprehension, is not simply scripted by their repressed conception and is wholly exempt from the narrator's smirk about puberty. Further refinements in Byron's thinking about seraphic knowledge and eyelight shape this extraordinary character. In *Heaven and Earth*, Aholibamah, who, like Aurora, has seraphic knowledge but of a somewhat different kind, thus describes the result:

>   There is a ray
> In me, which, though forbidden yet to shine,
> I feel was lighted at thy God's and thine.
> It may be hidden long: death and decay
>   Our mother Eve bequeathed us—but my heart
> Defies it:
>   (*Heaven and Earth*, I.i.103–08)

This is seraphic love and light of a sort but it is linked with Promethean defiance and, as the speech continues, modulates into a desire to be embraced by the seraph as serpent:

> And shall *I* shrink from thine eternity?
>   No! though the serpent's sting should pierce me
>   thorough,
> And thou thyself were like the serpent, coil
>   Around me still! and I will smile,
>   (I.i.125–28)

As we might expect, Christian, the knowledge-ridden Byronic hero who has tried to return to love's paradise, dies in *exactly* this way even to the detail of the smile:

> He tore the topmost button from his vest,
> Down the tube dashed it—levelled—fired, and smiled
> As his foe fell; then, like a serpent, coiled
> His wounded, weary form, to where the steep
> Looked desperate as himself along the deep;
> Cast one glance back, and clenched his hand, and shook
> His last rage 'gainst the earth which he forsook;
>   (*The Island*, IV.334–40)

Aurora smiles too. It is her characteristic, though not continuous, expression. But it is the detail of the ray 'lighted at' God's and seraph's light which is transformed so remarkably in Norman Abbey. Juan catches 'Aurora's eye on his / And something like a smile upon her cheek' (XVI.92). This 'quiet smile of contemplation' makes Juan blush but 'she did not blush in turn' (XVI.93, 94). All the heroines in *Don Juan* blush, except of course Catherine the Great. Blushing demonstrates the glow of natural life and this therefore is not the cause of Aurora's attractiveness. She, like Aholibamah, has a different kind of light:

>   but her colour ne'er was high—
> Though sometimes faintly flushed—and always clear,
> As deep seas in a Sunny Atmosphere.
>   (XVI.94)

The imagery here is of clarity, depth, and buried but discernible radiance caught from without, 'lighted at' some other source. Byron has removed Aholibamah's stridency and gently detheologized the references.[23] If we, in our turn, thread our way somewhere between the two we will discern, despite Byron's independence of mind and the heterodox nature of his sources, a series of commonplaces which make his claim 'I grow more orthodox' (*Don Juan*, XI.5) seem less ironic in substance than in manner. Love and Knowledge, it appears, are opposed but connected. A radical misdirection of Love or Knowledge, or both, is a foundation experience. It occurs (or recurs) most tellingly in those who repudiate the truth or justice of such a diagnosis. We can recognize this but cannot find a right reaction to it or to them. Some, however, can do so. They can be indicated but cannot be straightforwardly described.

This is what the myths, demythologized, use Byron to say, but it is his own gigantic capacity to connect, transform and think through his fictions that makes us rediscover their force. We need to get both emphases right. Byron is not a myth-maker in the sense that became fashionable in transatlantic criticism some twenty-five years ago. Myths are not the means by which we escape from history into the private imagination and the desire-led forces of limitless indeterminacy. They are the regulating imperatives of conduct and the common foundations of our self-recognition. History, like Byron's poetry, makes space for their evolution and repetition. The distinction between seraphic and cherubic knowledge is a commonplace of mediaeval Theology,[24] but the concept of seraphs may have been derived from that of poisonous serpents.[25] Fletcher Christian did return to Toobonai and then Tahiti in 1789. Newstead Abbey was dissolved in 1539. Byron was fascinated by the accidental character of history but his poetry holds to, derives intelligibility and force from, given myths of explanation.

Aurora Raby has been our object of attention and we are not yet finished with her because, though myths explain by origins, conceptual thought such as literary criticism is properly retrospective in character. Juan lives forwards, the narrator understands backwards. It is both easier and better to interpret Cain and Manfred via Aurora rather than the other way round. We begin then with a figure who sits and mourns for another's crime by Eden's door, reads books more than faces, smiles, grows like a flower, endures like a gem, and is in touch with light that originates elsewhere. Innocent, experienced Juan moves to her and loses interest in other characters and what he has become. She is an emblem, clearly, of Love and

Knowledge, history's crime ('deemed that fallen worship far
more dear' (XV.46)), and seraph's transcendence. If she bears
history as consequence, and she alone in Norman Abbey does
so consciously,[26] she accepts this consequence with patience
and sits smiling upon the monument 'of another's crime'. She
bears Cain's terrible 'But with *me*', but has transmuted the
fearful look of her predecessors into grave and pleasing
composure. But are they her predecessors as, once again, I
suggest? Let us continue our multiplication of transformed
instances. Here is Lucifer's advice to Cain:

> Think and endure,—and form an inner world
> In your own bosom—where the outward fails;
> So shall you nearer be the spiritual
> Nature, and war triumphant with your own.
>   (II.i.463–66)

This is familiar advice. *Childe Harold* is full of it. Prometheus is
praised for carrying it out. Manfred praises himself on the
same account (I.i.153–57). The emphasis is on what Byron
calls in 'Prometheus' the 'concentered recompense' of inner life.
We may add to this a more exalted vocabulary yet. This is
Lara:

> His mind abhorring this had fixed her throne
> Far from the world, in regions of her own;
>   (I.349–50)

And, finally, there is intimacy with space, which Cain gains by
his travel and Manfred always claims with horror and pride:
'Space and eternity—and consciousness' (II.i.47). If we
assemble these marks of the Byronic hero together—inner
citadel of strength, intimacy with unimaginable space, immor-
tal consciousness, and poise as of one on a throne, we find
ourselves constructing Aurora Raby:

> She gazed upon a world she scarcely knew,
>   As seeking not to know it; silent, lone,
> As grows a flower, thus quietly she grew,
>   And kept her heart serene within its zone.
> There was awe in the homage which she drew;
>   Her Spirit seem'd as seated on a throne

> Apart from the surrounding world, and strong
> In its own strength—most strange in one so young!
> (XV.47)

To this concentered strength and throned poise we must add intimacy with space:

> The worlds beyond this world's perplexing waste
> Had more of her existence, for in her
> There was a depth of feeling to embrace
> Thoughts, boundless, deep, but silent too as Space.
> (XVI.48)

It is important that Thought(s) is embraced by a seraphic 'depth of feeling' which fills, lovingly fills ('embrace'), the unimaginable expanses of space. This is what a seraphic eye does with the same thought-filled spaces which appeared as Death and Nothingness to Cain's neo-cherubic eye.

If it seems odd or implausible that Aurora is a transformed Byronic hero and, in this quite different guise, brings back that Promethean strain of thought and feeling into *Don Juan* which seems precisely founded on its exclusion, there are two factors which may be adduced as supporting evidence for doubters. These are Haidée and Norman Abbey. The latter, with its *Childe Harold* concomitants of an eerie ruined history, we have already mentioned. Aurora functions as a heroine within *Don Juan* and as a guest within the satirical world of Byron's fictive Abbey, but she emerges out of the shadows of a real, despoiled, and mysteriously present history for she is loyal to the 'old faith and old feelings' to which the ruined building still testifies. In this, she and the ghost of the Black Friar are, however metamorphosed, embodiments of *Childe Harold* experience in the different world of *Don Juan*. She is, pointedly, an orphan. No forgotten Lambro will come and claim her for the tomb but, unlike Haidée, she remains permanently conscious of the criminal history of which she forms an untainted part and loyal to 'her sires' (XV.46). How then does Haidée resemble her? Byrons says that she doesn't:

> Juan knew nought of such a character—
> High, yet resembling not his lost Haidée;
> (XV.58)

Yet 'each was radiant in her proper sphere' and, rather as with Milton's list of gardens that are precisely not like Eden,[27] we are meant to associate what we are specifically told to keep apart. The grounds of difference are obvious enough so long as we think of Haidée before she encounters her returned father, but this is Haidée too:

> She stood as one who championed human fears—
> Pale, statue-like, and stern, she woo'd the blow;
>
> (IV.43)

Her prototype here is Manfred who, as we have seen earlier, claims that he 'can act even what I most abhor, / And champion human fears' (II.ii.204–05). The phrase 'statue-like' too is not used lightly. Byron deliberately compares Haidée just before her death to the statues saluted as frozen images of suffering, endurance, and beauty in *Childe Harold* Canto IV (*Don Juan*, IV.61). Haidée bears within her two images. One is 'A second principle of Life', Juan's child, 'a fair and sinless child of sin' (IV.70). The other is the buried image of her father who is her death and, as she imagines in her dream (IV.35), fuses with Juan's dead face. In this dream, and the past and future reality brought with it, Haidée encounters the shadow-side of her bright experience and the exaltation of horror which is the preserve of Byronic heroes. She becomes through this a marker against which to set Juan's apparent movement beyond *Childe Harold* as his ridiculous boat sails slowly past 'The shores of Ilion' (IV.85) and leaves Haidée's now tragic isle behind.

When Juan meets Aurora, however, whom he seems almost to recognize and yet 'knew nought of such a character', he re-encounters as a fusion the Life and Death which Haidée's existence experienced as wholly, punishingly, separate.[28] This is what happens to the light in *her* eye:

> Oh! to possess such lustre—and then lack!
>
> (IV.69)

Haidée is exalted and broken by this terrible transition. Aurora lives comically not in the 'very life in our despair' of *Childe Harold* (III.34) but the other side of it. Haidée begins in an island paradise and ends in an island 'desolate and bare' which now lacks even a stone or ruined building to mark it. Aurora draws sustenance from the ruined history of her ancestors, imaged in Norman Abbey itself and, though 'a flower', has the indestructible radiance of a gem (XV.58). Like the ghost, whose disinheritance she shares, she is an emblem of unattended punishment in the Amundeville's Vanity Fair but she is, too, a Romance heroine and a new Eve who, alone in Byron's verse, fuses dark knowledge and the 'bounding chrystal' of the mutineers' unreachable stream on Toobonai. She annihilates the split between cherub and seraph, love and knowledge, which withers Manfred and is the apparent structure, offered only to be superseded, of *Don Juan*. Byron's life and work is a meditation upon and witness, conscious and inadvertent, to the Fall. Most of the time, like Job, he is demolishing the comforters but, like the Book of Job, his poetry is itself a tale of comfort. Aurora recapitulates the long-absent Harold as well as lost Haidée, but, and this is the truth to which we have not yet grown accustomed, Conrad, Lara, Harold *et al.* pay deformed witness to the Aurora which they will become.

A circle, said Byron, makes 'A holiness appealing to all hearts'.[29] It does so because it is limited and limitless. Our expanding universe pays new tribute to this concept much as Byron in St Peter's finds his mind 'Expanded by the genius of the spot'.[30] If we were to put our arms around the unlimited, as Aurora's 'depth of feeling' embraces boundless thoughts and space, then this circle and this holiness would be ours too. All Byron's poetry is concerned with this sublimity and this limitation. He is always in some sense a religious poet. His rage for justice and his preternatural sense of immediate given life make it impossible for him to be anything else. Aurora Raby is not an accidental construct of his art, she is generated out of the whole of it as no other of his characters is. T. S. Eliot was quite right. She *is* 'the most serious character of his invention'. She is, and is fully understood as being, the limit of his fiction.

This point could be put in many ways. It is open to qualification. If it is resisted altogether, however, we are not following Byron's thought through and will misinterpret its earlier direction.

Aurora exists in two dimensions. She is an invented fiction

within a fiction but she seems also to exist outside it. R. B. England, who writes extremely well about Byron but is without metaphysical inclination and is thus a neutral witness, comments: 'Aurora is a fictional character that he has himself created but . . . he establishes the illusion that she possesses a life independent of his mind, a life of which he is not entirely the master'.[31] How can this be so? The easiest way would be for Aurora to be a historical character like Byron's Catherine the Great, but she is not. The processes involved in reading the last sentence postulate an immediate and easy reference to history and fiction as distinct territories peopled respectively by existences and essences. In so far as Byron emerges as Byron within and without *Don Juan*, conducting us through his partly historical fiction and thus not wholly a fictive device within it (the narrator or 'Byron'), then *Don Juan* itself preserves the familiar demarcations of history and fiction. Fictionalists may react with horror to this, but there must be at least some sense in which writing the poem is recognizably Byron's act[32] just as much as his stylized but actual intervention into Greek politics. The recipients of both (Greeks and common readers) encounter Byron who, though present as stereotype and contained within what appears, is acknowledged in that presence as coming from elsewhere.

Yet Aurora too seems to come from elsewhere. Her origin is mysterious. She is an orphan brought up in a song of Innocence by 'guardians good and kind' (XV.44). She gazes upon Juan and upon the activity within the Abbey as a contemplative outsider who remains in touch with 'worlds beyond this perplexing waste'. Yet it is precisely this 'perplexing waste' beyond Eden's door that is the object of her unillusioned attention.

It has sometimes been suggested that Mr Jaggers in *Great Expectations*, who, it turns out, knows all the characters in the book, and Iago, who is in a way the author of *Othello*'s plot and remains in some unreachable mode of continuance after its conclusion, are mysterious counters to the creative intelligence. They have, as it were, emerged from the other side of the fiction which claims to contain them and, instead, dispute control of it with the author. Aurora is like this but she is a contemplative and not an active presence. Her intelligence is seraphic not destructive. Nor is she simply an essence, for 'worlds beyond this world's perplexing waste / Had more of her existence'. If we ask, a little incredulously, 'where does she come from then?' the answer must be that the whole of *Don Juan* (and much of *Childe Harold*) are concerned with hinting, articulating, and showing the nowhere and the nothingness which remain represented in the life and thought which spring unmediated from them. If this is lapsing into metaphysics more than Byron would tolerate for long, it is so only in manner. Byron is more metaphysical than I am. Aurora is there because Byron very fairly and perspicuously agrees 'that what is, is' (*Don Juan*, XI.5). Critics such as R. F. Gleckner and Brian Wilkie,[33] who get this far but omit Aurora, tell us that Byron was a nihilist. Indeed, as we have seen, we encounter in Aurora the nihilism of her predecessors (Lara, Manfred, Cain) but she wears a smile which, like that of Buddha,[34] denotes plenitude.

The satirical observation of a historical society and the death into life clowning of Byron's blonde duchess, which terminate *Don Juan*, are enabled by and held within the religious circle of that smile. If such a circle is fiction's limit then the myth of the Fall, which is the presiding fiction of limitation for Byron's poetry, is, finally, neither fiction nor limitation.

NOTES

1. G. Wilson Knight, G. M. Ridenour, E. D. Hirsch, Bernard Blackstone, and R. F. Gleckner are amongst the major modern critics to insist on this emphasis, but of course it has always been noted. Lamartine in his early poem dedicated to Byron, 'L'homme' (1819), wrote as to one who understood:

Notre crime est d'être homme et de vouloir connaître:
Ignorer et servir, c'est la loi de notre être.
Byron, ce mot est dur . . .
Mais cette loi, dis-tu, révolte ta justice;
Elle n'est à tes yeux qu'un bizarre caprice,
Un piège où la raison trébuche à chaque pas.

(ll.43–45, 59–61)

[Our crime is to be human and to want knowledge:
Not to know and to obey is the law of our being.
Byron, this is hard to accept . . .

> But you tell us that this law appals your sense of justice;
> It's only, as you see it, a bizarre whim,
> A snare which reason trips over at every step.]

2. *Don Juan*, 'Dedication', 2.
3. *Childe Harold*, IV.72.
4. C. Kerényi, *Prometheus*, trans. R. Manheim (London, 1963), p. 93.
5. Byron offers a parodic version of poetic inspiration as Promethean suffering in *The Blues*:

> *Lady Blueb.* I feel so elastic—'*so buoyant—so buoyant!*'
> *Ink.*   Tracy! Open the window.
> *Tra.*   I wish her much joy on't.
> *Both.* For God's sake, my lady Bluebottle, check not
>   This gentle emotion, so seldom our lot
>   Upon earth. Give it way: 'tis an impulse which lifts
>   Our spirits from earth—the sublimest of gifts;
>   For which poor Prometheus was chained to his mountain:
>   'Tis the source of all sentiment—feeling's true fountain:
>   'Tis the Vision of Heaven upon Earth: 'tis the gas
>   Of the soul: 'tis the seizing of shades as they pass,
>   And making them substance: 'tis something divine:—
> *Ink.* Shall I help you, my friend, to a little more wine?
>   (II.131–42)

6. *Childe Harold*, IV.153.
7. Kerényi, *Prometheus*, p. 93.
8. *Byron's Letters and Journals*, ed. R. E. Prothero (London, 1898–1901), V, 554.
9. *Childe Harold*, IV.142.
10. *The Prophecy of Dante*, IV.64.
11. Byron later projected a similar redirection of a curse onto his Dante:

>   Great God!
> Take these thoughts from me—to thy hands I yield
> My many wrongs, . . .
> (*The Prophecy of Dante*, I.118–20: but see the whole passage).

12. McGann lists these in his edition: see *Complete Poetical Works*, IV, 494.
13. See J. Ruskin, 'Fiction, Fair and Foul', *The Works of John Ruskin*, ed. E. T. Cook and A. Wedderburn (London, 1908), XXXIV, 333:

> Now, I beg, with such authority as an old workman may take concerning his trade, having also looked at a waterfall or two in my time, and not unfrequently at a wave, to assure the reader that here *is* entirely first-rate literary work. Though Lucifer himself had written it, the thing is itself good, and not only so, but unsurpassably good, the closing lines being probably the best concerning the sea yet written by the race of the sea-kings.

Ruskin's original MS attributes Byron's fidelity of imagination here and elsewhere to his 'reverence for the Laws of God and pity for the creatures of earth'.

14. And the sky shows that very ancient gray,
    The sober, sad antithesis to glowing,
          (*Don Juan*, XIV.28)

15. When Juan does, for once, suggest an initiative, he is immediately dissuaded by Johnson (V.43).

16. About this time, as might have been anticipated,
    Seduced by youth and dangerous examples,
    Don Juan grew, I fear, a little dissipated;
          (X.23)

17. We are told in prospect that something 'Occurred' at the end of Canto XII (85), and as we meet Lady Adeline in the second stanza of the next canto we are bound to imagine that she is its occasion.

18. Amongst others, G. Wilson Knight's 'The Two Eternities' in *The Burning Oracle* (London, 1939), A. V. Kernan's *The Plot of Satire* (London and New Haven, 1965) and Bernard Beatty's *Byron's Don Juan* (London, 1985) are exempt from this sweeping castigation.

19. T. S. Eliot, 'Byron', in *English Romantic Poets*, ed. M. H. Abrams (Oxford, 1960), p. 270.

20. Lamartine, for instance, in the same poem quoted in n.1, also positions 'L'homme' by Eden's door:

Tout mortel est semblable à l'exilé d'Éden:
Lorsque Dieu l'eut banni du céleste jardin,
Mesurant d'un regard les fatales limites,
Il s'assit en pleurant aux portes interdites.
          (ll.81–84)

[Every mortal being is much the same as the original exile from Eden
When God banished him from the heavenly garden,
His eyes mark out the fatal limits,
Seated he weeps by the forbidden gates.]

Byron may accept the diagnosis but his heroes won't submit to it; and Aurora, who indeed 's'assit en pleurant aux portes interdites', does so on behalf of 'another's crime'. Lamartine gives us the myth straight but does not quite accept it. Byron dramatizes it less straightforwardly but, far more than Lamartine, seems concerned with its truth rather than its piquancy.

21. In 'Detached Thoughts'; see *Letters and Journals*, ed. Leslie A. Marchand, IX, 46.

22. *Heaven and Earth*, I.iii.461.

23. The imagery that Byron uses here is of very ancient provenance and, detheologized or not, may be found in traditional theology. A Christian neo-platonist like St Gregory Nazianzene writes in the fourth century thus:

Who is it that as yet surrounded by the gloom here below, and by the grossness of the flesh can purely gaze with his whole mind upon that whole Mind, and amid unstable and visible things hold intercourse with the stable and the invisible? For hardly may one of those who have been specially purged, behold here even the image of the Good, as men see sun in water.

(Quoted by R. R. Ruether, *Gregory of Nazianzus: Rhetor and Philosopher* (Oxford, 1969), p. 150)

24. Byron perhaps derived the distinction—as E. H. Coleridge seems to imply in his note on these lines—not from mediaeval or patristic sources but from Bacon's *Advancement of Learning* (I, 28): 'The first place is given to the Angels of love, which are termed Seraphim, the second to the Angels of light, which are termed Cherubim'.

25. 'The word comes from the root meaning "to burn" in a literal sense; the *seraphim* were therefore the "burning ones" . . . this does not refer to the burning of fire, but to the "burning" occasioned by the bites which these demons, who are in serpent form, gave. Thus in Num. xxi. 6 it is said: "And Yahweh sent fiery serpents (lit. *seraphim* – serpents) among the people, and they bit the people" . . . the Israelites regarded these *seraphim* as demons of the waste. In one direction they developed into angelic beings, as we see from the prophet's description of his vision in the well-known passage in Isa.vi; but their original character also persisted . . .' W. O. E. Oesterley and T. H. Robinson, *Hebrew Religion: Its Origin and Development* (New York, 1937), pp. 111–12.

26. The ghost does too but it is, after all, a ghost.

27. *Paradise Lost*, IV.268–85.

28. Juan has experienced them in a ghastly fusion of a different kind in Catherine the Great, which puts paid to Eros in the poem until Aurora Raby re-inaugurates, on a different basis, the possibility of love.

29. *Childe Harold*, IV.147.

30. *Childe Harold*, IV.155.

31. R. B. England, *Byron's Don Juan and Eighteenth-Century Literature* (London, 1975), p. 169.

32. The arguments of E. D. Hirsch in *The Aims of Interpretation* (Chicago, 1976) on this point seem to me unanswerable.

33. Brian Wilkie, *Romantic Poets and Epic Tradition* (Madison and Milwaukee, 1965), pp. 188–226; R. F. Gleckner, *Byron and the Ruins of Paradise* (Baltimore, 1967), passim.

34. *The Island* gives, as we would expect, a more overtly erotic basis for this kind of smile:

> Is love less potent? No—his path is trod,
> Alike uplifted gloriously to God;
> Or linked to all we know of Heaven below;
> The other better self, whose joy or woe
> Is more than ours; the all-absorbing flame
> Which, kindled by another, grows the same,
> Wrapt in one blaze; the pure, yet funeral pile,
> Where gentle hearts, like Bramins, sit and smile.
>
> (II.374–81)

My argument for Aurora Raby's importance in *Don Juan* is developed at greater length in my *Byron's Don Juan* (London, 1985). Charles L. Clancy, in a short but thoughtful article, 'Aurora Raby in *Don Juan*: A Byronic Heroine' (*Keats-Shelley Journal*, 28 (1979), 28–34) says that Aurora is a transformed Byronic hero.

Lyric Presence in Byron from the *Tales* to *Don Juan*

BRIAN NELLIST

Byron's authority as poet is constantly manifest to us in the process of reading his work, yet it seems as constantly to resist not only interpretation, but even description. If a stranger to his work, an unprofessional reader, asks what his poetry is like, then I can tell him or her what happens in *Childe Harold* or *Manfred* or *The Corsair* or even, save the mark, in *Don Juan*. I can describe some of the issues touched on and the shifts of style, but I am always left feeling that my account has missed what is important, more signally than if, with the glibness of a one word answer, I were to reply to a similar question about Wordsworth by saying 'memory' or 'the self', or about Shelley, 'vision', or Keats, 'feeling', which would indeed be crude but not entirely irrelevant answers. With Byron, the poetry leaves me feeling that I do not know what would constitute relevance. Paradoxically, perhaps, that is a kind of answer. It is as though the poetry were written to resist such circumscriptions by what Lawrence calls 'knowing in apartness'. Is 'unknowableness', however unlikely it at first seems, the word I would want then?

This sense that the poetry offers the reader 'too much' is reproduced even in his prose comments upon himself, but an entry from his Journal for 6 December 1813, is significant as a reflection on what he is writing at that very moment:

> God knows what contradictions it may contain. If I am sincere with myself (but I fear one lies more to one's self than to any one else), every page should confute, refute, and utterly abjure its predecessor.[1]

The entry witnesses to its own formulating process. What begins with the apparent accident of a gentlemanly profanity, 'God knows', with immense swiftness is adopted by the mind

and flooded with significance in the very act of uttering it—
that is, 'only God knows—I do not; if there were to be
knowledge of such a process, it would need "God" to know it'.
Similarly, the notion that there may be contradictions in what
he is writing (since he never re-reads the journal, he cannot
know) is overtaken by the insistence that the contradiction is a
moral obligation ('should') owed to sincerity. Yet in the middle
of that thought he is seized by the fear that his mind may be
tidying up the process of thought by lying, which is less what
one says to others than what one does to oneself. No wonder
when it was axiomatic that he is unknowable to himself, he
should have been so suspicious of the public's desire to know
him through his characters[2] and of the identity of being a
writer at all.[3]

To 'know' a Byron poem is a different experience from
'knowing' Wordsworth, then. When I read *The Prelude*, though I
may not be certain of the significance of what I am reading, at
least I know where to look in the poem, which involves not only
recognizing the so-called 'spots of time' and the reflections
upon them, but equally the sense in other parts of the poem that
the failure of insight, or the gradual deprivation of the
imagination's power, in Cambridge, or London, or France,
may be just as important. There is agreement among critics not
so much about the poem's meaning as over where its centres of
gravity in every way lie. But with *Childe Harold*, the closest
equivalent in some ways among Byron's work to *The Prelude*,
there is nothing like this consensus about even where to look in
the poem for its centres. Even if we were to agree, in its last two
Cantos, on some such succession as, say, the Field of Waterloo,
night on lake Geneva, the Coliseum and St Peter's, not only do
these vie with other moments for recollection but, unlike
Wordsworth, Byron himself does not internally specify them as
pre-eminent. It is as though significance overtakes these
moments in the poem from the inside, as in the passage from the
Journal. Place is dependent upon an 'I', of course, in Words-
worth, whereas in *Childe Harold* the 'I' submits itself to a space
that seems to dilate beyond the knowable. Space extends along
almost indefinite compass directions that could stretch beyond
their halting points, West to East in the first two cantos, North
to South in the last two, but in the address to the ocean are

rendered fictive by directionlessness itself. Time likewise
expands from a personal time, first offered at a distance
through the Childe and then more intimately through 'I' and
'me' (though never through memory registered as the locatably
specific), outwards to a time that includes the European past
but, again, beyond that to process itself, almost as the ground of
time, an immeasurable oceanic eternity where man's life is an
unobserved bubble and 'Time writes no wrinkle on thine azure
brow' (IV.182). If the ocean is, as here, made divine—human,
that is, with a brow but without human weakness, not subject
to wrinkles—one may think that if there is a knowledge in the
poem, only 'God knows' it, as he said in the Journal entry.

   If I take almost any stanza from *Childe Harold*, it seems in
reading the poem as if it could provide the centre I need from
which to read the whole poem, and this plurality of possibility
seems not a weakness but a strength of the poem. In short, the
poem is constantly inventing itself, bringing into being the
point of view from which it *might* be conceived but never from
which it *must* be conceived. It lives continuously in its own
presentness and each Spenserian stanza becomes the realiza-
tion of the moments that constitute that present. Time is
overcome, not as in *The Prelude* by a recollection of the past
which substantiates claims for the present, but by a process in
which the configuration of the moving present is always
altering an inconsistently remembered past.

   This conception of poetry as a continuously modified 'now',
a moment that contains its own before and after conceived
from the heart of its own imagining, is close in definition to
what we expect in the lyric mode, in song. 'Song' is a usual
word for all poetry in the period, of course, maybe influenced
by Milton's usage in a signally important moment at the start
of *Paradise Lost* when he projects his poem as 'my advent'rous
song' (*PL*, I.13). At the end of *The Prelude*, Wordsworth
confirms his poem's status as song: 'this Song, which like a
lark / I have protracted, in the unwearied Heavens / Singing'
(XIII.380). Inherent in this conception of song lies its con-
tinuance despite all odds, 'protracted'; it celebrates the very
process of creativity which is vital enough to leave the heavens
'unwearied'. If Wordsworth can claim this at the end of the
flight, it is to confirm what he maintains that his life shows, the

interior power which sustains even so long an individual
singing as this; song is inherent to the song-bird.

The equivalent claim in *Childe Harold* is probably the start of
Canto III: 'it may be, that in vain / I would essay as I have
sung to sing' (4). This is neither Milton's promise nor Words-
worth's recollection, but a precarious potentiality in the middle
of the activity. Moreover, the potentiality is immediately
overtaken by the discovery that it is happening at the very
moment of conceiving it as possibility, 'gaining as we give /
The life we image, even as I do now' (6). It is this constituting
of the poem at the point of its discovery which makes the
process lyric, song-like, in a way different from most of *Paradise
Lost* or *The Prelude*. The poetry in these lines is in the middle of
its own coming-into-being, surprised by its own recovered
potency. The self which is gained lies beyond memory (the life
is always *being* recovered, never steadily there as assumption;
the past tense 'sung' does not guarantee the present 'sing') and
beyond predication by rumour and report (he wants from the
poetry 'forgetfulness' (4) and invisibility as he journeys the
earth (6)). The trust lies not so much in the knowable self as in
what happens on the page when he picks up the pen. The 'now'
is a letting things happen, not an indication as in Wordsworth
of what has happened in the spaces of the poem and the life.

It is this constitution of the poetry at the moment of its
occurrence which seems to be the special mark of lyric as genre.
The very name 'song' involves an analogy with music which
insists more purely than poetry on the succession of moments
which gives it being. This is to assume that, though lyric is
often personal, that quality is not of its essence and indeed lyric
can accommodate itself to any shape or form of subject. The
characteristic brevity, that it is read at one go, seems more its
sine qua non and in literature space becomes time. If the
momentariness of lyric is often personal, that is because it
locates itself within a necessary 'I'. Stanza form reinforces that
sense of brevity as though a whole lyric were composed of even
shorter moments. Lyric is compelled by shortness then into a
kind of instantaneousness, cut loose from the extended process
of argument or reflection, though it may touch on both,
compelled to occupy a kind of present tense, even when
formally it uses the preterite; it belongs in the reader's moment

of comprehension as much as in the poet's moment of imagination. The uncontextualized moment of lyric is manifestly able to absorb other genres, descriptive, discursive, satiric, even epic, but only from the special viewpoint of the momentary. The advantage it offers the poet is that a collection of lyrics can image the metamorphoses of a mind without any individual poem needing to bear the responsibility for the series of changes observed overall. The result of such a collection of lyrics as Donne's *Songs and Sonnets* is to offer an arrangement of moments of affirmation, moments of doubt, often within the same poem, and typically to produce a critical reading that diverges widely in terms of relative weightings.

If that description of what it is like to read lyrics is accurate, then it seems to me to describe also what for me it is like to read a lot of Byron's longer poems. In other words, to read *Childe Harold*, or *Don Juan*, or the tales, is less like reading *The Prelude* and in a way more like reading Shakespeare's *Sonnets* or Tennyson's *In Memoriam*. In the relative brevity of the steady moment, the constant shift of implication from within the consistency of the style, in the refusal to imagine an ending that could be definitive, while at the same time never irresponsibly turning away from resolution, in the rendering of a kind of presentness so that the time of the poem is always becoming my time while I read it, thrusting itself into a 'now', *Childe Harold* seems more like a multiple lyric than it is like *Alastor*, or *The Ancient Mariner*, or *The Excursion*. But if that were so, one might ask what difference this lyricism of Byron would make to reading his poetry and what it would do to Byron's meanings?

To begin with, I think it makes a difference to how we see Byron's supposed digressions. 'Digression' implies a departure from some central subject, but if the centre lies in the poetry's potentiality for ever fresh moments of apprehension, then digression *is* the centre; or rather multiplicity, the preventing of the reader from settling into a single stance, becomes the major business of the poetry. Song is all digression, either because it denies context or because it can seize on any context that life offers and make out of it poetry, as with the lyricism of Ben Jonson. Even in the volume, basically of songs, with which Byron's career starts, *Hours of Idleness* (1808), the verses engage with their own resourcefulness rather than with the attempt to

find a single mode that would be the poet's own centre. Not all
the poetry in the volume consists of what we would ordinarily
call song. There are verse letters, like the lines to Dorset, an
imitation of the enraptured prose of Ossian, satiric epigram (to
'Damaetas'), German balladic tale ('Oscar of Alva'), poetry of
recollection. In fact the *Edinburgh Review*'s notorious critique
hits the mark but misses the point. Attacking Byron's imita-
tiveness, the review adds 'Comparisons (as he must have had
occasion to see at his writing master's) are odious'.[4] The author
is only turning into accusation the open avowal of Byron's own
Preface, 'I have not aimed at exclusive originality, still less
have I studied any particular model for imitation'.[5]

No indeed; instead we have a repertoire of English poetic
styles and subjects since 1740 or thereabouts, often so deftly
achieved that the collection is like a parody history of recent
British poetry. The remarkable strength lies not in the indivi-
dual composition but in the capacity to assume temporarily, to
touch for a moment, so wide a range of possible poetic
responses and styles from the inside. In the absence of a central
voice, the Preface perforce holds them together by yet another
lyric experiment, that of languid and diffident aristocratic
amateurism. It is only 'Jeffrey's' obsessively Whiggish suspi-
cions which could miss the point,[6] that the whole volume is a
digression around the subject of poetry itself, an *eclogue* of
potential Byronic voices, appropriate to a first offering in verse.
The most interesting poem in the collection, where something
close to a new voice is indeed heard, is the farewell to Lord
Clare, significantly the friend always closest to his constant
self. The lyric, which starts as a kind of elegy of separation,
develops into a letter announcing his new identity of love poet.
But this serio-comic claim puts him into the dangerous literary
company of Thomas Moore (Little) whose own love poems
have drawn the wrath of recent critics:

> Poor LITTLE! sweet, melodious bard!
> Of late esteem'd it monstrous hard,
>   That he, who sang before all;
> He who the lore of love expanded,
> By dire Reviewers should be branded
>   As void of wit and moral.
>
>   (ll.43–48)

The sentimental lyric to Clare suddenly turns back on itself and claims gleefully a kind of guilt by association with Moore before the bench of reviewers, almost taunting Jeffrey into the response he so obligingly gave, but in a key outrageously remote from the Lydian measure of the poem's opening. The rhymes have until this point preserved an anodyne decorum typical of the slight sense of ventriloquism in the whole collection—'loved/beloved', 'glow/below', 'hours/showers', and so on—when in a stanza praising melodiousness, we find ourselves faced with the rhyming *force majeure* of *Don Juan*— 'before all/moral'—where, significantly, it is the final word that is pushed into inverted commas by the rhyme.

Here then in a volume which consists so largely of vagrant voices is a quite distinct voice dissolving itself in the apparent redundancy of a digression. The freedom is acknowledged instantly and turned into an instruction to Clare on how to read the volume, which certainly modifies the earlier assumption that he is a love poet:

> Now, [Clare] I must return to you,
> And sure apologies are due;
>> Accept then my concession;
> In truth, dear [Clare], in fancy's flight;
> I soar along from left to right,
>> My Muse admires digression
>
> (ll.67–72)

As we read the page, from left to right, following the flying pen of the author, our own 'soaring' is being mocked by being forced to jump through the hoops of the successive styles of the collection. The muse, we should note, does not command or recommend digression, but 'admires' it, as a kind of exuberant athleticism.

What this kind of lyricism offers is a momentary entry into an experience, projected through its appropriate diction and characterizing reflection, but which claims no finality of affirmation. What the *Edinburgh Review*'s attack provoked was not lyric but the heroic pentameter line of satire in *English Bards and Scotch Reviewers*. Satiric reflectiveness is rooted reactively in time and occasion in a way alien to song. Byron's eager interest in his own times, the time outside the lyric's generation of its own moment, meant that he was always open to satire. Yet the stability of satire's reflections, which nails the casual in the coffin of purpose, came to make him regret *English Bards*, for all its resourcefulness, as a hostage to the past, and even to try to withdraw it from publication subsequently, not an act many poets who had produced so accomplished a poem would do. Later compulsions into pure satire produced his few 'unreadable' poems.[7] Song and satire, then, digression as against coercive continuity, dramatic voice and reflective directness, sustain what Byron is to write throughout his career, and the problem, how to accommodate reflection within the lyric moment, is what I want to examine in this essay.

Unless the lyric poet is to commit himself to multiplying collections of songs like the *Hours of Idleness*, he needs a structure to sustain the maximum flexibility of lyric voice within a continuous process of poetic invention. What Byron finds, which I think is even more significant to him, though not to us, than *Childe Harold*, is the narrative of adventure, the tale. The figure of the wandering outsider in *Childe Harold*, begun in a fiction and completed in a more personal voice, allowed the poet the freedom to see from whatever position he wanted the implication of images supplied by the European journey. The Childe is given a memory only that he may lose it; a past is adumbrated only for him to be turned away from it, so as to exist in a continuous present of ruins, reminders of the past in a continuous present. The adoption of this quest for an absolute presentness by something closer to the poet's voice is both fulfilled and judged by its realization as death, often enough; 'there is that within me which shall tire / Torture and Time, and breathe when I expire' (IV.137). The spirit will tire its torturers but the victory over time is to die into a kind of life— the familiar and intimate 'breathe' is only possible when the breath is given up in the formal and final 'expire', and only then.

The tales take over that process but, by restoring the fictionality surrendered in *Childe Harold*, reclaim a greater freedom. They seem at first unpromising material for a role so important in Byron's career. They were written largely in England during the period of his fame and it might seem as if the outsider of *Childe Harold* had become so popular that in the

tales the Byronic hero has become the enslaved insider of the
reading public. The remarkable thing about the tales, though,
is how Byron can pursue a shifting interest while remaining
apparently at the same point. Internally it was a matter of
claiming different metres for the lyric mode. Starting from the
octosyllabic fragmentation of *The Giaour*, what he called the
'lyric measure' of Scott,[8] he can go on to accommodate the
heroic couplet in *The Corsair*, to reclaim for song, that is, what
he had before used for the dangerous assertiveness of satire.
Jeffrey, getting it right this time, finds that Byron has given it 'a
spirit, freedom and variety of tone . . . of which we scarcely
believed that measure susceptible'.[9] But the very similarity of
their heroes turns the tales into a varied perspective upon an
agreed issue. Scott, Byron's most astute critic, thought the
most remarkable fact of the tales was that their 'interest was
eternally varying, and never abated, although the most
important personage of the drama retained the same lin-
eaments'.[10] The hero changes partly because the lady he loves
puts varying pressure on his identity, from her almost hidden
role in *The Giaour*, through her Juliet-like choices in *The Bride of
Abydos*, to the fierceness of Gulnare and the tenderness of
Medora in *The Corsair*. In this metamorphosis of love we have a
kind of preparation for the key-changes of *Don Juan*. In the tales
Byron is, as it were, composing Goldberg variations on the
theme of the *Liebestod*.

His mind moves fastidiously within an apparently gross
medium. But the spectacular and exotic landscapes, by remov-
ing familiar circumstance, set the stay-at-home imagination
free from its moral moorings, no less than later the locations
chosen by Conrad and Kipling. On the other hand, the raffish
or merely fashionable reader, ready to welcome the freedoms of
such vagrancy, must have been surprised to find the restraints
and laws and guilt to which the apparently daring outlaws of
the tales subjected themselves, or were made subject by the
poet. What had seemed at first in the tales to challenge the
stuffiness of England, offered in the end a form of life that made
received morality empty and unreal by comparison with its
rigour. Sir Egerton Brydges, considering the moral issues
raised by contemporary critics, came to feel that the remote-
ness of the setting removed the action from imitation but

turned it into an image of a certain order of mind: 'the splendour of imagery, beauty and tenderness of sentiment, and extraordinary strength and felicity of language, are applicable to human nature, . . . and convey . . . an impulse which elevates, refines, instructs and enchants'.[11]

It is the lyricism of the tales that makes this possible, since their moments of reflection are never offered as general moral laws by the poet, but as thinking evolved from within the narrative. Delight and promise on the one hand confront dole and blight on the other, the heroes appear to claim freedom of action yet find constraint. The effect is to produce a narrative like the Rubbin vase; we think we see the outline diagram of an urn and suddenly recognize that it is not this central space that controls the picture but the profile of two faces staring at each other from either side of the frame. We cannot see both simultaneously, as we cannot both surrender to the excitement of the exotic tale and to its dissolution of action into problem. To read the tales, then, is to undergo a vertiginous shift in perception; they are written to be easy, apparently, and suddenly turn difficult. By preserving the lyric present, Byron can offer them as graphic structures, leaving us, while we are attending to one interpretation, to be haunted by the memory that there was always another reading possible. If he were to tell the tales not as a present tense but from memory's point of view, with a narrator in command, the vertigo would disappear and he would set up as sage alongside Wordsworth and Southey and Coleridge. What he learned from them which affected *Don Juan* was how eventually to be both inside and outside the story. This refusal to place himself is neither an irresponsibility nor an irritated rebuff to the reader; it is more a continuous recognition that knowledge is not a single thing. The mind, by choosing to know under one set of priorities, excludes itself from knowing by another. But literature might, impossibly, preserve both, by finding a form with the sequaciousness of narrative and the fragmentariness of lyric. It is with this process in the tales that we should now be concerned.

* * * * *

What is it in *The Giaour* which gave such impetus to Byron's imagination that he stays with the writing of tales so long? It is a wild story of seduction, the husband's judicial murder of his unfaithful wife and the lover's revenge, told in such a fragmented way that the poet called it 'these disjointed fragments' in his Advertisement and Moore tells how it

> accumulated under his hand, both in printing and through successive editions, till from four hundred lines, of which it consisted in his first copy, it at present amounts to nearly fourteen hundred. The plan . . . left him free to introduce, without reference to more than the general complexion of his story, whatever sentiments or images his fancy, in its excursions, could collect.[12]

But to tell a strange tale as though it were familiar to the reader, so that it has to be gathered from hints and intimations within the poem, is only an extreme form of the epic formula of beginning *in medias res*, reinforced by influences like the border ballad and even the Heroical Epistle, as in Pope's *Eloisa to Abelard*. Coleridge's *Christabel* is the instance referred to by Byron's immediate predecessors, Scott and Rogers. In his *Columbus* (1812), Rogers, the dedicatee of *The Giaour*, claims he is translating all that remains of a Spanish original, which 'has here and there a lyrical turn of thought and expression. It is sudden in its transitions, and full of historical allusions; leaving much to be imagined by the reader.'[13] Lyric incompleteness turns the reader into a part inventor. In an additional note, Rogers claims 'now and then perhaps the imagination of the reader may supply *more than is lost*'.[14]

But Byron is not in *The Giaour* simply writing a good lay of yet another minstrel with the benefit of Greek scenery. Other than the account of the ambush of Hassan, the husband, by the Giaour in the Mainote wars some unspecified time after the main event, there is almost no action in the tale. Instead action is dissolved into lyric modes, description, elegy, reflection, memory. More than that, we do not as readers quite know where to look. The opening invocation of Greece might be political but presents the country sexually, a woman as inviting love but finding from man only rape, like the flower that 'sweetly woos him—but to spare' (l.57), and then through the analogy with the only just dead, 'Hers is the loveliness in death; / That parts not quite with parting breath' (ll.94–95). Yet the appeal to Greek independence that follows involves now a male imagery, still associated with death however: 'Freedom's battle once begun; / Bequeathed by bleeding Sire to Son' (ll.123–24). What relation does this sexual imagery of the land bear to the tale that follows? The reader's sympathies are constantly being redirected through the sequence of lyric stanzas. The story is told first by a speaker who is a Moslem fisherman, the bystander who sees the Giaour on his horse escaping from Hassan's house and who is forced to take Leila's body to be drowned. Yet this speaker who says of the Christian hero 'I know thee not, I loathe thy race' (l.191), describes the tale as Hassan's sufferings, with the subsequent desolation of Hassan's house. 'The lonely Spider's thin grey pall / Waves slowly widening o'er the wall' (ll.291–92) and associates it with the devastation inherent in the Giaour as 'o'er his soul / Winters of Memory seemed to roll' (ll.261–62). The account of the ambush of Hassan and his men is, moreover, followed by a terrific, specifically Islamic, curse from the speaker. The fisherman's account then subsumes the fate of Hassan to the condition of devastated Greece at the start of the poem, yet does it from a point of view that estranges the Christian reader. But when the scene shifts to the convent where the Giaour has retired, the friar's point of view is again partly estranged from us; the unlikely guest has been accepted for his wealth (l.816). The friar now partly turns the Giaour himself into a fair ruin, like Greece: 'Time hath not yet the features fixed; / But brighter traits with evil mixed' (ll.861–62). When the protagonist himself speaks to the friar he can sardonically, and to the reader alienatingly, present himself as the male liberator of the land from Hassan: 'Thou wilt absolve me from the deed; / For he was hostile to thy creed' (ll.1038–39). Mainly he finds in the loss of Leila, to whom his memory is constant, the cause of an inner wasting presented in terms once again of landscape:

> The keenest pangs, the wretched find
>   Are rapture to the dreary void—
> The leafless desart of the mind—
>   The waste of feelings unemploy'd.
>   (ll.957–60)

The feeling of not feeling and being dead yet alive returns us to the opening description of Greece as dead but not dead in the imagination of the beholder. The dying Giaour's vision of Leila—'I clasp—what is it that I clasp? / No breathing form within my grasp' (ll. 1287–88)—only reinforces that association, though it is Leila who is now the child that dies. This complicated setting of a purely personal story within a partly politicized context leaves the reader baffled as to whether the moribund land is more like Hassan, the Giaour, or Leila. Blame for what happens becomes secondary to the sheer fact of suffering. By not giving us more of a tale, with antecedents and explanations, Byron gives us an unresolvable sequence of destructive and self-destructive passions locked into the sequence of mutual revenge; the Giaour himself at his death sees how easily he might have been Hassan, 'Yet did he but what I had done / Had she been false to more than one' (ll. 1062–63). In the face of such desires, the ruin of Greece seems both a temporarily alterable yet inevitable condition of life itself.

Nothing less than the whole poem can describe the whole course of the action, and the action, through the consequences of revenge, is complete only in the deaths of all of the main characters. Through the succession of speakers the poem becomes a drama, but a psychomachia without any arbiter. Yet if this seems to accommodate the poem to some fashionably open, deconstructed meaning, we should also observe the undeniable exhibition of a stern morality of consequence. The fisherman's description of the Giaour as 'the curse for Hassan's sin' (l. 280) is maybe only piety's interpretation of all disaster, but the Giaour himself admits a language of punishment to the Friar—'I grant *my* love imperfect—all / That mortals by the name miscall— / Then deem it evil—what thou wilt' (ll. 1141–43). This is less an orthodox morality than a belief that the religion of Eros both saves and condemns its adherents who 'In madness do those fearful deeds / That seem to add but guilt to woe' (ll. 1153–54). It is, of course, slightly disingenuous to argue that this self-administered retribution in tale after tale is Byron's tribute to the seventh Mosaic commandment. Nor is it quite a tragic morality since the agents perform their actions wilfully with full consciousness and are seen at such distance anyway. It is more a morality of honour where the code by which the character lives is tested by his willingness to endure every part of its destined career. That the most valuable and powerful feelings are also destructive does not produce a morality of quietism, in the Schopenhauerian manner, but rather a stern resolution that in a world where that occurs, the consequences must be abided for the sake of the action. We are in a continuous present where redemption is impossible.

It is this which makes the use of the present tense so often in the work, and of the past tense largely as the recollection of the characters speaking in that present, so necessary and peculiar in the work. Scott uses the historic present occasionally in his tales. Coleridge uses it in *Christabel* intermittently; but Byron uses it consistently in tale after tale. The historic tenses are used to fulfil the historian's task, to show how things came about. The shifting present of the lyric mode allows only the event, as presently experienced, to offer itself to our eye. Indeed, to reinforce that fact Byron dissolves the narrative into a succession of strongly visual glimpses which make us try to see what the situation is, by guessing at its past and future, from what we see of it at that moment. The most famous instance is the opening sight of the Giaour on his horse, galloping fast but frozen in the eye of the fisherman for one moment: 'Though in Time's record nearly nought, / It was Eternity to Thought' (ll.271–72). The moment of the witness's sight coincides with the moment that determines the hero's life for ever; the feelings it generates do become the Giaour's punishing eternity. But the whole poem is organized round such visual disclosures and we are given no other mode of reflection. In such a cosmos of pain we might expect, I suppose, a greater degree of profanity from the characters that some contemporary readers thought they found in *Cain*, but the strange thing is the absence of blasphemy, the silence. The gods are not invoked with vulgar spite by the Giaour. This Job does not curse even the day of his conception. The intelligence here is not the mind in reflection upon life, an end-stopped process of detachment from action, but lyric thought held within the moment that gives it context.

The Byronic hero becomes in our memory a stable creature, a compound of passion and guilt, misanthropy and hidden warmth of feeling, but from his auspicious birth in *The Giaour* he is not a fixed creature but an instrument used to challenge the reader's simplifications, a figure who shifts in and out of our sympathy to question the nature of sympathy itself. The poetry is therapeutic not as cure but as diagnostic to a reader who refuses to recognize any disease within the reader's own structure of feeling. If the reverse of the sterling currency of respectability is Gothic horror, the Byronic hero attacks the value of both sides of the current moral coin. In *The Bride of Abydos*, for example, the first canto seems to offer a clear domestic image only slightly troubled—a wise father, Giaffir, an obedient daughter, Zuleika, about to be married to the chosen husband, and Selim the unworthy son, apparently indolent, apparently more interested in his sister than he should be, the outlaw again. Yet the domestic paradigm, preserved with only sparse hints to the otherwise in the first canto, in the second canto assumes a different shape. Giaffir, we find, is a concealed fratricide and Selim is the nephew sworn to revenge his father but in love with his enemy's daughter, a combination of Hamlet and Romeo. The idleness we hear about in Canto I is enforced on him by his adoptive father to deny him access to power, but Selim has resisted the embargo by joining the pirates. The story may seem absurd, even if its implications are easy to see, but neither story nor reflection stand in the poem's foreground. As in *The Giaour*, speech, the expression of a life through the words of the distinct characters, is what matters here, the varied voices that the narrative produces. In Wordsworth's narratives by contrast we find little room for the voice. In neither the *Lyrical Ballads* nor *The Prelude* do the characters, like Goody Blake or the wandering soldier, make extended speeches: in the tales, speech functions as *apologia*. The Selim who in the father's account in Canto I seems to blackguard the family, in Canto II in his speech to Zuleika reinterprets domestic propriety and foreign conquest, the father's standards, as a lawless hypocrisy besides which piracy and wandering independence become lawful enterprise. Significantly the long speech of Selim, in a basically octosyllabic poem, slips into pentameter couplets:

> Power sways but by division—her resource
> The blest alternative of fraud or force!
> Ours be the last—in time deceit may come
> When cities cage us in a social home:
>
> (II.434–37)

It is not simply that heroic couplets, with their greater space and Augustan balance, allow such reflection; the Byronic hero himself has a genealogy in Byron's own satiric voice. To question that domestic decency is synonymous with morality or the best human image on offer, as one of the functions of the tale-hero, becomes here almost too explicit. Fraud is the form of power used by those grown accustomed to the cage; it is fraud that invents the rules which make force the only alternative, yet to that even Selim and Zuleika 'may come'; age can turn the outsider into the belonger. No wonder Byron admired Scott.

Yet the point to note here is that this is not after all Byron's voice but Selim's; that the thought is not a generalization, though it tends to become that in the reader's mind, but is called forth within a moment of narrative, when Selim must persuade the daughter to disobey Giaffir, her father. The idea constitutes not a final comment on domesticity by a free spirit, but one among a range of images which has to coexist, with the usual Byronic nemesis, with the fact that Selim's attempt fails. Selim is shot by Giaffir (naturally he would have a pistol ready; the householder will defeat the heroic sword) and Zuleika dies, broken between the two of them: dies also because the gentleness that attracts Selim means that the obedient daughter cannot be transformed within the restraints of the poem into romantic heroine.

How seriously, however, do we take this cock-and-bull story—or, more pertinently, how seriously did Byron take it? Older readings of Byron, that he came to write *Don Juan* out of derision at the excesses of the tales, miss the point that the carelessness and ease of the style makes reading them a very different business from reading more purely narrative poetry. The composition of the poetry is mixed up with the life in Byron: the tales were a tiny part of a busily social existence and were offered as such, as though to guard against any sense that literature belonged to a separate place, to the sober apartness of the study. They offer not a slow meditative pace but what Byron called in regard to *Don Juan* the tiger's spring; 'I am like the tyger (in poesy) if I miss the first Spring—I go growling back to my Jungle'.[15] There are more ways than that of *Don Juan* to involve a suspicion of the solemn cant of literary men actually within the style of poetry; Byron's scorn for the self-engrossing exclusiveness of literature is well known.[16] That friendly critic, George Ellis, in defending the diction of *The Bride* over against *The Giaour*, adds:

> what is read with ease is read with rapidity; and that many beauties of style, which escape observation in a simple and connected narrative, would be forced on the reader's attention by abrupt and perplexing transitions.[17]

The interest still lies in local effectiveness, though the more evident lyric anthology of the earlier tale, 'abrupt . . . transitions', writes the consciousness of that into the structure itself. Coherence of narrative here, however, serves rapidity, as Ellis says, and a rapidity which delays the moment of reflection until the poem is over. Breaking the poem up into separate lyric moments, increased by the movement back and forth between octosyllabics, heroic couplet and different lyric rhyme schemes, reinforces the shock of the double narrative, in Selim's tale-within-the-tale of Canto II. By keeping reflection out (what *is* the author's point of view?) and by making the tale so extraordinary, realizing it in the moments of a past present tense, the tale involves a distancing perplexity within a charge of powerful feeling, as completely, though differently, as in *Don Juan*.

This process is even clearer in *The Corsair* and *Lara* since Byron now deliberately returns to the longer solemnities of the heroic couplet throughout. 'Not the most popular measure certainly', he acknowledges in his preface to the former, and reminding the reader along the way of the, as always, regretted *English Bards*. Nothing could be further from the reflective pause of satiric couplets than *The Corsair*.

> Far as the breeze can bear, the billows foam;
> Survey our empire and behold our home!
>
> (I.3–4)

(almost) starts the poem, with the song of the Greek pirates. The balance of the syntax and control of the caesura might prompt comparison with satire:

> Let observation with extensive view,
> Survey mankind, from China to Peru.

But Johnson's mind in this opening to *The Vanity of Human Wishes* folds in on itself and that scrupulous insistence on the interplay of related meanings—'observation', 'views', 'survey'—slows down the reading even in a couplet so comparatively rapid as this. Byron's couplet playfully moves between that opening 'far' and the final 'home' to make them for sailors the same thing. It cheekily remodels the contemporary sanctions of 'empire' and 'home', subjects of contemporary sea-songs, into the dangerously unknowable place of billows and breezes, and puts that claim not into the mouths of loyal Jack-Tars but a bunch of pirates. Much more is going on in the second line than in the first, but the brisk, cheerful confidence of the first line establishes the tone and the speed of the reading. If we miss the implications at a first go it really does not matter, since the tenor of the whole work will make the point clear.

Unlike a satire, the whole composition is a structure of lyric moments which demand from us the swiftness of mind to respond to the gaps between the paragraphs. The first stanza is a song which we might take as the purest tribute to British sailors, yet the second paragraph starts 'Such were the notes that from the Pirate's isle / Around the kindling watch-fire rang the while', and the pirates who have been 'they' and 'them' in stanza 2 become in the next section 'us' and 'our'. Everything that happens, happens now. 'Hoarse o'er her side the rustling cable rings; / The sails are furled; and anchoring round she swings' (ll.97–98); we see the movements on board the arrived ship as they occur. Even when the verse slips into the past tense as at the start of stanza 7, 'Him Juan sought; and told of their intent', it does so only to get us to the present tense of the conversation of Juan, the lieutenant, with the Corsair captain, Conrad. Story becomes juxtaposed moments.

This is the tale where Byron presents his most extended portrait yet of the misanthropic hero, but he shows Conrad in the present, turned away from the past which is psychological cause to that present; we are tantalized by a story we are never going to be told:

> His soul was changed, before his deeds had driven
> Him forth to war with man and forfeit heaven.

Warped by the world in Disappointment's school,
In words too wise, in conduct *there* a fool;
Too firm to yield, and far too proud to stoop,
Doomed by his very virtues for a dupe,
He cursed those virtues as the cause of ill,
And not the traitors who betrayed him still; . . .

                    (I.251–58)

The Timon shape of this past allows the poet to offer it to us
without further detail; 'oh *that* reason', we say. The manner is
immediately close to a portrait in Pope but the way in which
virtues become vices, 'Too firm to yield', does not like satire
provide a basis for straight rejection. By seeing Conrad's past
only through his present, we become interior to a permanent
habit of mind in him; it is not that he did, but that he always
does, choose to condemn himself rather than his betrayers, out
of a kind of pride. Betrayal would always have to be seen as his
own weakness and this habit of mind cannot be judged by the
reader as purely reprehensible. Indeed the oxymorons force us
to look with suspicion at the term 'virtue' that in satire would
be the source of the criticism; 'Doomed by . . . virtue', 'virtues
as the cause of ill'. The paradox that the man 'Too proud to
stoop' turns out to have been too subject to outside influence,
that the man devoted to the ideal of a strong self-sufficiency has
in being so been 'Warped by the world', all that is simply
present without either the reflective moral discriminations of
satire or the explanatory detail of a narrative past which would
account for it.

   In fact, in this tale even more than in the preceding ones,
Byron allows the assumptions we make about the hero to be
checked. Our willingness to be thrilled by a bold and lawless
violence in the hero is accommodated only by the bare fact that
Conrad is a pirate. Everywhere else our interest in a moral
truancy is checked by finding Conrad, within the tale's given
context, more responsible than we are. If he feels foreboding in
Canto I, before the attack on the fleet mustered to destroy
them, he resists it in the cause of his men: 'Nor shall my
followers find me falter here' (1.314); if, later, mastery is said to
be with him a more powerful emotion than love (1.554), what
we see is less the wilfulness of that than the sacrifice of love to
painful duty—'Ah! never loved he half so much as now! / But

much must yet be done ere dawn of day' (ll.582–83). When in the attack on the Turkish camp the enemy fleet is fired too soon, while he is still at the Pacha's table disguised as a dervish, he 'check'd the first despair / That urged him but to stand and perish there' (II.161–62): Conrad is always stoically ready for sacrificial defeat. The success with which the Pacha's palace is set alight is displaced immediately by further calls on the moral code by which the hero lives: 'A stern delight was fixed in Conrad's eye, / But sudden sunk—for on his ear the cry / Of women struck' (II.198–200). What the eye knows and the ear knows involve different kinds of knowledge which Conrad cannot put together. The man who in Canto I could 'forfeit heaven' by piracy, in the very heat of action produces the betraying words 'Oh! I forgot—but Heaven will not forgive / If at my word the helpless cease to live' (II.207–08), and he goes into the flames to rescue the ladies of the 'Haram'.

By turning the action upon lyric moment, Byron creates in the poem a kind of forgetting in the readers. As we shall see, this tale does incorporate a language of reflection, but the action runs counter to it. The action dramatizes the discovery that the self is bigger than can be contained by memory. Experience becomes the constant meeting with the self as alien, as helplessly beyond knowing-in-advance. The odd consequence for Conrad is that he feels guilty about that condition of being surprised by experience—'Oh I forgot'. The character who was 'In words too wise, in conduct *there* a fool', we remember, is still blaming himself because experience in the event does not measure up to the wisdom of the mind: 'I forgot—but Heaven will not forgive'. It is possible to imagine a stanza of reflection on this in *Don Juan*; the point of the tales is that they will not pause to offer it except through the agency of further action.

How could wise words, for example, be ready for Gulnare, chief lady of the harem, or how could Conrad ever have understood in advance the effect her rescue would have upon her, or do anything about it if he had? The excellence of *The Corsair* lies in its unbearable ironies. Saving Gulnare is an involuntary act to Conrad, yet she, the slave-bride, sees in his supposed generosity the action of the free man and loves him for it. It is Conrad's refusal to see more in her than a woman, with whose safety the security of his loved Medora is in his mind involved, that to Gulnare seems to offer her an intrinsic dignity which the Pacha's possessive (literally so) love never can grant her: 'The Pacha wooed as if he deemed the slave / Must seem delighted with the heart he gave; / The Corsair vowed protection, soothed affright / As if his homage were a woman's right' (II.265–68). The Pacha is still giving a heart, of course, where Conrad only proffers the duty of 'homage', the standard relation of 'homme' to 'femme', punningly. Yet that coolness also offers Gulnare the independence to fall in love with Conrad, and independently to kill her sleeping husband, the enslaver, when Conrad is overcome and thrown in prison. Yet Conrad, bound yet again by a further scruple that prevents him from killing any man asleep, is now further bound by obligation to a murderess, while his thoughts turn to Medora's vision of love totally beyond such bonds of obligation; 'He thought on her afar, his lonely bride: / He turned and saw— Gulnare the homicide!' (III.462–63). The ironies are completed by the discovery on his return that Medora too has, presumably, turned out to be too strong in love and died when she knew him captive. No reflecting voice enters the poem to indicate its connexions, though with that rhyme on 'bride'/ 'homicide' we seem at one moment to be almost inside a *Don Juan* stanza. The implications of the poem are so dense and the movement of the verse so rapid, that it is as though the Juanesque style is on the point of being generated by the poem itself.

The peculiar modification in the language of the tales made by *The Corsair* is the incorporation of many more evaluations of the hero than earlier, perhaps the consequence of using the pentameter line. Conrad, within the narrative, seems more responsible than the Giaour, more reflective than Selim, yet he is more severely judged by the poetry. The result is to replace that interplay of viewpoint in the earlier tales by a more direct address to the reader: are you prepared to accept this reading of Conrad? At the death of Medora we find

The only living thing he could not hate,
Was reft at once—and he deserved his fate,
But did not feel it less;—the good explore,
For peace, those realms where guilt can never soar:

The proud—the wayward—who have fixed below
Their joy—and find this earth enough for woe,
Lose in that one their all—perchance a mite—
But who in patience parts with all delight?
                              (III.628–35)

Two structures of oppositions overlap here. On the one hand there is the poetry's severity of tone, which demands the reader's extenuation; 'hate' is a harsh word to use of a figure whose relationships as we see them, save one, are simply chilled by responsibility. It *may* be right—those who are to us the source of self-imposed duty may become at least resented— but we do not actually see it in the poem. To demand that sort of defence of a figure we never thought to defend is constant in the poem. The other opposition offers us alternatives to Conrad and so substantiates, in a way, the purely verbal undercutting of the hero. The first four lines of the passage involve a *contemptus mundi* placing of Conrad which condemns him: 'he deserved his fate'. Ironically, the only figure in the poem really to articulate this attitude is Conrad, influenced by Medora, and later disguised as the Dervish at the Pacha's table. As usual, his scruple prevents him from joining the feast and breaking bread with the enemy he intends to attack, but in his role of holy-man what he comes out with is, 'Salt seasons dainties—and my food is still / The humblest root, my drink the simplest rill' (II.123–24). So, in this passage of comment on Conrad, instead of 'humblest root', the adventure, the humble exploration offered to 'the good', is only of 'those realms where guilt can never soar'. The alternative account, though introduced with the moral language of 'the proud—the wayward', is really simply an empirical description of life in the world, the *only* alternative to heaven. The necessary expectation that it might bring joy produces the discovery that it is 'enough for woe'. That 'enough' seems to me grimly typical of Byron. He might have written 'And find instead this earth their woe', but that would have been to miss the implicit protest of 'enough'; as though such people would always try to have what the world offered, and if not 'joy' then 'woe' would have to suffice. The one source of joy had always been a 'mite', surrounded by all that woe, but its loss is the one thing that finally cracks even 'patience'. What is odd here is that the language of Christian asceticism does not simply obliterate the other valuation, though it places it, and *vice versa*. The judgement words and the pain words survive to the end of the poem as if the Aristotelian pity and terror could be kept distinct. Conrad is both tender mother and weeping child (III.648–49), or he is both the petrifying stalactite and the steadfast granite (III.677, 673). The reflective language then is turned from authoritative commentary back into a debate in which the reader inescapably must join. We are offered a dialectic without a synthesis, always heading back to what it is we actually see happening in the poem.

Even more than *The Corsair, Lara* seems remote from the passionate lyric fragmentation of *The Giaour*; it does not even have the insistent present tense of its immediate predecessor. But what lyric gave to *The Giaour* stays true for *Lara*; we are enclosed in a series of moments and not allowed to see story from the stasis of reflection or even the security of clear implication. There is no wonder that early readers of *Lara* should have wanted to see it as a sequel to *The Corsair*, though I am puzzled why Leslie Marchand agrees with them—'Conrad, the pirate, now called Lara, was the same brooding lonely man'.[18] There is no hint of such a connexion in the poem, and the letters only indicate that it is the conclusion to the series of tales: 'its very likeness renders it necessary to the others'.[19] An early editor merely comments darkly, it 'has been almost universally considered as the continuation of *The Corsair*'.[20] The mysteriousness of the hero's past, and the insistence on it as key to his identity, assume the power of a riddle to which, however, we are given no solution.

The present of Lara is so fragmentarily revealed, so contradictory, that we seem able to understand it only with a history always implied and never described. Lara's reappearance on his estates after so many years is unexplained, but then so is his leaving them in the first place. What or whom he sees in the midnight gallery that makes this ferociously tough character faint is never disclosed; if it is Sir Ezzelin—and who is he anyway?—then why does Ezzelin recognize Lara so slowly at Otto's ball? And anyway, why does Ezzelin want revenge against Lara? Who is the girl we know throughout as Kaled, the page, who never does anything in the tale and whose female identity is not revealed till the close? The structure of *Lara* seems as though it would be the familiar one of the secret finally disclosed, with earlier indirections but also hints at the resolution, on the model of Balzac's *Sarrasine* in Barthes's account of it.[21] But Byron teasingly offers us only enough of this process to leave us finally aware of what he was not doing. Thus, when we first see Kaled he is described:

> Of higher birth he seemed, and better days,
> Nor mark of vulgar toil that hand betrays,
> So femininely white it might bespeak
> Another sex, when matched with that smooth cheek,
> But for his garb, and something in his gaze,
> More wild and high than woman's eye betrays; . . .
>
> (I.574–79)

The reader's assumed knowledge about women—white hand, smooth cheek—is first used to point in the right direction and then in the wrong, 'more wild and high', with the implication that it is the reader whose ideas of women are too narrow, or that within a woman there may be something 'high' that her eye does not give away. Yet if we conclude from this that the tale's resolution will be in the redefinition of the relation of man to woman, not impossible after all from our knowledge of the other tales, then we shall be disappointed; all that we definitely find out is that Kaled *is* a woman, but who she is, what her relation to Lara consists in, what that has to do with the tale, whether even he knows her sex (but of course he must), we never discover.

Lara is a strange poem therefore. We know for certain about the hero no more than we see, and we are forced, despite all our desires as readers, into the incalculability of the present, forced to reflect only on the present and limit reflection to the feelings, passions, actions, such as they are, lyrically held by that present moment. In 1814 Byron was caught in the compulsions of a social life which subjected him to wild rumour and to contemplating marriage to Miss Milbanke. There may have been relief in imagining another figure invented by suspicion and trying to force the reader to accept Lara only in terms of what we definitely know, though in that case he failed since contemporary readers accepted the suspicion as fact, as they

did with the author. Byron warns the reader in the same way as
Lara does his acquaintances, 'Not much he lov'd long question
of the past, / . . . But what he had beheld he shunn'd to show'
(I.85–91). We are led away from the satisfactions of narrative
and left estranged in a tale we want to read as romance but
where human action is realized instead in terms of envy, social
oppression, homicide, plots and class strife.

Nothing really happens here, compared with the other tales,
except that when Lara's unexplained enemy, Ezzelin, disap-
pears he is suspected of murder and eventually crushed by the
other barons. What we have instead is character as a style of
existence in Lara himself which could involve murder, but
might not:

> He stood a stranger in this breathing world,
> An erring spirit from another hurled;
> A thing of dark imaginings, that shaped
> By choice the perils he by chance escaped;
> But 'scaped in vain, for in their memory yet
> His mind would half exult and half regret:
> (I.315–20)

The erring spirits were thrown into Hell, of course, and the
world of this poem is a place of punishment. But the lines are
also the best description of what it is like to read the poem; we
are forced to live dangerously in it, courting our own dark
imaginings and haunted by them even when the poem does not
definitely confirm them. Our danger is to pursue a kind of
interpretative completeness which in effect condemns Lara as
guilty. The poem produces in us a Cain-like desire for
knowledge, in the same way as Otto's desire to take suspicion
as certainty leads him to destroy Lara.

Two passages in the narrative in particular test our willing-
ness to choose these interpretative perils and risk the chance of
escape. When Lara gives freedom to his vassals in Canto II we
are specifically told that he did this only to gain supporters in
his feud and out of no interest in their political condition itself;
a style of character-blackening like that in *The Corsair*: 'What
cared he for the freedom of the crowd? / He raised the humble
but to bend the proud' (II.252–53). The sentiment could be
confirmed by both Byron's own scorn for radical rowdyism in

Hobhouse and by his making the Doge enter into populist revolution on personally aristocratic terms in *Marino Faliero*. Yet throughout *Lara* there have been intimations of a futile political order, the absurdity of castebound manners among the principals, the use of political words largely absent from the other tales, 'The Magnates of his land' (I.98), 'wealth or lofty lineage' (I.384), the appeal to rank in this challenge (I.474–77), and so on. Suddenly, those minor references are caught up into the foreground of the tale:

> Within that land was many a malcontent,
> Who cursed the tyranny to which he bent;
> That soil full many a wringing despot saw,
> Who worked his wantonness in form of law;
>
> (II.157–60)

In the oppressive land the law itself, by which we might judge Lara, approaches a statutory arbitrariness (though that 'full many' is typical; Byron does not offer the absence of law as itself a law). Whatever the reason, and the explanation only comes later, what we see in Lara is that, 'By him no peasant mourn'd his rifled cot, / And scarce the Serf could murmur o'er his lot' (II.200–01); and in that, see also both the norm and the ineradicable pain, or grousing, of the serf. Has then Lara's refusal to play the aristocratic game, his furious unwillingness to grant Otto his life in the duel, all along included the knowledge of an injustice he scorned to accept? How far back into the poem do we read this discovery? As usual, reflection in this poem demands question instead of answer. If Lara uses the people in a personal battle, and the poetry sees carnage in a cause not understood by the butchered (II.241–55) as clearly as Canto VIII of *Don Juan*, no less do the people use this private war to satisfy their own grudges and desire for booty (II.288–89).

The other dangerous moment for the reader's judgement of Lara is, of course, the conclusion—with its clear indication that Ezzelin was murdered. So Lara was guilty after all, we say; the deed did decide how we see him (I.508) after all. But though the glimpse of the corpse, with the star on its breast, is enough to identify the victim, no such visual detail determines to the watching peasant who the 'dark stranger' is that disposes of the body. The passage ends simply with 'And charity upon the hope would dwell / It was not Lara's hand by which he fell' (II.596–97). We are trapped at the end then by our own desire for knowledge, which would here mean narrative resolution, and a capacity to live with no more than we see, which restores to us the theological virtue 'charity'. If we think Ezzelin's murder too coincidental to allow us to acquit Lara, and the latter's behaviour irrational enough where his dark past is implicated for him to murder Ezzelin, that is scarcely in itself evidence. What is said finally about Kaled involves all the principals; that she has died is certain, 'Her tale untold', as the final line of the tale almost witty in its paradox puts it, but, in her case, 'her truth too dearly prov'd' (II.627). The iambic flow prevents us from stressing the 'her' to distinguish her truth from her master's (lover's) falsity. What we know is little, the tale is untold, and nothing can be gathered from the silence. The alternative is to side with Otto and his neighbours in a community of gossip and innuendo.

George Ellis, who read the poem as a continuation of *The Corsair*, was shocked by the tale into protest: 'the light minded and generous Conrad, who had preferred death and torture to life and liberty, if purchased by a nightly murder, is degraded into a vile and cowardly assassin'.[22] Lara is scarcely generous but then, unlike earlier tales, we do not actually see him very much and very little of him in action. What Ellis more interestingly identifies in *Lara* is a use of changing viewpoint within the poem, which I have argued is inherent in different ways in all the tales, from *The Giaour* onwards: 'Lord Byron seems to have taken a whimsical pleasure in disappointing by his second Canto, most of the expectations which he had excited by the first'.[23] The criticism sounds piquantly modern. Maybe that is why Byron himself had written that the poem should be put last in the series, 'because it is necessary to the others'. Looking back from *Lara* we can recognize how important have been the questions of how we make judgement upon action, what constitutes knowledge of human beings, what significance the past has for the present (much in *The Bride*, little in *The Corsair*), whether moral categories are habits of assumption or principles of insight. He has never done the same thing twice in the tales. In *Lara*, responsibility for the judgement is left to the reader. The generosity of the lyric spirit, which knows no more than it sees, stays like Kaled with what it feels through the authority of the moment, remaining 'true' at whatever cost.

The later tales, with the exception of *The Island*, seem both slighter and on a different tack. We have always known who the hero was in the tales even though what to think of him has remained at issue. But with *The Siege of Corinth*, say, the reader is puzzled to find which character in the poem carries the weight of our gaze. We are adrift between Alp the renegade, Francesca who loves him but stays true to her Christian faith, and finally Minotti, the steadfast father who kills his daughter and then destroys both church and himself to defy the Turks. Yet this shifting focus is held within a constancy to place, Corinth, refracted through a succession of lyric pictures, in the present, at midnight, in the morning, in battle, in the process of becoming a ruin, surrounded by corpses. There is of course a historic context but that is confined to the preface, and from within the poem, as usual with Byron writing tales, history does not explain. In other words, tale here is restored back to its origins in *Childe Harold*, perhaps because the poet had reopened that poem by 1816. This distracting lyric unrest is at its most acute in *Parisina*, though even as late as *The Island* we are subjected to a double hero. In *Parisina*, even more than in *The Siege*, the past relations of the three characters are generated from within their present consequences to leave us both wanting to draw conclusions about them yet finding it impossible to do so. Again, history itself, which might determine sympathies, is placed outside the poem in the prose of a footnote translation. The lyric sequence of the basically octosyllabic paragraphs refuses to compose itself into an account comprehensible to intelligence. This is not to deny the evidence of the poet's mind working strenuously in the verse, but rather to say that the events of it can only be lived through, not intellectually contained in the mind delivering a judgement of Solomon.

If the reader had read the preface, for example, he would have realized from stanza 2 that the love of Parisina is 'guilty'; but the poem does not evolve from that assumption but from the lyric enchantment of love itself—'It is the hour when from the boughs / The nightingale's high note is heard'. It is not under the category of guilt that we follow the movement of the first three paragraphs but as a transit from being outside the paradise of love to full entry for Hugo and Parisina in stanza 3, in a momentary but perpetual present: 'Who that have felt that passion's power / Or paused or feared in such an hour? / Or thought how brief such moments last / But yet—they are already past!' (ll.43–46). In the very moment of defending the lovers' paradise the poetry offers us the past tense it is trying to avoid. The irony that consciousness destroys the very quality that it wants to honour is repeated for Azo in stanzas 5 and 6; the husband who tenderly admits the embrace of the sleeping wife discovers at that very moment the guilty history that destroys the marriage, which contains another guilty history even further back. His son, Hugo, is 'the child of one / He loved' (ll.101–02). For the moment the recession of the tenses puzzles us; 'loved' seems to belong to the historic present, until the eye moves on to the name of Bianca, 'The maid whose folly could confide / In him who made her not his bride' (ll.105–06). Just when historically we seem to have reached the very point of the story in Azo's treatment of his son's mother, the language complicates our dawning discovery by, bitterly and misleadingly, but with a point after all, shifting the gaze to Bianca's 'folly' and leaving neutral Azo's responsibility in the affair, 'who made her not his bride'. What becomes important as the poem proceeds then is how our attention shifts from one figure to the next, not to discover who is to blame, but rather to register different styles of pain. Azo, in condemning wife and son, keeps dragging his words back from the future and suppressing feeling as an irrelevancy to judgement in repeated anacoluthon—'My life must linger on alone, / Well—let that pass'. Whereas, Hugo commands the articulacy of a suffering past: he is the son not a son, child of a deserted mother, whose bride was taken from him by the father, because as base-born he was 'a match ignoble for her arms' (with that terrible play on pride of family, 'arms', against personal feeling) and had to see his intended bride supplant his own mother. Yet in the competition of male voices, setting suffering future against suffering past, it is the stance of Parisina herself, inhabiting this terrible present moment, which is after all the most eloquent:

'To speak she thought—the imperfect note / Was choked within her swelling throat, / Yet seemed in that low hollow groan / Her whole heart gushing in the tone' (ll.342–45). The poem's opening noise of nightingale's high note and whispers of lovers is rendered here in an inarticulate noise of pain, groan and later her shriek, more expressive than the explanations and rationalizing of words, 'Her whole heart gushing'.

That would have been a kind of point of understanding in the poem yet time flows on in it, with Hugo executed and Parisina vanished and the centre now claimed by Azo. All the witnesses have presented themselves as victims, but the final sufferer is the insider, the ruler himself, Azo who takes on Parisina's recognition of a pain, mute and unexpressed. The sons who are the fruit of the second marriage find no feeling from their father:

>   on his cold eye
> This growth but glanced unheeded by,
> Or noticed with a smothered sigh.
> But never tear his cheek descended,
> And never smile his brow unblended;
> And o'er that fair broad brow were wrought
> The intersected lines of thought;
> Those furrows which the burning share
> Of Sorrow ploughs untimely there;
> Scars of the lacerating mind
> Which the Soul's war doth leave behind.
>   (ll.534–44)

As with Parisina, so for Azo the pain transcends explanation or spoken regrets; its language is silence, 'smothered sigh', and the visible signs wrought upon the flesh. Experience is fruitful, yes, but fruitful mainly of pain, through the 'burning share / Of Sorrow'. Characteristically Byron offers the pains of memory, where Rogers wrote of its pleasures. The language of the passage hovers between the specific and the general. We are looking at Azo, but the lines on his brow ('*those* furrows') become the common human fate and its cause ('*the* lacerating mind'). The head does not lead here but picks up the consequences of action and bears the results of 'the soul's war'.

Parisina, like the other tales, consists of a series of self-contained glimpses on the action and each paragraph, as in them, is as long as the mood or the perspective needs it to be, but its angle on the other tales makes it instructive. Since it ends with Azo, we are bound to see in his final state parallels with the earlier heroes; *Parisina* breaks off, as it were, where a poem like *Lara* starts. We for once see personal history which explains how such a character comes into being held by the past but turned always away from it, for whom memory is always pain, who has buried inside him earlier relations with human beings which have been destructive, guilty, condemning and self-condemning, and so how he might be closed off permanently from trust, as Azo is with his sons. Though our interest is partly in the causation, it is also in the end, I think, the condition itself that seems exemplary. We see how human strengths, intelligence, sensitivity in Azo, exist haplessly alongside casual egotism and so become not agents of release but the sources of pain, 'the lacerating mind'. In reading the tale we do not start with the actions that caused it all to happen; so-called causes are discovered only when we experience the supposed consequences. Caution could not be anticipated by Azo—he lives secure till the trap is sprung; it remains the retrospective creation of the moment. Of him we could say what was said of Lara: 'He stood a stranger in this breathing world, / An erring spirit from another hurled', and the 'another' now becomes not only the past as it was once inhabited, with confidence and carelessness; the lost paradise is the assumption that the intelligence, consciousness, is capable for the tasks set it. That is to extrapolate reflection from *Parisina*, of course, which is like the other tales in resisting such moments of detachment, of generalization that breaks from the tethering context. Even to think that life can never be saved from the traps it digs itself is an articulation which, as such, prevents you living out that moment. In *Mazeppa*, the hero's long ride strapped to the horse's back is so rapid that its terror is swallowed up in the succession of experiences and it ceases, almost, to be punishment. At the end of it, by means of it, the page-boy now becomes the Cossack hetman, who is recollecting all this in the moment of apparent defeat and in old age. How are we in such a tale to put rings round punishment and success, to find any sequence that could be called cause and consequence?

This movement in tales like *Parisina* and *The Siege of Corinth* towards the lyric contemplation of multiple-centred narratives might 'explain' why Byron moved on to drama. When each character momentarily becomes the centre of the story, drama is the natural form to offer itself to mind, where each speaker tells the story in their own way, temporarily seizing the stage. Lyric narrative and drama seem historically related forms, as witness the tales of such dramatists as Marlowe, Shakespeare and Dryden. In drama also, reflection is never offered *ab extra* by the poet but as in the tales is born from the moment of action. But the greatest tales, *The Corsair, Lara, Parisina*, can hold together historical condition and metaphysical plight, while in the drama on the whole choices are made and there is both a *Manfred* line of descent and a *Marino Faliero* line.

* * * * *

The problem that more immediately and finally concerns me here is what it felt like to return to verse narrative in *Don Juan* as the poet who had written the earlier verse tales, in many ways so evidently different in character. The popularity of *The Giaour* and it successors when contrasted with the coolness awarded to *Don Juan* by the public prompted in Byron himself a reflection uncomplimentary to the earlier poems: 'as long as I wrote in the false exaggerated style of youth and the times in which we live, they applauded me to the very echo . . . Such is Truth! Men dare not to look her in the face, except by degrees: they mistake her for a Gorgon, instead of knowing her to be a Minerva.'[24] The tales are in the style of youth then and the new voice, age, is that of Minerva. Don Juan himself is the exaggeration of youth and the poem is in a way a new series of tales but uttered through the voice of age. Don Juan is like the hero of the tales seen back to front; if he has little memory, that is a testimony to his freshness of enterprise, not as with Lara or Conrad because he is permanently turned away from the act of recollection: 'But Juan! had he quite forgotten Julia? / And should he have forgotten her so soon? / I can't but say it seems to me most truly a / Perplexing question' (II.208). Juan seems at first the hero bent on cheating circumstance, on not getting lines on his brow like Azo, on being so busy with the moment that even when he does try to remember, pulling out Julia's letter as the ship sets sail in Canto II, present circumstance, even if only *mal de mer*, compels him to forget. The extended reflection in the poetry is only called digression because it is a kind of enormously extended version of the *way* reflection happened in the tales. When Wordsworth, after the adventure with the boat in *Prelude* I, follows with the address 'Wisdom and Spirit of the Universe', the passage is not usually called a digression because the style of the reflection claims to be definitive. But Byron's account of, for example, Juan's forgetting of Julia just cited, is to be followed by a reflection on inconstancy which makes no such claims; the thinking is, maybe, 'very serious and cynical' as Byron said of himself on a much earlier occasion,[25] but it springs from the moment as a parallel variation instead of detaching itself and ascribing its status to a wisdom outside process and time's effect. Reflection in the poem lives the intellectual life in the way Juan lives his adventurous life, true to what the shifting moment discloses; to claim more than that is to stay outside the only true way in which one knows anything. This only seems digression, in the sense of a diversion from the subject or surrender to the stream of association, if you believe that time can be apprehended as other than the succession of moments of which it consists. With all the changes made, the lyric thinking of the tales is still that of *Don Juan*.

The subject and situations of *Don Juan* seem, after all, curiously like the world of the tales revisited. In all the tales Byron's imagination travels East, indeed in the final tale of all, *The Island*, to the furthest East of all, Tahiti and the Pacific Islands. Juan travels from West to East and then as emissary of that East back to the West again. Byron's Western mind tends to make judgements that are political, more immediately conditioned by the actual names and events of history, as in the Venetian plays or the Waterloo stanzas of *Childe Harold*, whereas his Eastern imagination tends either to turn history into a generalized image of enemy, victim, and revenge as in the Mainote wars of *The Giaour*, or seeks an underlying landscape which contains the metamorphoses of the individual lives as in all the tales. It is too crude a summary, but it is as though in *Don Juan* the poet considers the legends of the East under Western eyes, but then travels West to see its political intrigue and pettiness from a gaze requiring a grander, Eastern, perspective.

The Juan who holds these new tales together even follows the sequence of the earlier narratives in a kind of rough order; not exactly, of course, but the discomforted husband of Julia finds a kind of Giaour in Juan, and Haidée is stolen from a possessive father who plays a kind of Giaffir to her and Juan. The Harem adventure has curiously two lovers for Juan like *The Corsair*, one tender, one fierce, though which of them Juan loves is not in doubt; and Juan's relation with Catherine begins to place him at last in something of the same kind of jeopardy with the reader that the tales reach with *Lara*. In the later cantos, as all critics recognize, something strange is happening within the poem and Juan's place in the poem starts to alter. When narrative returns in the closing cantos it does so through the kind of disorientation we find in the late tales such as *Parisina*; there are now three 'heroines', and which if any of them is to be the focus of narrative the tale itself makes difficult to see. It would be grotesque to suggest that Byron is in any way simply retelling the tales but from a comic perspective. My point is rather that Byron's narrative imagination obeys a kind of inner compulsion which means that it will always progress in a certain direction. Lyric narrative cannot be premeditated, but that does not mean that it does not find certain principles inherent in its way of looking at things.

In the tales we are always *in mediis rebus* but *Don Juan* starts from the beginning. That is typical of its method. Nothing shall be hidden. The events of the earlier narratives present themselves pictorially as a succession of images, of discontinuous moments. But in *Don Juan* the sheer detail of the 'now', the plethoric significance of each moment of action, not only for the characters in it, but for the mind of the poet composing it, means that an attempt to see on so grand a scale renders events not less but even more mysterious than they were in the tales. Let me give an instance: when Juan traverses the walls of Ismail in Canto VIII of the poem, amid the hubbub, he meets General Lascy and while the general harangues Juan in German, a language he does not understand, all around them rises the Babel of the battle;

And therefore all we have related in
  Two long octaves, pass'd in a little minute;
But in the same small minute, every sin
  Contrived to get itself compressed within it.
                                              (VIII.59)

If you are telling a story how can you avoid, by the process of
selection needed to tell it, giving, if not an untruth, at least a
selection so extreme that the truth of it goes missing? Even to
locate the story within the limits of the moment leaves the
telling of it baffled and pitches consciousness at the critical
point of what it is you are doing in telling a story at all. The
telling, the 'I' and 'me' of the writing, in this case the 'we', has
become a foreground in *Don Juan* in a way it simply was not in
the tales, and it is the necessary result of that concern to tell the
truth which in the letters Byron found peculiar about this
poem. This truth does not involve turning away from the
momentariness of the tales; rather it means we have to get
further in and allow for the fact that even the moment is not
stable.

The second half of Canto VIII is told in an odd way. 'The
town was entered', Byron says in stanza 60, and the thought
that the fall of a town is a part of its history disgusts him with
civilization as such, enough to allow his imagination a truancy
beyond the American frontier with General Boone; 'The town
was entered', he repeats in stanza 69. But if we thought that
meant victory was secured, again he holds us back with the
furious rearguard fighting of the Turks. 'The city's taken'
sounds more definite in 82, but eventually he adds 'only part
by part' and follows it with the subsidiary tale of the Russian
officer crippled by a dying Turk biting his ankle. 'The city's
taken—but not rendered' is the next version of the formula at
87. The saving of little Leila follows, but then we come to the
Tartar Khan and his five sons; 'To *take* him was the point' at
106, when at 107 'But he would not be *taken*' (Byron's italics).
By 122 we hear 'The town was taken', though its governor
smokes amid the smoking ruins, refusing to admit defeat; and
finally at 127, 'But let me put an end to my theme: / There was
an end of Ismail'. The writing then keeps jerking the reader
back to what is apparently the same moment.

'The town was enter'd', 'The town was taken' are to the

detached imagination of the Gazette, synonymous phrases descriptive of a moment; even in despatches, where truth would be more detailed, how can 'The town was taken' disclose the truth of its multiple meanings? Where is there an end to the unfolding of the 'moment's' significance? Only, in 127, in the need to 'put an end' to the story does that bring the 'end of Ismail'. 'Plain truth' (138) seems consistently elusive. The canto breaks off with the poet worn out by the siege as was the town itself:

> What further hath befallen or may befall
> The hero of this grand poetic riddle,
> I by and by may tell you, if at all:
> (VIII.139).

Once telling the truth becomes the issue it is as though writing itself becomes problematic. The narrative poet describes events as though they have happened, but really he is concerned with a future he is inventing, what 'may befall', as he chooses where to send his hero. That 'if at all' is the greatest riddle of all. Just as Byron has ended the account of the siege because he wanted to end his theme, so here he could simply let the poem lapse, though this dangerous moment comes in the middle of a stanza that ends with Don Juan going off to St Petersburgh with the despatches.

But this means more than that the lyric propulsion of the poem is kept going simply because, in a sense, Juan's insatiable wandering saves the poet from a kind of nihilist despair. On the contrary, I believe, it is precisely the dangerous sense that the song may at any moment fall apart which creates in the poet the need to find something that does hold the moments of the narrative together. In the tales, that sustaining power had been partly the sense of nemesis that overtakes each hero in turn. In the poem whose 'truth' depends upon the presence of the writer, 'nemesis' would mean not so much a disaster overtaking the hero, as a changed status for the hero in the poem, so that the writer presents him to us in a different way.

That change happens about this point in the poem. The love affair with Catherine the Great in that case becomes not primary cause, not what 'hath befallen', but what 'may befall', to find a reason for the poet altering his presentation of Juan.

What is Juan doing on the field of battle at the start of Canto
VIII? With Johnson he is 'Firing, and thrusting, slashing,
sweating, glowing, / But fighting thoughtlessly enough to win'
(19). The almost erotic energies of that first line are, of course,
'fighting' and fighting 'thoughtlessly'. To the accidental man
who accepts the lyric contingencies of life this moment is
enough and 'thoughtlessly' renders innocent again what looks
at first a misapplication of life's energies.

> But Juan was quite 'a broth of a boy',
>   A thing of impulse and a child of song . . .
>   (VIII.24)

The problem is whether it is quite enough by this point to be 'a
child of song', whether to swim one moment 'in the sentiment
of joy' and then 'if he must needs, destroy' may not need
something more constant than impulse, to account for it. To be
precise, the issue of Canto VIII is not, I think, simply a matter
of a pacifist tract against battle as such; that is the instance
maybe, but the problem is greater. To find life caught between
the rhyming of 'joy' and 'destroy' is the fate also of the heroes of
the tales. What we have seen in Canto VIII is no solution to
the problems posed by a life in moments but an anxious
recognition that there is a problem and a desire to hold that
problem steady, even if to do so almost dissolves the poem into
exhaustion, riddle, mockery, dismay, and whatever 'I by and
by may tell you, if at all'.

Canto VIII has been the first time in the poem other than
the shipwreck, and the two events are cognate, where the
narrative context has seemed bigger than the hero and his
priority has been displaced. In the Norman Abbey cantos,
what displaces him seems not more urgent than his life but less
important, as though a hero could be swallowed by compara-
tive triviality of event. Choice and a ground for choice is the
only basis from which impulse could be guided. The choice
would be not only for Juan himself but for the poet thinking of
what 'may befall'. Hence, narrative by the end of the poem is
discovering a context focussed upon Juan again but recogniz-
ing different possibilities inherent in the choices between Fitz-
Fulke, Aurora Raby and Adeline. That choice confronts not
only the hero but the reader and the poet. When the poetry

says, of Adeline's motive in wanting to keep Juan from considering Aurora as a possible wife, "'tis easier far, alas! / To say what it was not, than what it was', that seems significant of the direction of the lyricism of the whole poem. But it is not a complacent scepticism which goes on surrendering easily to the moment. It involves an exemplary refusal to simplify causation but a refusal also, at some cost, 'alas', to remain content with not knowing. By the end of the poem Byron has passed beyond the suspension of knowledge that brought the tales to an end with *Lara*.

NOTES

1. *Byron's Letters and Journals*, ed. Leslie A. Marchand (London, 1973–82), III, 233 (hereafter cited as *LJ*).

2. 'Some Observations upon an Article in Blackwood's Magazine No. xxix, August 1819', in *Lord Byron, Selected Prose*, ed. Peter Gunn (Harmondsworth, 1972), p. 336.

3. *LJ*, II, 175; IV, 92–93; V, 177; XI, 47.

4. J. O. Hayden, *Romantic Bards and British Reviewers* (London, 1971), p. 187.

5. *Byron: The Complete Poetical Works*, ed. J. J. McGann, volume 1 (Oxford, 1980), p. 33.

6. Although Byron thought the article was by Jeffrey, it is now attributed to Henry Brougham; see J. A. Greig, *Francis Jeffrey of the Edinburgh Review* (Edinburgh, 1948), pp. 149–50.

7. Bernard Beatty, *Byron, Don Juan and Other Poems* (Harmondsworth, 1987), p. 55.

8. *LJ*, III, 141.

9. Cited in *The Works of Lord Byron*, ed. T. Moore (London, 1832), IX, 335.

10. Cited in *Works*, ed. Moore, X, 24.

11. *Works*, ed. Moore, X, 141.

12. Thomas Moore, *The Life, Letters and Journal of Lord Byron* (London, 1866), p. 179.

13. *Poetical Works*, ed. E. Bell (London, 1875), p. 54.

14. Ibid., p. 92; my italics.

15. *LJ*, VII, 229.

16. *LJ*, VIII, 41.

17. *Works*, ed. Moore, IX, 255.

18. *Byron: a Portrait* (London, 1971), p. 168.

19. *LJ*, IV, 165.

20. *Works*, ed. Moore, X, 19–20.

21. Roland Barthes, *S/Z* (Paris, 1970).

22. *Works*, ed. Moore, X, 45.
23. Ibid.
24. *LJ*, IX, 173.
25. *LJ*, I, 241.

The Orientalism of Byron's *Giaour*

MARILYN BUTLER

Orientalism is a major theme of English Romanticism. Much, even perhaps most, of the best poetry of Byron and Shelley is set between Greece and the Hindu Kush, a region which in their day signified the crumbling Ottoman empire and the insecure overland route to British India. This was the Debateable Land between a Europe locked in a war involving at one time or another every major state, and the supposedly wealthy empire and trading monopoly which Britain had secured in the East. The geographical significations should be taken at face value, since these are materialist poets, for whom the place of a poem's setting means what it says, and the time is always in some sense the present. Hazlitt came to view Byron's contemporaneity as a reproach: 'his Lordship's Muse spurns the olden time, and affects all the supercilious airs of a modern fine lady and an upstart'.[1] John Hamilton Reynolds thought his friend Keats scored over Byron by getting away from specifics of time and place. Keats 'does not make a home for his mind in one land—its productions are an universal story, not an eastern tale'.[2] Whether these two are right about the value of what Byron did, they are surely not wrong as to the fact. Whatever the East came afterwards to represent as an abstraction—a paradisal religious region of the mind for German academics, a place of sexual release and fantasy for French artists—in English culture in the Napoleonic war period it is also the site of a pragmatic contest among the nations for world power.

When Byron left England for the Mediterranean on 2 July 1809 he surely expected the focus of his trip to be more European than *Childe Harold* I and II, considered as a single poem, actually is. He visited exotic lands now fallen into slavery, but showing symptoms of heroic resistance: first Portugal and Spain, afterwards Albania and Greece. Colourful freedom-fighters, present-day equivalents of Scott's highly saleable Border rievers and Highland chieftains, must have been the bait that took Byron initially to the Iberian peninsula. After the French invaded Spain and Portugal in 1807, some of the Spanish peasantry rose against them in the spring of 1808, and were supported that August by the landing of a British army. Byron a year later arrives not quite as a tourist, more as a literary type of war correspondent, an early Hemingway. The whole of *Childe Harold* I and II in its original form, most of it written in Greece between 31 October 1809 and 28 March 1810, has the stamp of investigative journalism, in which the poetic reporter looks for signs of rebellion and (since he is highly partisan) satirizes the natives when, as in Portugal and Greece, he finds them supine.

For Byron the exercise is decidedly not designed to help the British war effort. Conservative intellectuals had rushed to make capital for Britain out of these uprisings by peasants against the theoretically democratic French. Wordsworth in *The Convention of Cintra* and Coleridge in *The Friend* both extolled the Spanish people for confirming Burke's view of human nature as *naturally* religious, traditional, socially bonded to a little platoon rather than to the abstract concepts of liberty and fraternity. Liberals like Byron and Francis Jeffrey were correspondingly embarrassed by Spanish resistance to the French, which had to be acknowledged as popular, but was also rightist, Catholic, and ideologically uncongenial to them. Byron contrives to dilute the topic in his first two Cantos of *Childe Harold* by placing it in a wider context and even trumping it with the yet more glorious possibility of an uprising in Greece, the spiritual home of liberty.

Significantly, Byron was not alone in linking the Spanish struggle with matters further east. Three of the most serious older poets then writing, Landor, Scott and Southey, all chipped in with works on the Peninsula, managing to choose the very same episode, which had a hero, Don Roderick, who could claim to be the father of all Spanish freedom fighters through his resistance to the Moorish invasion in the early eighth century. The subject was made obvious by its analogies with recent events at the Spanish court. The Moors were invited into Spain by a traitor, Count Julian, as an act of revenge after his daughter, la Cava, had been raped by Don Roderick. King Charles IV of Spain, or his Prime Minister Manuel de Godoy, the Queen's paramour, made the Treaty of Fountainebleau which in 1807 brought the French into the Peninsula. Still, and perhaps by chance, by the time Landor published his tragedy *Count Julian* (1812), and Scott and Southey their long narrative poems on Roderick, in 1812 and 1814, the fact that they were describing the Islamic occupation of a Christian country looked up-to-the-minute for a quite new reason. It became increasingly likely that there would be a war of liberation in the eastern Mediterranean, and there, in Greece, the religions of conqueror and conquered were as they had been in eighth-century Spain.

Southey, the most hawkish as a war poet of these three, was also the last to publish, so that his *Roderick, the Last of the Goths* had less topical impact than most of his work. Already by 1809 Southey liked to represent war with Napoleon not simply as a fight against an alien despotism, but, more popularly, as a Christian crusade of later days. In July 1811, when Byron got back to Britain, he found plenty of signs of a more resolute war policy than when he had left, and signs too of a vigorous Evangelical campaign in favour of proselytism in the East. It was in relation to India that the Evangelical pressure-group known as the Clapham Sect first mounted the campaign that for Wilberforce even outdid the abolition of slavery as a national moral crusade. Hitherto it had been the policy of the British East India Company, strongly supported by Parliament, to leave the Indian social structure undisturbed, or if parts were defunct, as was the case with Hindu law, to revive them. It was a cornerstone of Company policy to respect the spheres of influence of Hindu and Moslem religious leaders. But as long ago as 1792 the Evangelical Charles Grant, a servant of the Company first in India, now at its London headquarters in Leadenhall Street, wrote a tract which challenged the old policy of religious coexistence not merely on religious but on moral and social grounds. Writing for the minister under Pitt responsible for Indian affairs, Henry Dundas, Grant argued that Hinduism was not, as Warren

Hastings and William Jones had argued in the 1770s and
1780s, a social creed rooted in immemorial village customs
which also found expression in an indigenous code of law. In
fact the laws of Manu, a code on which Jones as chief justice in
Calcutta expended immense labour, were, Grant asserted,
chaotic and in their origins despotic, an imposition on the
populace from above. The 'cruel genius' which pervaded them
was the ethos of Hinduism, and it encouraged fraud, lying and
the abuse of people of inferior caste.[3]

Grant's long paper, though not published until admitted as
evidence in the parliamentary debates of 1813, was circulated
in India House and Evangelical circles in 1797, and frequently
seems to have been echoed in the first decade of the new
century, as Grant's Evangelical faction struggled for control of
the London end of the company's affairs. From 1802 Southey
took up the campaign to allow Christian missionaries in among
the Indian population, initially in reviews for the Dissenter-
owned *Annual Review*, then in 1805 in his epic *Madoc*. The epic
first took shape in 1794 as a romantic tale of a twelfth-century
quest to the New World in search of social and religious
freedom—a historical analogue to the pantisocracy plan—but
Southey revamped it extensively between 1803 and 1805. The
final version makes a strong case for the mass conversion of
native peoples where, as in pre-Conquest Mexico, their own
religion was cruel and oppressive. Southey's Mexico worships
a serpent cult served by priests who practise human sacrifice
and keep a cruel despotism in power. It is a paradigm of a
socially unacceptable religion which has close resemblances to
Grant's portrayal of Hinduism in 1792, for both these analyses
of religions concentrate on their impact on the welfare of the
common people, what Grant called the tendency of Hinduism
to forge 'a life of abject slavery and unparalleled depravity'.
Indeed, in an article written a year before his Hindu epic, *The
Curse of Kehama* (1810), Southey draws attention to the simi-
larity between the two religions: 'Except the system of Mexican
priestcraft, no fabric of human fraud has ever been discovered
so deadly as the Braminical'.[4]

The Curse of Kehama is an extravagant Gothic epic about a
wicked Hindu rajah, or would-be emperor of the world, an
eastern *alter ego* of Napoleon Bonaparte. We meet him at the

funeral of his son, who was killed by the father of a girl he was
attempting to rape; a resisting child-widow and several slaves
are flung onto the pyre. After the ceremony, the Rajah uses
supernatural powers (which Hinduism allows bad men to
acquire) to punish the man who killed his son, a peasant called
Ladurlad. He must endure an eternal life in endless pain,
consumed with an inward fire which no natural element, not
air or water or earth, will have the power to cool:

> I charm thy life
> From the weapons of strife,
> From stone and from wood,
> From fire and from flood,
> From the serpent's tooth,
> And the beasts of blood:
> From Sickness I charm thee,
> And Time shall not harm thee,
> But Earth which is mine,
> Its fruits shall deny thee;
> And Water shall hear me,
> And know thee and fly thee;
> And the Winds shall not touch thee
> When they pass by thee,
> And the Dews shall not wet thee,
> When they fall nigh thee:
> And thou shalt seek Death
> To release thee, in vain;
> Thou shalt live in thy pain,
> While Kehama shall reign,
> With a fire in thy heart,
> And a fire in thy brain;
> And sleep shall obey me,
> And visit thee never,
> And the curse shall be on thee
> For ever and ever.
>
> (*Curse of Kehama*, 1810, I, 19–21)

Kehama's memorable curse, given in the languages of folk
poetry and folk magic, symbolizes Hinduism as Grant
describes it, a religion cruel in its ideas and relentlessly
despotic in social practice.

Kehama is eventually defeated by the peasant Ladurlad and

his daughter Kailyal, whose quest takes them allegorically through the experience of religious conversion. Though their final apotheosis translates them to a heaven too doctrinally unspecific to be certainly Christian, they end believing in one supreme Deity who cares for his human creatures, and can intervene on their behalf. Unlike the Hinduism sketched by Grant, and summarized indeed by Southey in a long, violent article in the first number of the *Quarterly Review*, the religion that Ladurlad finds upholds the socially-conserving concept of justice as well as the personally-consoling concept of mercy.

In July 1811 Byron thus found that a topic overlapping that of his new poem—the small Eastern nation absorbed into a foreign empire—had been recently used by a rival poet to advocate a nationalistic religious policy for the British in *their* empire. At first sight it could benefit the Greeks if they engaged the sympathy of a powerful and wealthy stratum of British public opinion. But Byron plainly saw mostly disadvantages in representing Greek liberation as a Christian struggle. One arose from what he knew of Greek politics: in return for religious freedom the leaders of the Greek Orthodox church operated, according to a modern historian, 'as guarantors of the loyalty of the Orthodox populations to the Ottoman empire'.[5] The second was longer-term and more telling. The imminent fall of the Ottoman empire was certain to lead to a scramble for pickings by the Christian European powers, who now in the later war years found the swelling religious revival handing them new moral justifications for annexing Eastern populations. If only to protect Greece's chances of real independence, it was most important for Byron to play down the religious implications of the brewing storm there. Within a month of his return, in August 1811, he sent a new note for *Childe Harold* II, stanzas 3–9, to his friend R. C. Dallas, who was helping him with arrangements for publication. Dallas advised him not to publish it, and Byron agreed; it appears in McGann's new Oxford edition in the version Dallas published in his *Recollections*:

> In this age of bigotry, when the puritan and priest have changed places, and the wretched catholic is visited with the 'sins of his fathers', even unto generations far beyond the pale of the commandment, the cast of opinion in these stanzas will

doubtless meet with many a contemptuous anathema. But let it be remembered, that the spirit they breathe is desponding, not sneering, scepticism; that he who has seen the Greek and Moslem superstitions contending for mastery over the former shrines of Polytheism,—who has left in his own country 'Pharisees, thanking God that they are not like Publicans and Sinners', and Spaniards in theirs, abhorring the Heretics, who have holpen them in their need,—will be not a little bewildered, and begin to think, that as only one of them can be right, they may most of them be wrong. With regard to morals, and the effect of religion on mankind, it appears, from all historical testimony, to have had less effect in making them love their neighbours, than inducing that cordial christian abhorrence between sectaries and schismatics. The Turks and Quakers are the most tolerant; if an Infidel pays heratch to the former, he may pray how, when, and where he pleases; and the mild tenets, and devout demeanour of the latter, make their lives the truest commentary on the Sermon of the Mount.[6]

In 1814, two years after publication, Byron added ten new stanzas to *Childe Harold* Canto II, which focus upon the danger that foreign intervention will lead to fresh enslavement, that the Greeks must free themselves, and that religion is not the issue.[7]

The first of Byron's oriental poems written under the influence of the new, more polarized attitudes to the East was *The Giaour*, composed late 1812–March 1813, published in its first state in May 1813, and added to throughout that year. These dates coincide with the height of the Evangelical campaign to mobilize public opinion behind missions to India, a policy still opposed by the majority of directors of the East India Company as well as by the majority of members of Parliament. It was William Wilberforce, an M.P. of great eloquence and great moral authority, who saw that the Administration and the Commons could not be carried without an extra-parliamentary campaign. Wilberforce organized support not merely among Anglicans and old, respectable Dissent, but among enthusiastic popular sectarians more genuinely given to proselytizing, such as the Baptists, who in the teeth of official disapproval had been sending missions to India for a decade and a half.[8] The campaign worked; the volume and the fervour of public support induced Parliament to include in the Charter Act of 1813 a 'pious clause' which permitted missions to be sent to India and allowed for the establishment of an Anglican bishopric there. Though the practical effects were much slower than enthusiasts expected, the symbolic consequences were great. The secular Enlightenment intellectuals who had advocated governing India by old, Indian ways were now to be steadily driven back by a coalition of middle-class ideologues, Evangelicals and utilitarians, who believed in changing India for something better.

Byron's concept of other nations' independence was that of an Enlightenment intellectual, who respected the autonomy of other cultures, but was inclined to admire them precisely for their otherness, their unreformed feudal 'romantic' features. The decisive shift in the British public's perception of an Eastern population which was signalled in 1813 irked him partly because, like the Spanish uprising, it exposed the fault line in late Enlightenment liberalism, its equivocal attitude to mass movements. By marshalling popular opinion at home, Christians had won permission to go out and teach a populace abroad. Southey, one of the leading advocates of this Christianized and popular form of imperialism, remained Byron's chief literary antagonist throughout his life, and it is of course a great mistake to accept unexamined Byron's portrayals of Southey in *Don Juan* and *The Vision of Judgement* as merely a paid government hack. Southey was the only one of the trio of 'Lake Poets' to remain a genuine populist, the more troubling because by 1810 he was a Tory populist, and Tory populism almost certainly commanded more general British support than 'jacobinism' ever did. His influence, and that of the campaign of 1813, is felt profoundly in *The Giaour*. It is telling for example that Islam in that poem is the religion of leaders as well as followers, and can be illustrated from elegant courtly literature, while Christianity has no spokesmen in the poem but ignorant zealots.

As learned annotated verse, set in part of the Ottoman empire, Byron's *Childe Harold* II and *The Giaour* have often been spoken of as formally indebted to the first of Southey's romance epics, *Thalaba* (1801). Byron does indeed share with this poem by Southey a format, a concern with Islam, and a battery of sources in eighteenth-century learned Western orientalism.

J. J. McGann lists other debts, some of them structurally or textually significant, such as the fragment form, which Byron found in Samuel Rogers's *The Vision of Columbus* (1812).[9] But images, phrasing and formalistic details do not necessarily get to the centre of a poem, nor distinguish it from others, nor explain why it had to be written. *The Giaour* opposes two men who love the same woman, one a Moslem, the other a (nominal) Christian, and it is concerned with their creeds' attitudes to sexual love, to death and to an individual afterlife. In his treatment of the social implications of different religions, Byron often seems to be matching the materialism and pragmatism of his newly evangelized opponent Southey, though Byron's tone remains jeeringly, perhaps by implication snobbishly sceptical, and his political drift is quite different. The argument of this paper is that for its central subject, and indeed for much of its power and urgency, *The Giaour* is indebted to a current controversy, in part outside 'literature' as narrowly conceived, but already reflected in literature. Texts by Grant and Southey, some in verse, represent the ideological attitudes and social interests to which Byron was opposed at a level far more fundamental than his taste for the orientalizing of, say, Beckford.

Unlike *Childe Harold* II, which precedes it, and the Oriental romances to come, *The Giaour*, a love story, appears to have nothing directly to do with Greek independence. The 'Giaour' of the title (the word means foreigner or infidel) tries to save his mistress Leila, a slave in Hassan's harem, from being tied in a sack and thrown into the sea as a ritual, socially-approved punishment for her adultery. When he fails, he joins a band of Albanian brigands in order to ambush Hassan and kill him. In spite of incidental resemblances to (for example) Scott's *Marmion*, *The Giaour* begins very emphatically in the present day and in a mood to reject the romance of history. The first narrator, an educated Westerner, contemplates modern Greeks under Turkish rule, and finds them so enfeebled that he cannot bring himself to tell a story of heroic Greeks in olden times (ll.143–58). At this point indeed his narration fails completely, and we switch to the 'Turkish Fragment' announced in the poem's subtitle, supposedly a popular ballad narrated by a Moslem in a coffee-house. The complex narrational method balances the Western and Eastern points of view and impedes the Western reader from reading Hassan with Western sympathies, since to the Moslem fisherman who witnesses the violent main action it is the Giaour, not Hassan, who is the alien—'I know thee not, I loathe thy race' (l.191). Byron's Oriental tale out-Southeys Southey by being 'naturalistically' anti-Western. This does not prevent him from framing the fisherman in a more educated and cosmopolitan context, or from overlaying his voice with the sardonic commentary provided in Byron's dense, witty and idiosyncratic notes.

Byron's notes, here more personal as well as more generally informative than in any other of the tales, put greater emphasis on the Moslem governors than on the Christian governed, for, in this story of Athens, the native Greeks are virtually invisible. Similarly, though the turbulent, tormented Christian Giaour is the poem's hero, it takes some while for him to become the focus of attention. For at least half the story we are exploring the religion and psyche of Hassan, his Turkish antagonist, and noticing that he is socialized in his world, while the Giaour seems friendless there, except for Leila. The notes convey undisguised admiration for the warlike qualities taught by Mohammedanism—the courage instilled in warriors, for example, by their belief that if they fall in battle they will be welcomed to Paradise by a beautiful woman, or houri. Byron also derives satisfaction from revealing to his readers the dislike with which Christians are regarded in the East. But his respect for Turks does not extend to their regime in Athens, which he roundly abuses—'A pandar and a eunuch . . . now *govern* the *governor* of Athens' (l.151n).

Byron often retains an urbane Voltairean detachment when he writes of the Moslem's conception of the afterlife:

> Monkir and Nekir are the inquisitors of the dead, before whom the corpse undergoes a slight noviciate and preparatory training for damnation. If the answers are none of the clearest, he is hauled up with a scythe and thumped down with a red hot mace till properly seasoned, with a variety of subsidiary probations. The office of these angels is no sinecure; there are but two; and the number of orthodox deceased being in a small proportion to the remainder, their hands are always full.[10]

But this at least is colourful, and thus, like the other Moslem superstitions Byron treats, relatively attractive. The notes are more consistently derisory where they touch on Christianity. 'The monk's sermon is omitted. It seems to have had so little effect upon the patient, that it could have no hopes from the reader' (l.1207n). It is noticeable, too, that Hassan dies consoled by the knowledge that he can expect rewards in heaven because he is killed by an infidel. The sympathetic Moslem fisherman takes pious pleasure from this fact (though Byron ironically defamiliarizes such piety by his sly emphasis on the non-Hebraic, non-ascetic notion of the houris). Mohammedanism performs at least two useful social functions, it seems: to console people and to draw them together. But from the monk who later in the poem attends the deathbed of the Giaour there is no such fellow-feeling. The monk views the Giaour as a damned soul:

> If ever evil angel bore
> The form of mortal, such he wore.
>
> (ll.912–13)

Any possibility of Christian solidarity vanishes when the Giaour rejects the monk's half-hearted consolation and takes over the burden of the narration, with a 'confession' as theologically perverse as that of Pope's Eloisa: he will not hear of a Heaven which omits the sexual happiness he has known and lost on earth:

> Who falls from all he knows of bliss
> Cares little into what abyss.
>
> (ll.1157–58)

In his philosophy it is not the monk's transcendental Deity, but Leila, who is

> My good, my guilt, my weal, my woe,
> My hope on high—my all below.
>
> (ll.1182–83)

In a dying vision which echoes the Mohammedan belief in the houri, he sees the ghost of the drowned Leila. Unlike Hassan, the ungodly Giaour is loath to believe in apparitions, yet he begs her to stay and let him share her fate, even bodily, rather than leave him to enter some future existence without her:

> But, shape or shade!—whate'er thou art,
> In mercy, ne'er again depart—
> Or farther with thee bear my soul,
> Than winds can waft—or waters roll!
> (ll.1315–18)

As a love story, one of those classic late-Enlightenment triangles of the *Werther* type that oppose the free and intuitive behaviour of illicit lovers to the religious propriety of the legal husband, *The Giaour* achieves a greater simplicity and intensity than the tales which succeed it, *The Bride of Abydos* and *The Corsair*. However accidentally it was put together, the effect is elegantly compact. To withhold the Giaour's own voice, to deny us entry to his consciousness, until he comes to utter his fiercely heterodox dying 'confession', is to give him the special status of one speaking from the grave, the domain long since of the only people he has cared about, his mistress and his enemy. As a humane and personal morality, the Giaour's creed is plainly Byron's: he sincerely hates a religion that instructs a man to tie his wife in a sack and throw her into the sea for infidelity. Hassan's pious docility puts him in the same category as two of the Old Testament's Just Men Byron later depicted, Abel, who loves God better than his brother Cain, and Noah, who lets drown the girl his son loves, because she is not on the list of those God wants saved from the Flood. Byron's morality prefers the personal and human to the abstract and divine, a point he characteristically makes by redeeming a character technically criminal through the trait of total sexual loyalty to a single individual. (Women may have this reckless sexual loyalty too, especially in his later work— Myrrha in *Sardanapalus*, Aholibamah in *Heaven and Earth*.) But nowhere perhaps is there a study of the Byronic humanist so concentrated, intense, and personally felt, so skilfully central and unimpeded, as in the last five hundred lines of *The Giaour*, where the intellectually superior hero confronts the dense priestly bigot trying to prepare him for a Christian afterlife.

For all the elaboration of its fragmented format, the poem achieves simplicity through its ferocious concentration on one moral issue—whether love between human beings is not superior to and perhaps incompatible with belief in either of the two great monotheistic religions. The two halves of the poem can be seen in the end as equally preoccupied with this issue. Byron enforces the point by symmetrically ending the first 'Moslem' part with a meditation on the afterlife, first as the pious Hassan will encounter it, then, anticipating the end, as the Giaour eventually should. The Moslem section ends with the fisherman's curse, a pronouncement which rises to the strange fanatical intensity so characteristic of this poem, and, in Byron's perception, of the discourse of religion itself:

> And fire unquench'd, unquenchable—
> Around—within—thy heart shall dwell,
> Nor ear can hear, nor tongue can tell
> The tortures of that inward hell!—
> But first, on earth as Vampire sent,
> Thy corse shall from its tomb be rent;
> Then ghastly haunt thy native place,
> And suck the blood of all thy race,
> There from thy daughter, sister, wife,
> At midnight drain the stream of life;
> Yet loathe the banquet which perforce
> Must feed thy livid living corse;
> Thy victims ere they yet expire
> Shall know the daemon for their sire,
> As cursing thee, thou cursing them,
> Thy flowers are wither'd on the stem.
> But one that for thy crime must fall—
> The youngest—most belov'd of all,
> Shall bless thee with a *father's* name—
> That word shall wrap thy heart in flame!
> Yet must thou end thy task, and mark
> Her cheek's last tinge, her eye's last spark . . .
> Wet with thine own best blood shall drip,
> Thy gnashing tooth and haggard lip;
> Then stalking to thy sullen grave—
> Go—and with Gouls and Afrits rave.
>
>   (ll.751–72, 781–84)

In gloating over the Giaour's hell to come, in the arms of human loved ones, the fisherman ironically anticipates his voluntary dying preference of eternity under any conditions with Leila. But the curse is also a religious statement, though it represents the dark underside of religion, its primitive super-stition and its cruelty. Rhetorically it makes the centrepiece of the poem, though only Byron's note fully reveals how ideologi-cally appropriate this is. His source for the folk belief in vampirism, common to the Balkans and the Levant, is a note to Book VIII of Southey's *Thalaba*, a work which overall main-tains the kindliness and orderliness of monotheistic religions. But the notion of the curse and some of its details, for example the perpetual fire about the victim's heart, also recall the most celebrated moment in the more recent *Curse of Kehama*, where the very same author accused polytheistic religions of a peculiar tendency to superstition and cruelty. (It is strange, all things considered, that the motif of the vampire was released into nineteenth-century Western literature by two competing progressivist critics of regressive religions.)

Poems inevitably take on the ambivalences of the human consciousness in which they are moulded. But, viewed as polemic, *The Giaour* is hardly muddled or likely to be practi-cally ineffectual. The story 'proves' Turkish rule ethically unacceptable to civilized Westerners, without ever showing the Christian church in a more favourable light. The plain fact is that the poem has good Moslems but no good Christians. The poem's villains are the two great monotheistic codes, Christianity and Islam, *comparable* instruments of personal control over the lives of men and women, and potentially of political control by great powers over the destiny of small nations.

Byron's next oriental romances, *The Bride of Abydos* (1813), *The Corsair* (1814) and *Lara* (1814), deal more directly than *The Giaour* with the theme of Greek liberation, but lack its psycho-logical intensity and rhetorical power. Their political contribu-tion is to familiarize a British (and, rapidly, a European) readership with the idea that the fight within Greece would not be led by 'respectable' leaders of society, churchmen, land-owners or wealthy merchants, but by irregulars of little or no social standing, the bandits or 'klefts' in hill country, and pirates on the sea. Rigas Velestinlis (1757–1798) was a real-life revolutionary who was also the associate of bandits, Lambros Katzonis a real-life pirate. Byron alludes to both in his note to

Canto II, l.380 of *The Bride of Abydos*, and, however lightly stressed here, it is of course no accident that all his eastern Mediterranean heroes fight the Turks as either bandits or pirates:

> Lambro Canzani, a Greek, famous for his efforts in 1789–90 for the independence of his country; abandoned by the Russians he became a pirate, and the Archipelago was the scene of his enterprizes. He is said to be still alive at Petersburg. He and Riga are the two most celebrated of the Greek revolutionists.[11]

It must be because of clues of this kind that Francis Jeffrey, reviewing *The Corsair* and *The Bride of Abydos* in the *Edinburgh Review*, suddenly refers in a rather coded, unspecific fashion to the historical probability that modern poetry (like Byron's) will be political:

> This is the stage of society in which fanaticism has its second birth, and political enthusiasm its first true development—when plans of visionary reform, and schemes of boundless ambition are conceived, and almost realized by the energy with which they are pursued—the era of revolutions and projects—of vast performances, and infinite expectations.[12]

But the trouble with these sequels is that in them Byron develops what was probably the most titillating theme in *The Giaour* for its not very politicized drawing-room audience, the hero's terrible sense of sexual guilt and loss. An action presumably intended to simulate a heroic national struggle reads like a trumpery and undermotivated yarn in a colourful setting, a vehicle for a hero who could have been encountered in a Western drawing-room. Byron lacked what both Southey and Shelley had, a positive belief in political change. His difficulty is graphically demonstrated by his love of leaders who have nowhere to take their followers to. His Conrads and Laras are as much strangers, as socially isolated, as the Giaour, and Sardanapalus could have been an admirable ruler, but only if he had not been born millennia before his time. Byron's best sustained nationalist writing is probably in the *Hebrew Melodies*, that collection made direct, accessible, popularly Zionist through being set to the genuine folk and religious music collected in the synagogues by Isaac Nathan.[13]

It was only by chance and in a travestied form that any of the Oriental tales made their way into English popular political mythmaking. Peter Manning has surveyed thefts made of Byron's copyright by the radical publisher William Hone, who began in 1816 by pirating especially the more political, pro-Napoleonic poems of that year. It was not until 1817 that Hone brought out a sentimentalized prose paraphrase of *The Corsair* (for fourpence, in contrast to Murray's edition of the poem at five shillings and sixpence), prompted, Manning suggests, by its sudden notoriety in October 1817. In June 1817 a group of Nottinghamshire working men from Pentridge mounted a protest which, partly through the efforts of government *agents provocateurs*, turned into an uprising. It was quickly put down, and the leaders were brought to trial at Derby in October, charged with high treason. Manning recounts how Byron became implicated in the defence:

> Jeremiah Brandreth, the 'Nottingham Captain', who had in the course of the rising killed a man, was found guilty on the eighteenth [of October], as was William Turner on the twenty-first. Faced with these convictions, the defence sought to exonerate the third man charged, Isaac Ludlam, by arguing that he had only 'Yielded to the overpowering force of their extra-ordinary leader.' No doubt remembering Byron's maiden speech in Parliament in 1812 against the death penalty for this very same class of rioting Nottingham weavers, Denman, a Whig, attempted to establish the irresistible magnetism of Brandreth by comparing him to Byron's Corsair: '. . . I have . . . found him so wonderfully depicted by a noble poet of our own time, and one of the greatest geniuses of any age, that I shall take the liberty of now reading that prophetic description. It will perfectly bring before you his character, and even his appearance, the com-manding qualities of his powerful but uncultivated mind, and the nature of his influence over those that he seduced to outrage.'[14]

Denman proceeded to quote to the court some thirty lines of *The Corsair*, including the description (I.179–82) of the 'spell' Conrad cast over his followers, but the tactic failed, and Ludlam was condemned along with the other two. In November, a week after the execution of Brandreth and the others, the papers were full of accounts of the prosecution of the radical bookseller Richard Carlile for publishing radical parodies by Hone; in December, Hone himself was on trial for that offence. It seems to have been at this point that Byron's Corsair entered the popular consciousness, shorn of his foreign nationalist specificity, and thus of the characteristics that meant most to Byron and to liberals of his type. Hone's prose love-story preserves little but the invitation to the reader to identify with an idealistic criminal, a modern Robin Hood, an ill-defined, non-socialized focus for political discontent not unlike the modern urban terrorist.

In the long run, Byron was to be successfully attacked more as an anticlerical writer sapping the faith and morals of individuals than as a misleader of the riotous masses. After he left England for good in 1816, a sustained campaign began, not ended even with his death, on the Gothic self-projection perhaps most tellingly pioneered in the vampirish Giaour. Coleridge connects Byron with the subversive Gothic taste in *The Courier* in August 1816. This is that curious, deeply revealing and pregnant passage, afterwards absorbed into the *Biographia Literaria* as chapter XXIII, in which Coleridge, by contrasting Byron's self-absorbed and self-absolved demon-heroes with the properly-punished sinners of Christian literature (such as Don Juan), seems incidentally to have incited Byron to reply with his greatest poem. Lesser critics (Coleridge's nephew J. T. Coleridge, Southey, Reginald Heber) from 1818 mounted an intensifying campaign on his Satanism that led equally logically to the most spectacularly heterodox of all his works, *Cain*.[15]

If *The Giaour* represents the aspect of Byron his religious antagonists most wanted to attack, this is not only because of its protagonist, but because of its wholesale critique of Christianity as a social creed, an instrument of government at home as well as abroad. Byron did not often deal with such topics on a level of generality, but he did eventually return to this one in the mythological tragedy which is also a pre-Shavian comedy, *Sardanapalus* (1821). Here the monarch concerned is a debauchee and a divorcee who cavorts with his mistress in a newly-built pavilion. He also has the misfortune, as a secularist and pacifist, to be king of a nation seized with belief in a divine mission to conquer India. Sardanapalus is thus both the newly-crowned George IV, unhappily cast as leader of a serious, professional, efficient middle-class nation, and the equally déraciné Byron, whose role in the public limelight requires him to take up uncongenially responsible positions. A study of a post-religious consciousness, *Sardanapalus* is the most complex and searching of Byron's self-projections. But it is also the most social and political. In returning to the type of national dilemma he first properly confronted in *The Giaour*, how to determine the goals of government among the sometimes contending and sometimes collusive forces of religion, nationalism and progressivism, Byron if nothing else added a dimension to his studies of private disaffection and existential despair.

NOTES

1. William Hazlitt, 'Lord Byron', *The Spirit of the Age* (1825); reprinted in *Byron: The Critical Heritage*, ed. Andrew Rutherford (London, 1970), p. 269.

2. J. H. Reynolds, review of *Endymion* in *The Alfred*, 6 October 1818; reprinted in *Keats: The Critical Heritage*, ed. G. M. Matthews (London, 1971), p. 119.

3. Charles Grant, 'Observations on the State of Society among the Asiatic Subjects of Great Britain, particularly with respect to Morals, and on the means of Improving It. Written chiefly in the Year 1792', *Parliamentary Papers*, 1812–13, X, Paper 282, p. 66.

4. [Robert Southey], 'Periodical Accounts, relative to the Baptist Missionary Society, &c', *Quarterly Review*, 1 (1809), 194. Cf. Grant, p. 44.

5. Richard Clogg, *The Movement for Greek Independence, 1770–1821* (London, 1976), p. xiii.

6. Byron, note to *Childe Harold*, II.3–9, published in R. C. Dallas, *Recollections of the Life of Lord Byron* (1824), pp. 171–72; reprinted in *Lord Byron: The Complete Poetical Works*, ed. J. J. McGann (Oxford, 1980–), II, 283.

7. Cf. especially Canto II, stanzas 27, 77–83, 89–90.

8. For the controversy over renewing the Company's charter, and especially over the insertion of the 'pious clause', see Eric Stokes, *English Utilitarians and India* (Oxford, 1959), pp. 28ff., and Ainslie Embree, *Charles Grant and British Rule in India* (London, 1962), especially pp. 141ff.

9. McGann, *Complete Poetical Works*, III, 415.

10. McGann, III, 420: Byron's note to *Giaour*, l.748.

11. McGann, III, 441: Byron's note to *Bride of Abydos*, II.380.

12. Francis Jeffrey, 'The Corsair: a Tale and the Bride of Abydos: a Turkish Tale', *Edinburgh Review*, 23 (1814); reprinted in *Byron: The Critical Heritage*, p. 55.

13. For the *Hebrew Melodies*, and especially Byron's concern for the

authenticity of Isaac Nathan's music, see Frederick Burwick, 'Identity and Tradition in the *Hebrew Melodies*' and Paul Douglass, 'Isaac Nathan's Settings for *Hebrew Melodies*', in *English Romanticism: The Paderborn Symposium*, ed. R. Breuer, W. Huber and R. Schowerling, *Studien zur Englischen Romantik*, I (Essen, 1985).

14. Peter J. Manning, 'The Hone-ing of Byron's *Corsair*', in *Textual Criticism and Literary Interpretation*, ed. J. J. McGann (Chicago, 1985), pp. 112–13.

15. For this campaign and its implications for Byron's dramas of 1821, see my 'Romantic Manicheism', in *The Sun is God*, ed. J. B. Bullen (forthcoming, Oxford, 1988).

Beppo: The Liberation of Fiction

J. DRUMMOND BONE

Leaving aside its ottava rima, *Beppo*'s digressive narrative method, frequent use of lists, and almost equally frequent use of bracketed phrases, are three of its most immediately striking formal qualities. Roughly half of the complement of 99 stanzas (really 100, for one should include the note to stanza 46) is concerned with matters not strictly necessary to the plot—43 stanzas in fact, by my count, though there is clearly some area for disagreement.[1] I was prepared to acknowledge as a list some 30 constructions, and this somewhat conservatively, since I was deliberately sceptical of runs of three or, of course, less.[2] McGann's new Oxford edition prints more than 23 bracketed phrases—'more than' because I have only counted what I considered the more interesting examples, though they do form the substantial majority. In terms of the content of the poem, most readers are struck, I think, by the frequency of references to art in general and the mechanics of writing in particular, especially so if these are taken together. I recorded references to art in 14 stanzas, and references to the process of writing in 16, a grand total of thirty instances of some sort of reflexivity. Moreover, there are in addition 19 stanzas which could be said to contain some reference to the existence of language as constructed medium (as opposed, that is, to absolute expression).[3] One could argue then that not far short of half of the poem's stanzas, even allowing for overlap, are in part concerned wih the business of the artist.

If these features characterize the texture of *Beppo* as we read, what effect do they cumulatively produce? It seems reasonable to introduce the critical question this way round in this case since the surface of *Beppo* appears so transparent as to render interpretative criticism redundant. Without interpretation as an obvious task we have rather to ask—not where(-else) one can find the meaning or centre of the poem, and what in the poem's structure leads us there—but simply, what effects do the surface textures produce? I have to admit that the one can look remarkably like the other, since the articulation of response or effect appears as meaning; but a recognition of the difference is crucial, because just such a perception is what enables us to respond with enthusiasm to late Byron.[4]

Let us start with the digressions considered in abstract. Self-evidently they reduce the importance of the plot in the poem by continually distracting our attention from its development. The actual core of the action, taken from the story of the Turk recounted in front of an embarrassed Hobhouse by Pietro Segati and referring rather less than obliquely to the happy arrangement between Pietro and Marianna Segati and Byron himself, takes up a mere 18 stanzas. It would be wrong however to leave it at that. Rather the plot is never allowed to seem central in the first instance—it is either stanza 10 or stanza 21 before it begins, depending on one's point of view, and if 10 it promptly vanishes again until the latter. Nor can it facilely be claimed that somehow the reader has an inbuilt expectation of a plot which is never properly fulfilled, for the genre is far too uncertain for that. It is not so much the avoidance of plot as its introduction which gives *Beppo*'s digressive structure its own peculiar quality. If there is an unfulfilled expectation of plot it is introduced by the poem itself almost subliminally in stanza 10—'at the moment when I fix my story'—and more definitely in 21—'But to my story.— 'Twas some years ago, . . .', and again in 50:

> But to my tale of Laura,—for I find
>   Digression is a sin, that by degrees
> Becomes exceeding tedious to my mind,
>   And, therefore, may the reader too displease—

or in 63:

> To turn,—and to return;—the devil take it!
>   This story slips for ever through my fingers . . .

The poem then from time to time reminds us of what it has not done and is not doing. Stanzas 50–52 in particular could almost be called a digression on the bad habit of digressing. This makes the reader aware of the contingency of what is being read—it could have been otherwise, maybe should have been otherwise. The effect is unsettling in a pleasantly comic way. Comic and unsettling because we have discovered ourselves to be in a different conceptual frame of reference from the one in which we believed ourselves to be—we are the man on the banana skin laughing at his own fall from free-will into the laws of gravity, though here the conceptual direction is the other way round. Pleasant because Byron has provided us with a safety net in that the subject—art—is one which we recognize, though too late to avoid the joke, as being quite at home in a relativistic conceptual frame after all. That is, when we read art as life we expect it (though goodness knows why!) to behave as an absolute system, but when we read it as art we are quite content for it to behave as a relative one.[5] Byron shifts us from the one to the other, and the shift is unsettling, but the landing, already as it were prepared, is soft. It is not a fall into the unknown.

The digressive structure speaks then of relativity—through how the poem could have been different, and is only relatively this or that. It also makes us aware that plot is not the central issue that it might be, and this prepares us for certain features of the ending of the poem, broadly its 'happy' ending and Byron's 'arbitrary' close which I shall discuss below. It qualifies our expectations of final resolution—given the possibility of plot there is the possibility of conclusive, perfect in the musical sense, resolution, but given that that possibility is only sketchily realized, we cannot expect too much. It is this sense of qualification which is conveyed.

Leaving the abstract structure, let us turn to the lists. I shall look first at two rather marginal cases, in the sense that they are barely lists. In stanza 8 the poem tells those who are 'curious in fish sauce' to make sure that before they cross the sea they 'bid their cook, or wife, or friend / Walk or ride to the Strand' and buy lots of their favourite sauces. 'Cook, or wife, or friend' works comically, it seems to me, in two ways, one specific to itself, and the other less concerned with its specific content and more with its abstract structure as a list.

In the first we are struck by the implications of the equation of cook to wife, particularly following the verb 'bid', and then more subtly quizzed by what we make of the equation of wife to friend. The comedy comes from the unexpected associations—or, to put it in the same rather Germanic vocabulary as our discussion of digression, from the shift from one framed set of conceptions to another. This category- or register-shifting is of course one of the standard ploys of satire. In straightforward satire the object is created as believing itself to belong to one category, and is then shown to belong to another. But here the technique seems used as it were for the purely formal pleasure; it would be difficult to assign a satirical object, unless it is the narrator himself, or just the abstract possibility of narrator or reader confusing two categories which are normally thought of as separate.

In the second, more general, way the register-shift is not between one lexical item and the next, but between the expectation of a single item and the number we are in fact given. There is a redundancy or an excess in terms both of grammar and sense—'bid their cook walk to the Strand and buy in gross . . .' conveys the matter every bit as well, or better. The extra details have the irrelevant excess of conversation. That this is perceived as a register-shift is interesting, and somewhat remarkable, but few I think would disagree. It is remarkable because in a poem so colloquially framed as *Beppo* one might have suspected that it would appear as realistic rendering of the spoken manner, only faintly strange in the general perception of this in itself as unusual in highly wrought rhyme. That it does strike us like this is probably owing to the admixture of the specific qualities noted in the paragraph above. As we look at Byron's use of lists we must therefore note that in so far as the technique seems to repeat itself, it is in danger of losing part of its force as it loses its disruptive surprise, unless other measures are taken to support this. In the case of stanza 8 the faintly dotty irrelevancy is extrapolated in the next line in the alternative 'Walk or ride', in the next two by the additional information presented in brackets about forwarding the sauce, and lastly by the climactic listing of the sauces themselves—'Ketchup, Soy, Chili-vinegar, and Harvey'. All of this ensures the humour *because of* the conversational irrelevance, and does not allow the detail to be merely conversationally irrelevant. The question of conversational irrelevance being read *not* as irrelevant, or rather not wholly as irrelevant, but as carrying crucially a surprising shift of conceptual frame becomes of central importance in Laura's response to Beppo's return, as I shall discuss below.

My second preliminary example seems even less of a list than the first, and indeed I counted neither in my enumeration. It appears just two stanzas before the passage above:

> 'Tis as we take a glass with friends at parting,
> In the stage-coach or packet, just at starting.
>
> (6)

Humour is here only a marginal response. If it is there at all, it would derive from the most general and nebulous of the reactions described above, namely that between the context as rhymed poem and the specific content as mundanely conversational. But there does seem to me to be a Byronic timbre to the phrase, not only because of the note of parting. The alternative removes the phrase from the illustrated abstract and presents it as an attempt to be comprehensively illustrative. That is, two or more specifics seem to function in a qualitatively different way from one. Their concrete existence becomes almost more important than their illustrative function. One example is enough to carry the illustration, and given more than one we read the presence of the second as important *per se*, since to interpret it solely as further illustration, unless it is appropriately further qualified, is clearly redundant. The additional illustration, therefore, moves us to respond to the represented thing, rather than the thing as representation. This movement, let us notice, has some similarities to that discussed above, in that it involves a realignment of the reader's expectations, a minor refocussing, in the recognition that the text has become concerned with the concrete and not only with the illustrative. But the transition is not sufficient to be called comic. The direction of the movement, however, towards the particular and material, is of considerable importance, and I hope to convince that it is one of the characteristic sounds of *Beppo*. Talking of sounds, it would be foolish not to remark on the way in which the additional mode of transport allows Byron to produce a symmetrical alliterative pattern—p . . . t/st/p . . . t/st. Rarely, as again we shall see, is lexical diversity *not* underpinned by sonic structure.

From these perhaps marginal but also simple examples let us turn to some of *Beppo*'s more obvious lists. One of the most striking is the list of England's good qualities in stanzas 47–49. This in fact forms part of a long digression beginning in stanza 41 with Byron's reasons for admiring Italy, itself a list though diffused over 5 stanzas, and ending with the digression on digression of stanza 50.

The beginning of the English list turns the poem from high-flown speculation on the poverty of the word when compared to the plastic arts back to the autobiographical particular:

> [Italian Beauty] . . . in what guise,
>   Though flashing from the fervour of the lyre,
> Would *words* describe thy past and present glow,
>   While yet Canova can create below?
>
> 'England! with all thy faults I love thee still,'
>   I said at Calais, and have not forgot it;
> I like to speak and lucubrate my fill;
>   I like the government (but that is not it); . . .
>   (46–47)

The shift over the stanza break is not, however, a disturbing one. Nevertheless, the later stanza does comment quietly on the preceding one, or rather is commented *on* by it.[6] From Italian Beauty which can only be captured by the higher art, we have moved to the beauties of England, and these are introduced as associated rather with mere speaking and 'lucubration', not even with the 'fervour of the lyre'. I take it that the word 'lucubrate' has a comic overtone of excess, and we do of course embark on a list which has at least some of the qualities of the conversational excess we have already mentioned. It is, however, a little difficult to be definite about the usage—OED, unhelpfully from our point of view, quotes this as its contemporary example. The point is underlined by the quotation from Cowper which Byron adopts as his own: *this* is all the lyre can muster in praise of England (in contradistinction to Canova's art and Italian Beauty, let me repeat), and it is further lowered in register by being given an autobiographical setting (removed, that is, from the higher world of 'art'), and further still by it being suggested, in the saying that he has not forgot it, that he might possibly have forgotten it. Byron had initially given the attribution—'So Cowper says—and I have *not* forgot it'—but decided to go for the specific time and place of the autobiographical reference.

The following line also changed in character. There the first thought had been 'I like St Paul's Church and Ludgate Hill', which would have moved the reader immediately into the kind of context now given by the following stanza (48). Byron postpones this by the revision's dual function of referring back to the idea of the previous stanza, and of introducing the long ramble of opinions by way of praise for England's freedom of speech. The satire of stanza 47 at least starts by seeming serious in intent, aimed at the vaunted advantages of British government. But it could not be said to be sharply focussed. The line 'I like the freedom of the press and quill' has no undercutting bracketed comment, as do the preceding and succeeding lines, and the satire of the final line, if in fact it has any aim at all, is directed rather at the speaker than at any institution:

> I like a parliamentary debate,
> Particularly when 'tis not too late; . . .

The satire of 48 is less 'serious', in that the issues it addresses are more domestic, and the satiric purpose is arguably abandoned totally in lines 3 and 4. One might ask again here, in what exactly does the comedy lie? And again the answer would, I think, be that we perceive the list as having lost direction as satire, and now existing only as personal, conversational opinion. What the reader experiences is not, however, primarily the sense of irrelevance, but the sense of the change of context. The modulation starts with line 8 of the previous stanza quoted above, is held in suspense in line 1 of this stanza, is underway again in the first half of line 2, and is completed in line 3. The movement is reinforced by the racy elimination of the pronoun subject of line 4:

> I like the taxes, when they're not too many;
>   I like a sea-coal fire, when not too dear;
> I like a beef-steak, too, as well as any;
>   Have no objection to a pot of beer:
> (48)

Indeed, and not surprisingly, the verse also carries the point: lines 1, 2, and 5 are broken before the undercutting phrase at the perfectly reasonable poetically 'regular' 4+6, 6+4, and 4+6 syllable points in the pentameter line, while line 3 is punctuated to read 5+1+4, though it could be slurred as two phrases only, and line 4 supports its racy grammar with the first uninterrupted ten syllables of the stanza. In other words the change in line-structure highlights the two 'conversational' lines, and when in line 5 we seem to return to the satirical mode, though still very much on the domestic level, the verse returns to its more rhetorical form—by way of preparation in fact for the fireworks of the stanza's concluding lines. Up to this point then—the end of 48.4—the list has moved us not directly but nevertheless steadily towards personal opinion on concrete material objects (if steak and beer can be so described!), which have no relevance to anything other than that personal opinion on them. I suggest that the experience of reading this passage is at least as much an experience of that movement as it is of political or cultural satire.

But of course the list does not end there, and, as noted in passing, line 5 at least returns us to satire, if only on the weather. However, the progression over the remaining lines of this stanza and through the next is actually broadly parallel to the foregoing. The shift once more into the political is smoothed by the symmetry of lines 6 and 8 as glosses on the lines preceding them, while the scattered pauses of 6 and 7, more noticeable against the restored 'regularity' of 5 noted above, hold up the progress of the verse in anticipation of the throw-away ironic indiscrimination of the last line, which also lurches with an extra syllable into the separation of 'every-thing'.[7]

> I like the weather, when it is not rainy,
>   That is, I like two months of every year.
> And so God save the Regent, Church, and King!
> Which means that I like all and every thing.

The list then reaches its climax in stanza 49, lines 1–5, now detailing those 'faults' the speaker is prepared to forgive. In this speeded up enumeration we again start from the 'serious' and progress to the domestic. Of course, it is standard practice in satire to introduce the personal or trivial as a bathetic reduction of the object of satire. Even if not precisely focussed, the existence of the object of satire in a climate of humour has some satiric effect. There is no doubt that this is to some extent descriptive of the way in which this passage works. But it also works by dissolving the satire itself in the multiplicity and increasingly tangential relevancy of the list. From 49.2, where the interpolated 'my own' introduces a note of simple comedy, referring not only to his debt but also his reform, the force of the political attack on Regent, Church and King is dissipated with increasing speed, and it is this dissipation which takes centre stage in 5. This line is another miniature masterpiece of control, worked hard for in revising, in which the 'cl' of 'cloudy climate' is apparently picked up in 'chilly' to carry on the subject of the weather, except of course that the eye deceives the ear and the speaker the expectation of the sense—the subject is sex, and not the weather. The effect of this formal 'failed-symmetry' is to accentuate the apparent inconsequentiality of the logic of the speaker's encyclopaedic list of failings. A logic is as it were postulated but then strikingly avoided.

The ensuing line returns to the 6+4 format, but now the undercutting phrase undercuts the seriousness of the satire, and the sonic symmetry helps reveal the relationship of forgiving political horror and forgetting sexual coldness which devalues the former. The 'accepted' explanation of this as satire is that the reader laughs at the speaker's equation of politics and sex, and in that laughter in fact perceives the seriousness of the former which the poet has ironically devalued. But is 'devalued' in this case the correct word? I rather doubt it. The repeated movement of the poem's rhetoric in the same direction tends to establish that movement itself as the value-generator of the poem. The reader is surprised but increasingly reassured by the speaker's seeming lack of discrimination of register. At least part of our response here is not satire arrived at as it were through the speaker's naivete, but rather a delighted acquiescence in the collapse of categories. 'Devaluing' is barely to the point, but something is certainly happening to the distinctions upon which values are based.

Our list is brought to a full close with the emphasis of two lines both opening 'And . . .'. These apparently tie up the loose ends of both the satire and the grammar, though in fact in the latter case this is rather more appearance than fact, trailing on as they do after the stanza's main verb in line 6, 'forgive'. They do, however, bring us back to the political issue, if in a bewilderingly complicated way, still owing a lot to our recognition of this as a recognizable conversational sentiment, but scarcely an argued case. To cut the knot and somewhat state the obvious—we are to be left feeling that either he does *not* venerate what he calls 'our recent glories'; or if he does, then he feels that good has by chance sprung from ill. How far the reader experiences an identification with or an understanding of the poet's point of view here, and how far he 'merely' experiences an understanding of the speaker's way of feeling, seems to me to be a real question. I should certainly like to emphasize the latter as a possibility—that what we read is pleasure at the illogical position in which the speaker finds himself, and that we do not read this as 'merely' anything, but as a perception of value.

I have not explicitly mentioned in the above the nature of the 'identity' of the first person singular, but it will have become clear that this is an ambiguous matter. In 47.2—at Calais—the speaker can reasonably be identified with the historical Byron himself. Elsewhere there is a distance between the speaker as producer of irony and the speaker as apparently 'unconscious' carrier of that irony, though of course self-irony depends on just this projection of a transparent naive mask, and this is no reason to introduce the concept of a 'narrator-character' interposing between the historical Byron and his story. The problem, if it is a problem, occurs throughout the poem, of course. The 'I' who does not 'believe the half' of Beppo's stories is clearly in one sense at least fictional, as in a different way is the 'I' of '. . . if I once get through my present measure, / I'll take another when I'm next at leisure'. The 'I' who thanks God that at least Turkish women do not 'deal in mathematics' is, however, clearly a very close relation of the Byron of the biographies. For the first person singular to function it only has to refer to a set of characteristics which are not flatly materially self-contradictory—they can be as intellectually self-contradictory as they like and more or less still not disrupt the grammatical function. This is more easily seen in the usage of the third person, where for example we are quite used to seeing slippage in a novelist's use of free indirect style. But it is also almost equally feasible in the first person. This is not to say that the slippage, in either case, goes unnoticed, but it does not lead to the question 'what is the truth of the pronoun's identity?'. We react to the change in much the same way as we react to the change of register discussed above: that is, the appearance of the autobiographical 'I' is mildly comic in itself as a disruption of the expectation of fiction and of the narrator's sometime apparent objectivity; and this moves the text from the representative to the particular, making it seem to partake more of the casual and occasional than of the planned and inevitable.[8]

I intend to treat one other major list-like structure at length—Laura's gabble of questions—but for the moment turn our attention to some other more manageable examples. The technique is brought to our attention by three notable examples in the first three stanzas of the poem:

> The people take their fill of recreation,
> And buy repentance, ere they grow devout,
>   However high their rank, or low their station,
> With fiddling, feasting, dancing, drinking, masquing,
> And other things that may be had for asking.
>
> And there are songs and quavers, roaring, humming,
> Guitars, and every other sort of strumming.
>
>   Masks of all times and nations, Turks and Jews,
> And harlequins and clowns, with feats gymnastical,
>   Greeks, Romans, Yankee-doodles, and Hindoos; . . .

In the first two cases the major effect lies in the comic bathos of the sexual innuendos as climax to the lists. Apart from anything else this establishes a major fact of the poem—that in the end, as here at the conclusion of these stanzas, and with particular irony in the 'farewell to flesh', everything comes down to sex. In all three cases the lists produce the sense of fertile multiplicity which characterizes the Carnival. This is helped by the randomization of the lists—thus fiddling is separated from dancing by feasting, and feasting likewise from drinking by dancing. What takes precedence over organization by sense is organization by sound—most obviously the alliterative pairs in this case—and this produces the odd sensation of liberation from the conventional way of looking at things combined with the pleasure of feeling that the now apparently uncategorized can in fact be fitted into a pattern. Thus the sound patterns both help reveal the random organization of the content and create a fresh pattern themselves. It is as if the components of the list were freed to be solely themselves, and yet in a different dimension unfold from one to the other a new pattern. This is an effect related to, but not the same as, the shift of lexical register. The shift here is from lexis as the prime categorizer to sound. A similar if less striking process can be heard in the second example, the penultimate line of which again caused Byron some thought.[9] In the last example it can almost rather be seen than heard in the pairing of Yankee-doodles and Hindoo. To sum up this abstract account then: the reader does not experience randomness, but does experience the sense of a multiplicity of things surprisingly allowed to be only themselves; and does experience the humour of a category shift, but not a shift which has any definable content. Always remembering nevertheless that there is *also* in the first two cases the more usual 'surprise' of the sexual ending.

Sound patterns are not just a matter of alliteration, of course, and in the above examples we find the pre-echo of the 'd' alliteration in 'fiddling', the weak rhyming of the entire line after the first word, and the double-rhyme 'masquing'/'asking'. The second example is more subtle, with echoes forward and backward in the 'r' and 's' of 'quavers' (at least with a rolled 'r'!), and the rhyming only in the last two words, though again setting up the double rhyme with the next line. In stanza 10—

> For dance, and song, and serenade, and ball,
> And masque, and mime, and mystery, and more
> Than I have time to tell now, or at all, . . .

—the effect of the increasingly obvious sound patterning is thrown into further relief by the enjambement of 'more/Than', which not only enacts the idea of overflow, but also deflates the growing expectation of some climax to list and sound, by leading it into the next line only to abandon it. In stanza 71—

> Their days are past in doing nothing,
> Or bathing, nursing, making love, and clothing.

—the awkward double rhyme sets off the comic equation of making love and making clothing, while from 'doing' onwards the lines are strung on the (as we have seen common) '-ing' rhyme, with the second line itself enclosed by the '-athing/ -othing' variation of its double first and last rhymes. In this case the disparateness of the activities is, I think, actually part of the line's effect (that is, one feels not that they are separate and by chance together but that they are actually incompatible). This disparateness arises partly out of the contrasting absence of sound pattern other than the '-ing' rhyme in the central portion of the line.

Now, clearly this kind of sound manipulation does not occur only in lists, and it might be said indeed to be itself one of the characteristic devices of *Beppo*. What I would like to suggest is that it characteristically plays a role which is complementary to that of the list, or if one prefers, vice versa. The general tendency is to substitute formal pattern *or* unexpected existential pattern for expected existential pattern. In both cases the reader's normal taxonomy of experience is comically displaced, and in the former case it is replaced by a system which does not seem to have any *meaning*, though in so far as it *is* pattern it is perceived as significant. Moreover, in the latter case the characteristic movement is in fact from class to particular. The result of all this is to free items from both their representative and constructive function—they no longer stand for their class nor are primarily means towards a larger structure of meaning—and to allow them to stand in their own particularity. At the same time, to repeat, partly because of the various abstract patterns, this particularity is not perceived as disintegration.

If the foregoing has to any extent convinced, it will be easy to see that in this context the device of the bracketed phrase will tend to function in something of the same kind of way. Like the list it intrudes on the text with information which might seem 'irrelevant'. Frequently what it contains shifts the category of what has gone before it, usually in the direction of the material or the materialistic. To emphasize these general tendencies is not to deny the specific satirical effects in most usages. It is simply that the repeated process of these usages produces the characteristic colour or tone of the poem, and this overall colour or tone is at least as much the poem as the individual brush stroke or note.

The bracket takes the place of the dash we find in Byron's letters, and correspondingly loosens the syntax. This, on repetition, becomes noticed as an effect-in-itself. The grammar of Byron's letters and of the ottava rima poems is characteristically appositional. In fact this could easily be said of much of *Childe Harold* and the Turkish Tales as well, the difference being that the sense in the latter tends to gloss over the grammatical looseness, whereas in the prose, and in particular in *Beppo* and *Don Juan*, the sense underlines the grammatical disjunctions. Up to a point this might be more accurately described the other way round—that the grammatical disjunction serves the disjointed sense. But as the structure takes on the recognizability of a trope, this effect can be at least momentarily inverted, and the dash or bracket waves the flag of its own reappearance, signalling the poem's freedom from grammatical restraint as the poem's very essence—for the instant. Differing degrees of this effect can be seen in stanzas 52, 58, 77, 83, and 98, but it has to be emphasized that the effect is cumulative, and that by the time of this example in 52 there have been at least 17 previous bracketed phrases:

> But I am but a nameless sort of person,
>   (A broken dandy lately on his travels)
> And take for rhyme, to hook my rambling verse on,
>   The first that Walker's Lexicon unravels. . . .

The interjected gloss bobs along on the ideas of 'broken' and 'rambling', and helps create that sense of the random, but its very appropriateness transforms the random into the free. This effect is emphasized by the variety of the structure's repetitions. To be more precise, the effect is the sense of the random surfacing of structure, and of this randomness being transformed into freedom as the expression is recognized as a (repeated) structure. Of course, this example exaggerates all of this by its reflexive content, making the reader hyper-conscious of its faux-naïveté.

There is less obviousness in 58, where the punctuation is strikingly reminiscent of a Byron letter in full flood:

> They went to the Ridotto,—'tis a hall
>   Where people dance, and sup, and dance again;
> Its proper name, perhaps, were a masqu'd ball,

But that's of no importance to my strain;
   'Tis (on a smaller scale) like our Vauxhall,
     Excepting that it can't be spoilt by rain:
The company is 'mix'd' (the phrase I quote is,
   As much as saying, they're below your notice);

Once again the conversational tone springs from the self-proclaimed irrelevance—the 'that's of no importance' immediately being followed by an equally unimportant gloss parallel to the first (''tis a hall . . . 'Tis (on a smaller scale). . .'), only made more irrelevant by its excess of qualification—'on a smaller scale . . ./Excepting that . . .'. But the irrelevance is conditioned by the recognition of the figure, and of course a degree of explicit self-awareness does reappear in the next line, where the bracketed phrase reveals the presence of euphemism as a figure used to give expression to, yet at the same time to conceal, snobbery. The revelation of the figure of course not only renders it ineffective, but makes us aware of the shiftiness of language, and aware of the poem's awareness. It is this last which helps us read the disruptions and quick turns of thought—well, scarcely thought—in this stanza as the spaces of freedom rather than the emptinesses of 'mere' conversation. Note that the 'serious' satire of the last line and a half is carried in the same kind of aside as the irrelevancies earlier in the stanza. I am not denying the social point of this satire, but I do want to suggest that its vehicle also has significance for our response to the texture of the poem beyond the particular case. Whether the sense is irrelevant or pointless or neither, the awareness of the bracketed aside as a tactic is an awareness of freedom in the linguistic moment—though it is recognized as freedom and not randomness by it being perceived as a variation of a repeating structure. As I have said before and shall have occasion to say again, explanation can very easily distort by its very explicitness. What the reader experiences is a feeling of freedom. The 'linguistic moment' does not come into it—the feeling is empty of content, but full of value.

However, it is only too easy in analysis to ride one's hobby-horse. The effect I am detailing is more noticeable in cases where either some reflexivity is involved or where Byron calls to our attention the relationship between the narrator and the known biography of the poet himself. I put it in this tortuous way deliberately in order to avoid the deceptive clarity of identities, which only produces the will-o'-the-wisp search for certainty discussed above. The comic effect we have noted in 78—'Nor deal (thank God for that!) in mathematics'—or even in 83—'And then I looked, (I hope it was no crime) / To see what lady best stood out the season'—comes from the uncertainty of whether we are dealing with a character who is contained wholly within *Beppo*, or whether with one who also exists elsewhere. In so far as the method of the aside contributes to this uncertainty it also contributes to that sense of dizzying disregard for categories. The categories in question are essentially formal—part of our matrix for reading. Thus the biographical interjections function in roughly the same way as those referring to the process of writing. But there are many cases where this effect is minimal, really only present in so far as any case adds to the sum total. The example of 'mix'd' above is clearly an example of a common satiric technique—an unlooked-for explanation which reveals an unquestioned act as valueless or immoral. Another would be the second line of 98:

> His wife received, the patriarch re-baptized him,
>   (He made the church a present by the way);

Here the bracket really works only by marking off the relevant 'explanation' through presenting it ironically as an aside. The real 'bracketed phrase' effect in this stanza comes in the last phrase following the dash, '—but *I* don't believe the half of them', which gratuitously as it were places the whole storytelling operation in doubt.

It would at least be fair to say that there is an obvious analogy between the digressive narration and the grammar of the bracketed phrase. As well as their particular places in local structures, they produce a sense of freedom and of multiple possibility in the narration of the poem taken as a whole.

This might be the moment for a short pause to list the suggestions of my description so far. The digressive progress of the narrative initiates the reader into the possibilities of plurality, and prepares us for inconclusion. The lists continually disrupt our categories of comprehension, and seem to work against category without substituting chaos. The bracketed phrases are also disruptive and also usually suggest that all is not what it seems. Both suggest that the pleasures in encyclopaedic particularity are of more value than the pleasures of intellectual coherence. The identity of the first person pronoun is fluid. Various kinds of sonic structures work against the disruptiveness of subject and grammar, though in doing so they may also ironically emphasize it. All of these devices then have effects related to each other. We need to be aware, however, that in this general categorization we are going against the tendency of the devices we are categorizing to value the particular and even the material over the general and the intellectual. The poem's characteristic movement is from the abstract to the particular, whereas our analysis, perhaps inevitably, wants to move in the opposite direction.

The last of the poem's textural features I noted in my first paragraph was its interest in art. This could be subdivided—as in paragraph one—roughly into three: art in general, writing in particular, and 'difficulties' with language. I shall take them in reverse order.

Frequent references to the mechanics of language give the reader a growing awareness of the medial quality of the stuff of communication. It is not a given absolute, but depends upon interpretation and is thus necessarily contingent. The gloss as a satiric figure can produce this sense as a by-product, but only in a context which already suggests it. The example of 'mix'd company' is a case in point—the poem's 'the phrase I quote' certainly does make explicit the mechanics of what is going on, but it could barely be said to make that explicitness the main object of the communication, and if it is present at all it is because there is a context which alerts us to it. Similarly, in stanza 6 'the Carnival, which being / Interpreted, implies "farewell to flesh" ' helps to presence language per se, but the main impact is clearly satiric by way of irony. On the other hand,

> The gentle reader, who may wax unkind,
>   And caring little for the author's ease,
> Insist on knowing what he means, a hard
> And hapless situation for a bard

is here in 50 essentially being reminded that what he is presented with is an artifice with its own difficulties of construction. The humour of stanza 1, ' 'Tis known, or at least it should be', also really arises out of the surprising refusal to take the phrase simply—it is revealed as a cliché, a kind of empty clearing of the throat. The poem opens with a qualification of its own opening words, and this is itself comic in its immediate moving of the poem from the register of authority to that of uncertainty—assuming that one agrees that poetry is provisionally at least in the authoritative key. It also of course announces the qualified and the provisional as in the musical sense a theme for development.

In stanza 2 this gesture is made more narrowly linguistic in aim in the unpicking of the cliché 'dusky mantle':

> The Moment night with dusky mantle covers
> The skies (and the more duskily the better)

Again there is the refusal to take the phrase at its accepted value, and it is the gesture of refusal, rather than what is revealed by it, which has the main impact. Another similar example is to be found in 28:

> 'Tis said their last parting was pathetic,
> As partings often are, or ought to be . . .

As McGann points out,[10] there is subtle comedy with specific reference in this stanza, but here the humour lies once more in the qualification of the cliché—and the effect lies in this process of qualification and not primarily in the fairly trite scepticism which is the lexical 'meaning'. And again this is to a more than marginal degree dependent on surrounding constructions of a similar kind.

There are numerous examples of concern with the successful and otherwise workings of language. In stanza 5 the issue of Italian versus English is first raised:

> And even in Italy such places are
>   With prettier names in softer accents spoke,
> For, bating Covent Garden, I can hit on
> No place that's called 'Piazza' in Great Britain.[11]

This uses the familiarity of place names in London in contrast with Italian exoticism to devalue the London places, and riding on the back of this devaluation attacks the pretentiousness of calling the Covent Garden square a 'Piazza'. But it also detaches the name from the place and the accent from the word and there is gentle humour too from this allowing of meaning and form to free-float. The being of the places is put in the same conceptual frame as the enunciation of a name, which has the odd effect of potentially separating them, and it is this potential separation which comes as a surprise. This explanation is necessarily cumbersome; the effect described is light and indeed lightening. This implied separation of form from meaning is found in other musings on Italian. The Count knows

> Music, and dancing, fiddling, French and Tuscan;
> The last not easy, be it known to you,
> For few Italians speak the right Etruscan.
> (31)

Though the fact is accurate the effect is to give the reader a peculiar sense that native speakers have not mastered their own language, and in this comedy again lies a separation of language as meaning from language as spoken form. Forms of language are again under scrutiny in 37:

> The word was formerly a 'Cicisbeo,'
> But *that* is now grown vulgar and indecent;
> The Spaniards call the person a 'Cortejo,'
> For the same mode subsists in Spain, . . .

The phrase is now 'Cavalier Servente' in 'politest circles'. This discussion contributes once more to the reader's awareness that in *Beppo* the mechanics of speech are easily detachable from the meaning with which they are normally thought to be identical.

I cannot emphasize too much, however, that my account of this process not only in its length and insistence but also in its abstract quality actually violates that which it is trying to explain. The reader of *Beppo* is not being asked to speculate on the ontology of language, nor indeed to 'speculate' on anything. Rather the poem produces a sense of delightful and multiple particularity. The linguistic digressions have something of the quality of a collector's savouring of a cache of his peculiar obsession. We have noticed this too of course with the lists, and indeed the brackets also have in their cheery intrusiveness the sense of a delight in encyclopaedic detail. The process is one of diffraction, one might say. The forms of language are teased loose from their content in order to be delightfully displayed. It is the delight which the poem communicates, not the disjunction nor even the elements themselves. Relish reaches some kind of climax in 44:

> I love the language, that soft bastard Latin,
>   Which melts like kisses from a female mouth,
> And sounds as if it would be writ on satin,
>   With syllables which breathe of the sweet South,
> And gentle liquids gliding all so pat in,
>   That not a single accent seems uncouth,
> Like our harsh northern whistling, grunting guttural,
> Which we're obliged to hiss, and spit, and sputter all.

But the pressure to be open to this device, if one can call it that, is there in all kinds of locutions, reminding us of the facts of language alongside the facts of life:

> Stopp'd by the elements, like a whaler, or
>   A blundering novice in his new French grammar
>   (61)

> . . . for fear the press
> Should soil with parts of speech the parts of dress.
>   (57)

The self-reflexive references to the business of composition are probably the most treated aspects of *Beppo*. Though it would, in my view, be quite wrong to isolate them as a kind of 'key' to some 'meaning' or other which the rest of the poem is designed to conceal, taken together they do reinforce the effect of the references to language. The reader is made aware that what the normal convention of reading presents as given fact can be seen as more or less arbitrary artifice. The mechanics of the poem are separable from the content:

> And so we'll call her Laura, if you please,
> Because it slips into my verse with ease.
>   (21)

Oh that I had the art of easy writing
What should be easy reading! . . .
(51)

This story slips for ever through my fingers,
Because, just as the stanza likes to make it,
  It needs must be—and so it rather lingers;
This form of verse began, I can't well break it,
  But must keep time and tune like public singers
(63)

There are many other examples, and one might note in particular stanzas 50 and 52 which I have quoted above in other contexts. A recognizable texture is apparent: 'several oaths (which would not suit the Muse)'; 'and that's the cause I rhyme upon it so'; 'as I have said, / Some six and thirty stanzas back'; 'One hates an author that's all author'; 'My pen is at the bottom of a page'; and so on. There is also the stanza 'note' to stanza 46.[12] This self-reflexiveness amounts to another category shift—what we normally regard as reality or a representation of reality is revealed as fiction. Presented in this way this could be the material of despair or cynicism—a world view which sees life's value as *mere* fiction. But of course this is not what emerges in *Beppo*. On the contrary, the writer's intervention as writer is felt as gently, liberatingly comic. Why, or rather, how? Partly because it exists in the context of the other qualities we have described. These condition us to read each in terms of the shared quality of 'liberation from'. Partly, too, because the personality of the writer is insisted upon. This provides the reader with the comic safety net. It is not a question here of *all* life necessarily being 'fictional', only of *this* particular set of circumstances surrounding the person of this narrator. Or so the fiction of the insistent first person pronoun can make us believe. But there is also a characteristic wistfulness about these passages. In this the reader feels not the loss of epic reality, but rather the sense of effort involved in the making of fiction. This seems to me crucial to the experience of *Beppo*. It is this sense of effort and only relative success which gives value to the life of the text. The writing of *Beppo* is not presented as a business of resigned cynicism, but as a gentle effort with necessarily limited success. This feeling, together with the freedom of its ease of movement, permeates the moral being of the poem. Look at stanza 63 quoted above, or 51 and 52, or of course the last stanza. All enact the breach of the convention of fiction as reality by discussing the limitations of fiction in the necessities of its form, either intellectual or, as in the last stanza, simply physical. The fiction of the text may be free from the hypocritical convention of reality, but this does not mean that it is a shapeless chaos, nor is it easily come by. And all this is presented as a personal struggle—and that is almost too emphatic a word—with particular material.

Some of *Beppo*'s most famous stanzas deal not with writing but with the other arts, or the arts of performance. Once again they provide a pervasive background colouring. Italy is festooned with vines 'much like the back scene of a play' (41), and the poem has a similar backdrop of things artistic. Laura at the Ridotto is

> Fresh as the Angel o'er a new inn door,
>   Or frontispiece of a new Magazine,
> With all the fashions which the last month wore,
>   Coloured, and silver paper leav'd between
> That and the title-page . . .
>   (57)

On a somewhat higher artistic plane, though possibly not much, the Count is a connoisseur of the opera and the Improvisatori, and could

> . . . himself extemporize some stanzas,
> Wrote rhymes, sang songs, could also tell a story,
> Sold pictures, . . .
>   (33)

All of this sets the scene of sophisticated Venice, a society of the arts and of artifice. It also provides an ideal vehicle for satire on the pretensions of society at large. The fiction in Shakespeare's *Othello* lies not in its suspicion of women but in the melodrama of poor Othello's reaction. This is not the way people actually behave—rather:

> When weary of the matrimonial tether
> His head for such a wife no mortal bothers,

But takes at once another, or another's.

(18)

The reaction of the hero in the play is here the 'natural' one, whereas that of the Venetian is 'artificial'—and the fact that the play itself contrasts Othello's innocence with Venetian sophistication provides an added richness. These usages, however, establish a general ease of movement between art and life. We have another recognizable figure. Note that we cannot say that the boundaries between art and life are dissolved, for if that were true we could not appreciate the movement across the boundaries as unusually easy, or indeed as anything. Dissolving, perhaps, but dissolved, no. Artifice, art, and life interpenetrate the same existential and moral plane. Venetian society is full of artifice, but the Carnival is in fact the last place where the needs of the flesh are forgotten. On the other hand, 'decent', 'natural' behaviour seems to have intellectual sham and hypocrisy built in.

Two of the most famous examples of artistic reference come between stanzas 11 and 15, and in stanza 46. The Venetian women have pretty faces

> Such as of old were copied from the Grecians,
>   In ancient arts by moderns mimick'd ill;
> And like so many Venuses of Titian's
>   (The best's at Florence—see it if ye will)
> They look when leaning over the balcony,
> Or stepp'd from out a picture by Giorgione
>
> (11)

The comparison of beauty with classical art is no more than a cliché. But there is a distinctive quality in the comment 'copied', and in the further elaboration 'by moderns mimick'd ill'. These emphasize the material as opposed to the expected ideal qualities of art, and the point is underscored by the plural 'Venuses', sounding faintly comic no matter how accurate—or rather, *because of* its factual accuracy. The culminating thrust of this movement comes in the bracketed phrase, which shifts us resolutely from the ideal world of Grecian beauty to Murray or Baedecker. It is the particular and material which is surprisingly found in the conventionally ideal, and, as in the linguistic examples discussed, the means are at least as emphasized as the ends. But this barely has the effect of reminding us of the Venetian women's artificiality, if at all. It simply sets up an amusing dialogue between the two aspects of art—amusing in the awkwardness of the juxtaposition of the two categories of material and ideal involved. Not, let us note, a dialectic, but a dialogue.

This dialogue continues over the next three stanzas:

> Whose tints are truth and beauty at their best;
>   And when you to Manfrini's palace go,
> That picture (howsoever fine the rest)
>   Is loveliest to my mind of all the show . . .
>
> Love in full length, not love ideal,
>   No, nor ideal beauty, that fine name,
> But something better still, so very real . . .
>   A thing that you would purchase, beg, or steal,
>   Wer't not impossible, besides a shame . . .
>
> One of those forms which flit by us, when we
>   Are young, and fix our eyes on every face;
> And, oh! the loveliness at times we see
>   In momentary gliding, the soft grace,
> The youth, the bloom, the beauty which agree,
>   In many a nameless being we retrace,
> Whose course and home we knew not, nor shall know,
> Like the lost Pleiad seen no more below.
>
>   (12–14)

In the first stanza quoted we notice again the brackets from Baedecker, as well as the possible implications of the balancing of 'beauty' and 'truth', though in the contemporary usage of Byron's circle these were probably readable as virtual synonyms.[13] The second stanza starts materialistically, and proceeds to become almost shockingly so—particularly in that word 'thing'. But the third turns us immediately from 'thing' to 'forms', and from the substantiality of consumer goods (as it were) to transience in the terms 'flit', 'at times', 'momentary', 'gliding', and even 'soft grace'. This is a strange balance of the ideal presenced—the lost Pleiad for a moment visible if not capturable by naming—and of the existence of the ideal precisely *as* transient, all the while of course apparently claiming that it is still the real and not the ideal which is being described. The words 'One', 'fix', and the suggestion of static composition (in eighteenth-century terms) in 'agree', serve to insinuate the feeling of permanence in the passing moment (as I have written elsewhere[14]). The effect of all this is to come close to eliding the difference between the real and the ideal, the permanent and the transient, while surrounding this elision resolutely with the material and with a sense of loss. In the course of the three stanzas, art is seen in material terms, as valuable in so far as it is like life, and then some of the more usual attributes of art are allowed to creep back as it were, but only in so far as they remind us of an absolute ideal which does not exist—or at least not on earth. A further twist is added in the next stanza when the 'lost Pleiad seen no more below' is echoed in the sentiment that 'beauty's sometimes best set off afar'—the implication being that no ideal withstands scrutiny. We are losing the point of course in this abstraction. The point is that the discourse of art as artifice includes both art as ideal and life as physical fact. It is this discourse which the reader experiences.

I have already to some extent discussed stanza 46 in my earlier treatment of the list beginning in 47. It is riddled of course with sly humour—even if Italy is still Paradise, Italian woman is still Eve, and Raphael's death in the embrace of beauty has an innuendo other than the ideal. But it also deals in the growing notion that there are arts higher than the literary, though characteristically *Beppo* will have none of the abstraction of music, proposing the plastic materiality of Canova. Here art is seen as approaching a possible ideal, even if not the art of words, and even if art is actually inspired rather by life than by the ideal—and even if there is the feeling that actually life is all we might want (the word is 'desire'):

> . . . didst thou [Italian beauty] not inspire
> Raphael, who died in thy embrace, and vies
>   With all we know of Heaven, or can desire,
> In what he hath bequeathed us? . . .
>   (46)

The qualifications of my analysis are a pathetic attempt to approach the comic delicacy of the text—of course. It is life which inspires the ideal, though the ideal is not the less ideal for that; nor is Canova's ideal the less for it being material, nor Raphael's materiality less for it presenting an ideal—in both cases, quite the contrary. One of the sensations of reading this stanza is the implied failure of the narrator—here once more is the sense of the effort of the poem. It tries and to some extent fails, because words fail—but this does not render the effort meaningless. The explicit effort writes the value. And the humour works for the reader as the complicit wink of success. That art encompasses life is not a devaluation. It is the only envaluing.

Beppo, by a happy coincidence after a process of accretion, ends on the appropriately unround number of 99 stanzas, with the even more appropriate qualification that the uncounted note to stanza 46 makes 100—so it is neither one thing nor the other. As the last stanza tells us, ends are not in themselves important:

> My pen is at the bottom of a page,
>   Which being finished, here the story ends;
> 'Tis to be wished it had been sooner done,
> But stories somehow lengthen when begun.

Not even 'the' page—'a' page. But there is a quietly smiling elegiac tone here nevertheless. Beppo's 'stories' of the previous stanza, which keep his friends amused, and the first person pronoun's story here are closely related. Neither are totally to be believed—perhaps. The narrator has 'heard' that the Count and Beppo were always friends, and yet this is in the very next line a story which ends at the foot of a page. Life and art run together as art. The 'it' of the penultimate line, referring to the story as a task, has then about it a broader shrug of the shoulders. Stories expand 'somehow'—with life's irrelevance. But the reader does not understand by 'stories' only those which are written. Significance does not lie for this poem in the definite, the abstract or the general, but in the variable, the material, and the particular, and in the process of dealing with their fertile multiplicity.

A death would be the most inappropriate close imaginable, since it would gather the meaning of the poem, its moral world, into the meaning of its end alone. The *envoi* has a sense of parting, but it cannot be absolute. I hope we have agreed that the texture of the poem, the nap so to speak, makes us live in the feeling that the general is always diffracted dynamically into the particular, that the apparent monolith of the real kaleidoscopes into the variegated structures of the artificial, and that value is not a matter of absolute revelation, but of contingent effort.

In the essay to which I have referred in note 14, I suggested that the list of questions which pours from Laura in stanzas 91–93 liberated the poem from the expectation of a dénouement for eternity. At what would have been the appropriate moment in a Turkish Tale for the climax of the plot in a duel, time is allowed to flow over the need for a definite resolution. This reading of an outburst of essentially irrelevant 'conversation' has been subsequently indirectly supported by Ann Barton in her reading of Raucocanti's verbal incontinence as a means of modulating the return from the impossible ideal of Haidée's silent island to the real world of change and noise.[15] Irrelevance ensures an outcome which is not tragic. As we have seen, irrelevance is rarely without value in *Beppo*. It returns the moment which invites the definite to the world of the relative and unresolvable. I am tempted to gloss this analysis by saying that it returns the potentially serious to the comic. But if that were to suggest the 'merely' comic, it would be misleading. The wistful vision of time and the particular as humane value, not even in themselves but as the result of always compromised effort, does not *lead* to comedy, but has the gentlest of comedy as a precondition. Those who read

> They entered, and for coffee called,—it came,
> A beverage for Turks and Christians both,
> Although the way they make it's not the same . . .
> (91)

as an image of the brotherhood of man underneath their apparent differences; or those who read

> He then threw off the garments which disguised him,
> And borrowed the Count's small-clothes for a day . . .
> (98)

as an image of *maison-à-trois* tolerance are either monstrously tasteless or without humour or love—or without all three.

Those who can marvel at the perception of the lending of underclothes in the idea of tolerance, or can taste another's favourite coffee in the thought of brotherhood, will understand *Beppo*'s radiant sadness.

NOTES

Quotations from *Beppo* are from *Lord Byron: The Complete Poetical Works*, ed. Jerome J. McGann, volume IV (Oxford, 1986): hereafter, McGann. Unless otherwise specified, all references are to stanzas.

1. Stanzas I have counted as 'plot' are: 21–35, 53–59, 63–69, 81–82, 85–99.

2. Examples of lists can be found in stanzas 1, 2, 3, 8, 10, 16, 22, 31, 32, 39, 40, 42, 44, 47, 48, 49, 55, 60, 62, 64, 66, 71, 72, 73, 78, 89, 91, 92, 93. There are also other notable uses of alternatives, apparently for their own sake—for example in stanzas 6 and 8.

3. References to art can be found in 11, 12, 13, 14, 15, 17, 18, 31, 32, 33, 41, 46, 46 note, 57. The following have references to the process of writing: 7, 10, 12, 21, 50, 51, 52, 56, 63, 75, 76, 94, 96, 97, 98, 99. The following are the references to language 'artificialized': 1.1, 2.3, 5.6–8, 6.1–2, 7.5, 21.8, 22.2, 28.2, 31.4, 37.1–3, 40.1–2, 44.1–8, 50.7–8, 57.8, 58.7–8, 59.1–2, 61.3–4: clearly there are also cases of overlap with the list above.

4. I am aware that this line of thought may be felt to conceal in its lack of technical vocabulary a covert 'anti-dualist', closet 'deconstructionist', tendency.

5. Note that it does not matter whether plot or digression are considered the ground absolute—either is so until relativized by the modulation into the other.

6. Stanzas 44 and 47 were composed before 45 and 46, with 46 added last of all (see McGann, pp. 481–82); and it should indeed therefore properly be said that from Byron's point of view, though not from the reader's, stanza 46 comments on stanza 47. This relationship capitalizes on an inherent possibility which a revision to stanza 47 discussed on p. 103 above may have made more apparent, since the revision precedes the composition of 46, and the transition from 45 to present 47 or unrevised 47 would have been much looser than it now is.

7. The elision of *a* syllable is aided in line 6 by the 'y–y' juxtaposition of 'every year', and militated against here by the awkwardness of 'every thing'. This is an area for disagreement, without doubt, where analysis inevitably loses the fluidity of the effect.

8. There is a note to stanza 64 on the fair copy MS sent to the printer, somewhat oddly, dating—wrongly—the narrator's visit to the Ridotto. McGann's note to this note simply identifies Byron and narrator (McGann, p. 489). This is the only sensible way of proceeding, given that the note no

longer forms part of the text we read. If it did, the literal biographic response would be only part of our whole response to the note.

9. It saw two revisions in search of the right euphony; see McGann, p. 129.

10. The identification of Laura with Ariadne, abandoned by Theseus, but in some versions of the legend finally married to Bacchus, has a nice double edge; see McGann, p. 486.

11. These lines were revised, probably by Hobhouse, but the changes do not involve the place names; see McGann, pp. 130, 483.

12. Byron asked that this should be printed at the foot of the page, to form an integral part of the text, and it is a strange editorial choice in McGann that it is banished to the Commentary on pp. 487–88.

13. Apart from Keats's problematic identifications, one thinks of Shelley, in *Defence of Poetry* for example. For another view, see Stuart Peterfreund, 'The Truth about "Beauty" and "Truth" . . .', *Keats-Shelley Journal*, 35 (1986), 62–82.

14. 'The Rhetoric of Freedom', in *Byron: Wrath and Rhyme*, ed A. Bold (London, 1983), pp. 166–85.

15. Anne Barton, '*Don Juan* Reconsidered: The Haidée Episode', *Byron Journal*, 15 (1987), 11–20.

'The Platitude of Prose': Byron's vampire fragment in the context of his verse narratives

DAVID SEED

The ghost story which Byron began in 1816 is virtually unique in being the main surviving piece of prose fiction by the poet. However brief, it gives us a fascinating glimpse of how he might have developed a narrative in prose as distinct from verse, and it also has the added historical importance of representing (together with John Polidori's *The Vampyre*) the first fictional treatment of vampires in English fiction. Byron was an insatiable reader of novels. His comments on and allusions to the overlapping genres of Gothic fiction and oriental romance will be used to set up a context for the abortive vampire-story. This should demonstrate Byron's impatience with simple linear narrative and clarify his experiments with different structures in several poems, particularly *The Giaour, Manfred*, and *The Island*. First, a brief rehearsal of the familiar circumstances surrounding the vampire story.

In the summer of 1816 Byron, his doctor Polidori, and the Shelleys were briefly staying near each other in the neighbourhood of Geneva. Since the weather was impossibly cold and rainy that June, the group passed the time by reading from a collection of German ghost stories translated into French under the title of *Fantasmagoriana*.[1] Byron suggested that each member of the party should write a ghost-story, whereupon Shelley began a piece 'founded on the experiences of his early life', Mary Godwin (inspired by a dream) produced the narrative which was published as *Frankenstein*, and Claire Clairmont began a story which she abandoned and which was subsequently lost. Mary Shelley describes Polidori's plan as follows: 'Poor Polidori had some terrible idea about a skull-headed lady, who was so punished for peeping through a key-hole—what to see I forget—something very shocking and wrong of course . . .'.[2] Led into difficulties, Polidori abandoned his story. We would expect the instigator of the scheme to have had a definite plan himself, and in fact Byron's intentions were outlined by Polidori in the introduction to his novel *Ernestus Berchtold* (1819):

> Two friends were to travel from England into Greece; while there, one of them should die, but before his death, should obtain from his friend an oath of secrecy with regard to his decease. Some short time after, the remaining traveller, returning to his native country, should be startled at perceiving his former companion moving about in society, and should be horrified at finding that he made love to his former friend's sister.[3]

Byron got as far as the friend's death and then abandoned the project. It was the subsequent activities of Polidori which complicate this account.

At the suggestion of Countess Catherine Bruce, Polidori took over Byron's subject and wrote a full novel, *The Vampyre*, based on what he called Byron's 'ground-work'. The manuscript was then sent by an unknown hand to Henry Colburn, the editor of the *New Monthly Magazine*. In 1819, entirely on his own initiative, Colburn published the novel in that periodical and then as a separate volume as a 'tale by Lord Byron'. Colburn's bad faith is amply demonstrated by the fact that he cancelled the introductory note showing that Polidori was the author, and by his grudging later emendation that the work was a 'tale related by Lord Byron to Dr. Polidori'.[4] When Byron first heard of the publication he exclaimed, 'Damn "*the vampire*" . . . It must be some bookselling imposture . . .'; and three days later he wrote a letter of refutation to *Galignani's Messenger*, where he declared, 'I am not the author and never heard of the work in question until now'.[5] Part of Byron's indignation was caused by Colburn's inclusion of an entirely spurious account of the former's residence in Mytilene, and when John Murray sent him a copy of *The Vampyre* he insisted: 'I need not say it is *not mine*'.[6] To confirm his position Byron

ensured that his own fragment was published along with
Mazeppa and there the matter ended. It seems quite clear that
Polidori took over Byron's subject but not with any plagiaristic
intent. As we shall see later, he was a derivative writer rather
than an out-and-out thief. *The Vampyre*, then, is a work on the
margin of Byron's corpus. The subject is his but the treatment
is Polidori's. As Byron subsequently noted, 'I scarce think that
any one who knows me would believe the thing in the
Magazine to be mine . . .'.[7]

Byron would have found a precedent and potential model for
his planned story in a verse tale by Robert Southey. The first
substantial mention of vampires in English Literature occurs
in *Thalaba the Destroyer* (1801), whose eponymous protagonist is
a spiritual seeker fated to follow out a certain course of action.
Vampirism emerges in the poem's love-theme, where Thala-
ba's betrothed, Oneiza, is stricken on their wedding night by
the Angel of Death. Her form then reappears to torment
Thalaba at midnight:

> It was She . . .
> Her very lineaments, . . . and such as death
> Had changed them, livid cheeks, and lips of blue;
> > But in her eyes there dwelt
> > Brightness more terrible
> Than all the loathsomeness of death.[8]

The verse-form, which Southey describes as the '*Arabesque*
ornament of an Arabian tale', imposes its own formality on the
scene, introducing pauses, local climaxes, and isolating
phrases for emphasis. The metre thus supports the episodic
nature of Southey's narrative and heightens effects which
might seem ludicrous in prose. Southey has carefully prepared
this scene by introducing a hiatus in the narrative. Thalaba's
repeated haunting can then be described by an observer before
we see the event for itself. Oneiza's reappearance marks both a
dramatic climax and a frustration to Thalaba's romantic
yearning because she has been transformed into a being
neither alive nor dead. Only after he pierces her with a lance
can her spirit be liberated in anticipation of the resolving union
of the lovers in death which closes the poem.

Byron knew *Thalaba* and incorporated references to it in his notes to *The Giaour*, a work which clearly belongs within the genre of oriental tale in spite of its huge differences from Southey's poem. Unlike the latter, it relies far less on verbal exoticism and replaces episodic sequence with an astonishing narrative complexity. The advertisement to *The Giaour* puts forward a contrast between Byron's 'disjointed fragments' and the 'entire' story on which it is based which does not do justice to the poem. The character of the Turkish fisherman is introduced as a device for limiting the point of view and for limiting the amount of narrative information which Byron is willing to release. The whole poem skilfully exploits an alternation between action and stasis, between story and static image. One crucial result of this is to gesture repeatedly towards an act which is never described explicitly and to shift the poem's emphasis onto the process of narrating and onto consequences. Like Wordsworth in 'The Thorn', Byron uses questions and reporting ('some say'/'others say') to build up both the reader's curiosity and the mystery at the core of his narrative. It is no surprise that Byron admired Coleridge's *Christabel*, which he called a 'tale' and therefore linked with this genre since that poem too builds up an atmosphere of mystery by simultaneously referring to a pivotal event and refusing to specify it.[9]

Byron's techniques in *The Giaour* expand the subject from the individual experiences of a Turkish girl who takes a Christian lover, and transform it into a series of fated actions where passion leads to death, or worse. Hassan goes to woo a second fatal bride in battle; Leila 'sleeps beneath the grave'; but the Giaour is doomed to tell his story. His confession to the monk radically alters the previous perspectives of the poem which have demonstrated Byron's instinctive realization that point of view plays a crucial role in constituting the very nature of the narrative. The Moslem perspectives on the Giaour have depicted him as a monstrous satanic figure, but once he begins to tell his own story, casting himself as the victim of his own fate, he becomes more humanized and more a figure of pathos. Byron refuses to resolve his poem with an unambiguous conclusion like Southey's. The Giaour simply 'passes', leaving us uncertain about his ultimate end. Narrative discontinuity, by now accepted as a norm in modern fiction, here helps to build up a swift-moving tempo. Byron cuts rapidly from section to section in order to produce a local rhetorical climax. Line 689 establishes the perspective of Hassan's mother waiting to hear of her son's death; the arrival of this news then leads us straight into the image of his tombstone; the tone shifts at line 747 with the introduction of a Moslem curse on the Giaour, one phrased in terms of vampirism:

> But first, on earth as Vampire sent,
> Thy corse shall from its tomb be rent;
> Then ghastly haunt thy native place,
> And suck the blood of all thy race . . .
>
> (ll.755–58)

This powerful passage is a narrative prediction (unlike Southey's static description) of how love can be perverted into consumption. Since the poem is working so extensively through image, there is no need for Byron's story to substantiate these lines (and this is one of the advantages of verse over prose here) because their main point is to foretell the Giaour's exclusion from common humanity. The sign of this exclusion, here and in Byron's other poems, is the mark of Cain borne by the Giaour. Far from being 'foolish fragments', as Byron remarked,[10] this poem looks forward to the experiments of Browning and Henry James in partial narrative perspectives. Indeed, the perspectives of *The Giaour* are not only unresolved; they are so extreme in their opposition to each other that they almost tear the poem apart.

Byron was an admirer of the oriental tale in part because of its distance from realism. As the reviewer of *Lalla Rookh* noted, Moore's temperament was well fitted to the expectations of the genre 'in which we are prepared to meet with, and to enjoy, a certain lawless luxuriance of imagery, and to tolerate a certain rhapsodical wildness of sentiment and passion'.[11] Byron would probably have agreed with these sentiments since he was a great admirer of the most famous English oriental tale, *Vathek*. In March 1818 he wrote to Samuel Rogers asking him if he could secure copies of the unpublished episodes of that work, and to Medwin he exclaimed: 'What do you think of the Cave of Eblis, and the picture of Eblis himself? There is poetry.'[12] This is a reference to the Cave of Despair in the last episode of the novel where Beckford sets up awe-inspiring architectural images whose perspectives challenge the eye's capacity to register scale. Application is one of the most sincere proofs of enthusiasm, and Byron by his own admission drew on *Vathek* for *The Giaour* and *The Siege of Corinth*. His choice of title, too, may have been influenced by Beckford whose own Giaour functions as a demonic tempter. True to the genre, *Vathek* is exotic, episodic, and appeared in English (being written originally in French) with a cumbersome textual apparatus in Samuel Henley's footnotes. Byron avoided this scholasticism in *The Giaour*, preferring the oriental tale for its heightened poetical effects. In 1813, on completing *The Bride of Abydos*, he suggested that he had been writing 'to wring my thoughts from reality'. By 1817, in spite of the fact that he had applied the term to his own writings, his opposition to the word 'tale' had hardened. Under the mistaken assumption that the sub-title to *Lalla Rookh* was to be 'A Persian Tale', in March of that year Byron wrote to Moore: '. . . I wish you had not called it a *"Persian Tale"* [it was in fact called an "Oriental Romance"]. Say a "Poem", or "Romance", but not "Tale". I am very sorry that I called some of my own things "Tales", because I think that they are something better. Besides, we have had Arabian, and Hindoo, and Turkish, and Assyrian Tales.'[13]

Byron's dislike of this term appears to reflect a suspicion that the oriental tale had become a discredited genre, but this did not mean that he stopped writing tales himself or that he could not appreciate a new work like *Lalla Rookh*. Moore acted on the genre's capacity to cut across prose and verse (in 1813 Byron himself was planning a 'tale in prose' after finishing *The Bride of Abydos*) and produced a work where verse tales are framed by the prose narrative of a wedding journey from Lahore.[14] In his characteristically forthright way, Byron declared to John Murray that he did not like the prose at all and thought 'The Fire-Worshippers' the best tale.[15] This narrative resembles *The Giaour* in dealing with two star-crossed lovers, one of whom is a Moslem and the other an Infidel. Hafed, the hero of the piece, is a fire-worshipper and one 'of that ancient hero line' defending liberty against the encroachments of Islamic tyranny. When Hafed's small army is defeated he leaps defiantly onto his own funeral pyre; his lover sees the fire from a boat near the shore and springs into the sea as if to embrace Hafed. The narrative structure of the poem, however, could not be more different from *The Giaour*. Moore uses an omniscient voice not a limited angle of vision, and breaks the poem into four verse 'chapters' through brief prose passages which describe the reactions of the main listener, the princess Lalla Rookh. The role of the narrative voice is to punctuate and highlight the different sections of the poem, which in turn establish the passion between the two lovers, Hafed's defeat in battle, and the sombre consequences. A rhetorical stylization of the narrative is made possible by its oriental subject and also by the fiction that the poem is delivered orally by the bard Feramorz. His declamatory rhetoric is offset in the prose passages by another character called Fadladeen. For the most part these passages function as a purely practical expedient to demarcate the episodes clearly, but in Fadladeen we may find the true reason for Byron's dislike of Moore's prose. The former character acts as a one-man audience, a potentially hostile critic who can attack the rhapsodies of Feramorz for producing a poem which is a 'slight, gilded thing, sent adrift without rudder or ballast, and with nothing but vapid sweets and faded flowers on board'.[16] Moore's self-consciousness at incorporating such a figure as a means of anticipating and deflecting criticism suggests that he was as aware as Byron of how stale the oriental genre had become by 1817.

In spite of Byron's reservations about the genre of the oriental tale, he consistently found opportunities for structural innovation in his verse narratives. The intricate organization of *The Giaour* is extreme but its complexities are not unique. *The Bride of Abydos* presents a story-within-a-story occasioned by the disguised identity of Selim. *The Corsair* alternates the perspectives of an external narrator, one of Conrad's men, and of Conrad himself so that the latter never emerges as simply a hero or a villain. Similarly, *Parisina* retards the flow of events by assembling the viewpoints of spectators, Parisina, her husband, and her husband's bastard son Hugo, who has been her lover. The poem asks what sort of judgements are possible on their incestuous love, thereby delaying the sequence of judgement and punishment. Hugo's execution is a crucial event which this time Byron describes in great detail in order to raise unresolved questions of justice at the end of the poem. In *The Island* (1823), we encounter comparable shifts of perspective which cut across a linear narrative.

In the year of the poem's publication, Byron wrote to Leigh Hunt that on the one hand he wanted to avoid repeating the style of *The Corsair*, on the other hand the danger would be '*not to run counter to the reigning stupidity altogether—otherwise they will say that I am eulogizing Mutiny*'.[17] The specific mutiny was that which took place on the *Bounty* in 1789, but interestingly Byron makes no attempt to retell this story. Rather the facts of the mutiny, no doubt familiar to Byron's readers, were to function as a 'foundation' to the poem according to its advertisement. Indeed, the first canto positively hurries to get it out of the way, shifting rapidly from Captain Bligh's peaceful slumbers to the achievement of the mutiny, already a *fait accompli* by the third section of the poem. Once Bligh and his faithful remnant have been cast adrift, Byron explicitly pulls the narrative focus away from them ('But 'tis not mine to tell their tale of grief') and onto the South Sea islanders. The second canto now recapitulates the calm of the poem's opening, this time composing an island idyll through the perspective of a local native. The timeless rituals of the islanders have been corrupted, however, by the incursions of outsiders who brought warfare with them, and here the central subject of the poem is introduced—the problematic nature of civilization. Byron temporarily adopts the voice of an islander who is capable of remembering the lost peace of the islands and of recognizing the cultural claims of European conquerors. He is caught within an adulterated society, the worse of two worlds ('the sordor of civilisation, mixed / With all the savage which Man's fall hath fixed' (II.69–70)). This voice places the events of the poem within the larger perspective of history, thereby establishing an ironic context for the extended lyrical present of the two lovers, Neuha and 'the fair-hair'd Torquil'.

Here again the fact that Byron is writing in verse enables him to be very selective about narrative information. The details of Torquil's past are not to his purpose. Instead he evokes a romantic situation which is then disrupted by the arrival of Ben Bunting, one of the mutineers. His profane voice erodes Byron's paradisal analogies and re-enacts the corrupting of the islands, for a consciousness of time is expressed through recurrences in this poem rather than through simple temporal sequence. Bunting forces us to revise our estimate of Torquil from romantic youth to an individual within a historical sequence of events.

The mutiny-narrative, which has been suspended, is now reactivated at the end of the second canto with preparations to fight a newly arrived man-o'-war. Once again Byron skates over important events to push the reader straight on to consequences. The defeat of the mutineers takes place between the second and third cantos, and two narrative questions are now raised: what is to be the fate of the surviving mutineers?, and can the island paradise be recaptured? The two questions overlap with each other as long as Torquil is seen with Christian and the other mutineers, and for this reason it is crucial that the tale should separate them. Although the lovers have returned at the end of the poem to an island 'no more polluted with a hostile hue', the conclusion is heavily charged with ambiguity since the consciousness of time cannot be blotted out. The lovers will pass 'such happy days / As only the yet infant world displays' (IV.419–20) and within the set of oppositions which the tale has established between innocence and corruption, youth and age, 'infant' clearly carries positive connotations; but it also implicitly anticipates its own demise. By not confining himself to recapitulating the mutiny story, Byron has ingeniously balanced the notion of recurrence against that of narrative sequence. The repeated pattern is of peace being disrupted by violence, the idyllic island being marred by sexual pollution. The intermittent plot-line enables the perspective to be as varied as that of *The Giaour*, and enables Byron to use the myth of the Fall almost as a literal event. While the specific sequence of events relating to the two lovers does conclude, the tale also glances forward to yet another possible fall, yet another possible disruption of the island as idyllic retreat.

We have already seen cases of Byron adapting prose narratives—*Vathek* and Bligh's account of the mutiny—to his own poetic purposes, and John Moore's novel *Zeluco* (1789) made such a strong impression on Byron when he read it in his youth that he subsequently considered its hero as a possible model for Childe Harold.[18] Moore gives a study in the working out of a domineering impulse which has swayed Zeluco from his childhood and which leads him into 'wild and rakish' behaviour. The novel does not present a narrative so much as a pathological case-study where all emotions are reduced to a common physiological level. The structural unit is the episode within which false impressions and schemes are allowed to run their course, ultimately so as to confirm the general wisdom of the narrator. Moore levels an unremitting irony against the postures of romantic love in particular, as in the following lines: 'Signora Rosolia, when she heard of Zeluco's having sailed for Spain, immediately fainted, as is usual with young ladies when they are abandoned by men who pretend to be dying for them, and whom they consider as the only men who can make them happy—'.[19] Moore sets up a distance between the events within his narrative and a narrating consciousness which interprets every episode as a typical example. A principle of depression is at work here, where drama is constantly reduced to self-deception and where Zeluco's stature is radically confined. His very name would lead us to expect an overweening Gothic hero, whereas Moore's method reduces him to a cruel and egotistical epicure and muffles our interest in his ultimate fate by demonstrating the typicality of his behaviour. Since his life will not reveal new facets of his personality, the reader waits for more and more extreme confirmations of his cruelty and its social reception. Zeluco's life becomes in effect a pretext for the moral survey indicated in the novel's subtitle, *Various Views of Human Nature taken from Life and Manners, Foreign and Domestic.*

Just as Moore's reflections play around a central unchanging character, so Byron uses Childe Harold to set up meditative episodes in his poem. The latter's progression comes partly from the sequence of the journey. Harold's apostrophe to his bark on leaving England ('With thee . . . I'll swiftly go . . . / Nor care what land thou bear'st me to') anticipates other departures later in the poem and appears to suggest travel without a specific goal, but arrival in Greece in Canto II marks a topographical climax since the poem has reached a land so rich in historical resonance. The piety and purpose implied in the poem's title now become realized, and indeed later in the century the notion of the tour as pilgrimage was taken up as an ironic and anti-Byronic trope by Thackeray (in *From Cornhill to Cairo*) and Mark Twain.[20] When Francis Jeffrey complained that 'the narrative and description' were of 'inferior interest' to the moralizing passages, he was forcing a false separation between the poem's closely interwoven elements.[21] Narrative transition from place to place is intermittent, but once it is suspended the eyes take over as a source of movement. Verbs of looking and surveying are crucial in this poem because they then occasion meditations on transience, vanity, and history. One form of progression shades into the other so that the physical landscape becomes charged with more and more potential subjects for the roving eye and the meditative imagination. The accelerations of tempo are more dramatic and promise more variety than Moore's relentless insistence on his own wisdom. Literally and metaphorically there is always new ground to cover:

> Away! Nor let me loiter in my song,
> For we have many a mountain-path to tread,
> And many a varied shore to sail along . . .
> (II.36)

The pronoun 'we' strategically draws the reader in as a companion on these travels which, although they resemble a leisurely tour, are actually marked by an urgency to compete with Time itself. It is a landscape dotted with ruins and we shall now see how the ruin and travel to the Levant figure in Byron's vampire-narrative, contrasting his treatment of the subject with Polidori's.

The Vampyre contains two pieces of preliminary matter which importantly affect the reader's reactions to the narrative proper. The first, 'Extract of a Letter to the Editor' (probably not written by Polidori), performs the same function as Mary Shelley's preface to *Frankenstein* in outlining the circumstances of the novel's origin, but with the difference that it pays overwhelming attention to Byron's presence. The result is to minimize Polidori's participation (he is simply 'the physician') and to associate Byron strongly with the novel as if he were the author, although this is nowhere stated as such. The introduction serves a different purpose in relating the narrative to the genre of the oriental tale and in taking explicit literary bearings from Southey's *Thalaba* and from *The Giaour*. Once again Byron is given prominence. Polidori is also clearly attempting to bolster the authenticity of his own narrative, which he does by repeating almost verbatim Southey's quotation from Joseph Pitton de Tournefort's *Voyage into the Levant* that appears as a note to *Thalaba*.²² The quotation is unacknowledged, as is Polidori's erudite listing of the Greek terms for 'vampire' which are taken from Byron's note to *The Giaour*. The same derivative spirit can be seen in the narrative itself where Polidori has taken his Greek maid Ianthe straight from the introductory poem to *Childe Harold's Pilgrimage*.²³ On this evidence *The Vampyre* proves to have an even closer relation to Byron's writings than was suspected.

The novel revolves around a contrast between its two central characters. Aubrey is young, naive and prone to romanticize Lord Ruthven: 'he soon formed this object into the hero of a romance'.²⁴ Ruthven himself is unpromising material, however, being very withdrawn from society. Polidori describes him in a curiously negative way as if consciously weaving a variation on the domineering look of traditional Gothic heroes: he possesses a 'dead grey eye, which, fixing upon the object's face, did not seem to penetrate, and at one glance to pierce through to the inward workings of the heart; but fell upon the cheek with a leaden ray . . .'.²⁵ The implication here is that Ruthven is a jaded rake, but in his excitement Aubrey is more swayed by the compliment of Ruthven agreeing to accompany him to the Levant. *The Vampyre* works on the basis of retarded revelation and Aubrey's role is to observe but to display a reluctance to draw inferences from his observations. The status of Lord Ruthven slides gradually towards the monstrous as more information is released about him. He anticipates Dorian Gray in being a corrupter of youth and Dracula in being a sexual predator. On the verge of his death in Greece, Ruthven extracts an oath from Aubrey to conceal his death, a stratagem which further delays his unambiguous exposure to the reader. Aubrey is horrified to see his 'dead' companion apparently circulating freely in London society, and horrified again when he discovers that he is betrothed to his sister. Under the pressure of helplessly observing his sister going to her doom, Aubrey collapses into an illness from which he recovers sufficiently to recount his story to her. Having performed his narrative function, he can then give up the ghost and Polidori can state what any reader worth his salt has already guessed, namely that Ruthven was a vampire.

Byron's prose fragment begins quite differently. He also introduces two male characters not so much to contrast as to partially mirror each other. Where Polidori's narrator is constantly looking over Aubrey's shoulder to ironize the intensity of his reactions Byron makes his young character the narrator. Since he is unnamed he represents a more youthful version of Augustus Darvell, 'a man of considerable fortune and ancient family'.[26] Darvell has passed through the same school as the narrator but at an earlier date, so that Byron appears to be presenting the latter in a role similar to Mary Shelley's Walton, who is a possible Frankenstein-to-be. Where Polidori's narrator distances us from Aubrey and discounts his view of Ruthven even before we learn the truth about the latter, there is no check on Byron's and therefore his account carries more potential for discovery. His judicious antithetical sentences bear testimony to a penetrating analysis of character. In short, the narrator's very style validates his comments on Darvell, who, like Lord Ruthven, is also an enigma and a 'being of no common order'. As rumours circulate around Darvell the narrator makes a point of standing aloof from the popular assumption that mystery suggests evil. As far as the latter is concerned, he states: '[I] felt loth, as far as regarded himself, to believe in its existence'.[27] James B. Twitchell is undoubtedly right to argue that 'Darvell seems simply another Byronic Hero who . . . is driven by some inner demon, some mysterious force, into a life of exile'.[28] His very character implies a hinterland of unspecified experiences which apparently work through to their ultimate conclusion when the narrator and Darvell travel to the Levant. On the journey the latter falls prey to a wasting disease and he finally expires in a Moslem graveyard, where, to the narrator's astonishment, 'his countenance in a few minutes became nearly black'. Interestingly, the journey is also a recapitulation for Darvell. In other words Byron begins with an ending and throws out indications that his plan was partly to work backwards into the narrative past, perhaps to shed light on the origins of Darvell's destiny.

Both Polidori and Byron demonstrate that place is crucial to the very possibility of dealing with vampires. In 1818 a writer in the *Quarterly Review* surveyed the traces of the legend in Northern Europe and remarked that 'in England vampires seem to have been long forgotten'; whereas in his notes to *The Giaour* Byron writes that 'the Vampire superstition is still general in the Levant'.[29] Byron's shift in the fragment from England to Western Turkey thus introduces new fictional possibilities. The Levant was to Byron what the Apennines were to Mrs Radcliffe; and where Polidori introduces within his narrative an exposition of the legend to the startled Aubrey, Byron takes his two characters on an 'excursion' to the ruins of Ephesus. We are already familiar with the symbolism of ruins from *Childe Harold's Pilgrimage*, the third canto of which Byron was composing at this period (his fragment is dated 17 June 1816); and the landscape which his characters traverse (from Christian to Moslem ruins, and then to a 'city of the dead') seems to be taking them metaphorically towards the bounds of humanity itself. The choice of setting and some of the descriptive details indicate traces of the oriental tale in Byron's narrative, particularly as he develops the dialogue between his characters and thereby allows Darvell to reveal himself more directly and more dramatically than Polidori's depiction of Lord Ruthven, where report and rumour are all-important. Just before his death Darvell swears his companion to secrecy (compare Polidori) and also to perform certain ritualistic acts such as to throw an Arabic ring into a spring near the Bay of Eleusis. The ring talisman and the mysterious images of the stork and snake are probably taken from *Thalaba*, where the ring has an important part to play in the destiny of Southey's protagonist and where the latter enters the ruins of Babylon. By transposing these details into a more realistic context of a journal-narrative Byron increases their mystery which, tantalizingly, he never developed.

The oath which Darvell demands gestures towards the supernatural without ever quite reaching it, and James Twitchell has used this fact and others to argue tendentiously that Polidori was the true originator of the vampire-story. He points

out that Darvell's strange death does not fit the body of vampire
lore and that Polidori, not Byron, has used the supernatural in
his narrative.[30] This argument can be faulted on a number of
grounds. Firstly, on each occasion Byron's plan is referred to the
supernatural figures. Polidori himself wrote to Henry Colburn
in 1819 that 'it was his [Byron's] intention of writing a ghost
story'.[31] Shortly after the original scheme had been devised
Monk Lewis visited Byron in Switzerland and Mary Shelley
recorded in her journal: 'we talk of Ghosts; neither Lord Byron
nor Monk G. Lewis seem to believe in them'. And she com-
mented dryly, 'I do not think that all the persons who profess to
discredit these visitations really discredit them'.[32] Whatever his
actual beliefs, Lewis exploited the supernatural for all it was
worth, not only in *The Monk* (which Byron told Medwin was the
best romance 'in any language, not excepting the German'),[33]
but also in his later collections, *Tales of Wonder* (1801) and
Romantic Tales (1808). By the same token Byron's beliefs would
not necessarily debar him from using supernatural materials in
his works. *Manfred*, which he began at this time under the
influence of Lewis reading him translations of *Faust*, is packed
with spirits. Twitchell also exaggerates the presence of the
supernatural in *The Vampyre*, where lore is expounded as pure
information. The crux of mystery in this novel has nothing to do
with subsequent developments of the vampire-figure but occurs
when Aubrey sees Ruthven alive after his death. Aubrey's
reaction is to suspect that he is hallucinating: 'He roused
himself, he could not believe it possible—the dead rise again!—
He thought his imagination had conjured up the image his
mind was resting upon'.[34] Two perfectly plausible experiences
are brought into collision so that Aubrey's sense of the real is
questioned, and it is a weakness of *The Vampyre* that Polidori
makes so little of this epistemological theme.

The last aspect of the vampire-story which should be
considered is its sexual dimension. Aubrey temporarily parts
company with Lord Ruthven over whether his intentions
towards a certain Italian lady are honourable or not; and when
the corpse of his Greek maiden, Ianthe, is discovered, 'upon
her throat were the marks of teeth having opened the vein'.[35]
Polidori keeps his innocent victim firmly contrasted to his
villain whereas James Planché's stage adaptation, *The Vampire*

(1820), complicates this relationship by introducing sexual response. When Lord Ruthven seizes the hand of Lady Margaret, a potential victim, she exclaims: 'Heavens! how strange a thrill runs through my frame'.[36] In Byron's fragment, however, he is careful not to simplify Darvell into a mere rake and must have been conscious of the danger that his personal notoriety would lead his readers to take Darvell as a self-portrait if he was presented as dissolute. Perhaps for this reason the sexual element in his characterization is reduced to the slightest of hints, one of a whole series of possible explanations why he should be so mysteriously shifting in mood. The vampire-rake analogy was certainly not limited to fiction. In 1814 Harriet Shelley complained to Catherine Nugent that 'Mr. Shelley has become profligate and sensual, owing entirely to Godwin's *Political Justice* . . . the man I once loved is dead. This is a vampire. His character is blasted for ever.'[37] It was not until later in the century, however, that Le Fanu's 'Carmilla' and *Dracula* could use the vampire story as a covert means of dramatizing female sexual responsiveness.

In Byron's fragment the narrator resists the popular suspicion of Darvell by setting up his viewpoint as an alternative, but there is no indication of how this viewpoint could be varied once established. Here we may meet another reason why he did not pursue the project since, as has been shown above, Byron delights in varying perspective and presenting subjects under different aspects. *Manfred*, for instance, which resembles *The Giaour* in some of its structural facets, does precisely this. In the same year that Byron's poem was published, one 'P.F.' sent to *Blackwood's Magazine* an account of a tradition supposedly obtained from a Swiss monk because its subject so strongly resembled that of *Manfred*. The sketch describes the determining results of a temperament, fixed from youth, of one whose 'soul was wild, impetuous, and uncontrollable' and who was burdened by a 'peculiar melancholy' which separates the man from average humanity.[38] He lives with an older brother, a 'young female relative', and a guardian. The guardian dies, whereupon the older brother and the 'relative' begin to live together as man and wife. Returning from his travels, the younger brother rhapsodizes over the Alpine landscape and realizes that the 'relative' embodies his ideal of beauty.

Horrified that his brother has beaten him to it, he wanders off into the mountains and is only saved from committing suicide by the timely arrival of the 'relative'. They then go to live together in a deserted cottage where the girl wastes away under the burden of guilt. The younger brother 'wandered among the forests and the mountains' and is later found dead but with no signs of violence on his body. The similarities with *Manfred* lie in both works presenting temperament as a fatality and in numerous details (the brother's tower, his near-suicide, and so on). It is in its treatment of sexuality that the sketch differs radically from Byron's work since the incest is made quite explicit and a moral perspective on the brother's actions is established as their consequences emerge. There are reasons for doubting the authenticity of the sketch, however. Far from being a neutral account, it is intensely literary in its metaphorical opposition between light and dark, day and night; and it twice quotes Wordsworth to portray the brother as a Romantic solitary. It is also completely implausible as a narrative since the only way it could have been transmitted would have been via the confessional, as happens in *The Giaour*; and there is no suggestion that this ever happened.

When we turn from the prose narrative to *Manfred*, the most immediate and striking difference is that Byron's dramatic arrangement of his materials complicates our sense of narrative sequence. Like his prose fragment, this work begins near to the ending of an action whose beginning is never fully described. One reason for this is Byron's evident desire to throw the enigmatic character of Manfred himself into maximum prominence. Like Darvell he is a solitary, a member of the 'brotherhood of Cain'; and Leslie Marchand has pointed out that the story of Cain took a very early hold over Byron's imagination, appealing to a Calvinistic belief that certain individuals were predestined to commit evil and to face damnation.[39] Transpose this notion into narrative terms and we have a group of characters doomed to pursue an unchangeable fate of which they are only dimly conscious, and at the same time, as in Manfred's case, display some culpable complicity of will.

In Act II of Byron's poem (which he insisted was to be read and not performed, 'for it has no pretense to being called a drama')⁴⁰ Manfred becomes his own narrator, recounting the story of his life entirely in terms of negatives and exclusion:

> From my youth upwards
> My spirit walk'd not with the souls of men,
> Nor look'd upon the earth with human eyes;
> The thirst of their ambition was not mine,
> The aim of their existence was not mine;
> My joys, my griefs, my passions, and my powers,
> Made me a stranger; though I wore the form,
> I had no sympathy with breathing flesh . . .
> (II.ii.50–57)

What is astonishing in this account is how much story is missing. There are no transitions from one age to another, but rather a self-dramatizing and basically static portrait of an extraordinary temperament. Two exceptions are hinted at. The first is Manfred's 'researches' into ultimate courses, and here he suggests the Faustian theme of the over-reacher seeking a knowledge beyond the bounds of ordinary humanity and suffering a penance as a result. But Manfred never makes a Faustian compact and only hints in general terms at the sequence of transgression and punishment. The second possible exception lies in the issue of incest which 'P.F.''s sketch described unambiguously. In the case of *Manfred*, however, our desire for narrative certainty is doomed to frustration because Manfred himself is our main source of information and the details of a female mirror-image (which it would be too naturalistic and too reductive to call 'sister') have to be extracted against his will by the Witch of the Alps. Manfred tantalizes the reader by identifying this relationship as the 'core of my heart's grief' but never spells out the exact nature of his distress. The poem, in short, leaves origins calculatedly vague so as to build up the awe-inspiring drama of consequences and Manfred's ultimate end. It assembles a collage of perspectives on Manfred—those of the chamois-hunter, the spirits, the abbot, his defendants, and of course himself—without ever resolving them, and these perspectives raise narrative possibilities without ever authenticating them. The chamois-hunter wonders whether 'some half-maddening sin' has brought Manfred to this pass; the abbot retails local rumour (once again Byron uses the ' 'tis said' device), but as soon as we try to summarize the narrative element of the poem enormous problems arise from the restriction on information and from the poem's repeated tendency to express events in metaphors of mind, especially in the repeated figures of rising and falling.

One of the few critics to confront the nature of Romantic narrative, Karl Kroeber, has argued that simple narrative structures belong to the apprentice phase of Romantic poetry and that 'Romantic invention and rearrangement of subject-matter tends to stress three factors: pictorial beauty, timelessness, and stylization of character'.[41] In the case of Byron this list needs considerable extension since Kroeber implies that the rearrangement of materials has consequences in areas other than plot. All narratives contain gaps and it is a striking testimony to the sophistication of Byron's experiments that he should exploit such an opportunity to shift point of view or imply an event without ever describing it. Traditionally in prose fiction the gaps between chapters are taken to contain action of no great importance, but Byron sometimes uses the greater liberty offered by verse to do the very opposite, to omit a central event as in *The Giaour*, or to shift the very register of his language from, say, description to narrative or monologue. Kroeber points out that verse narratives played an important part in the development of the novel and argues that during the Romantic period there was an 'ultimate connection between verse and prose story telling'. Certainly Byron's example bears out this assertion since he began several other novels in addition to his one surviving fragment. He planned a 'pretty little Romance' in 1804; in 1807, while at Cambridge, he wrote 214 pages of a novel since lost; and in 1813 he began a satirical epistolary novel in collaboration with Robert Charles Dallas and contributed his efforts to the latter for use in his novel, *Sir Francis Darrell*. At the same time as the vampire fragment he also began a 'romance in prose' which was intended to 'shadow out his own matrimonial fate', probably as a rejoinder to Caroline Lamb's *roman à clef*, *Glenarvon*; and Byron also started a novel describing the adventures of an Andalusian nobleman called Don Julian.[42] This was begun in 1817 and, to judge by the fragment reproduced by Thomas Moore, was a first-person narrative dealing with Julian's marital difficulties which have become a subject of public discussion.[43]

We have also seen examples of how prose works influenced Byron's verse tales, and how the genre of the oriental tale, straddling prose and verse, influenced his vampire narrative. Although his argument is an important pioneering statement, one problem in Kroeber's discussion of Byron lies in a rather schematic opposition which he mounts between the novelistic and the poetic. Here he is describing the structure of *The Giaour*:

> Byron manipulates and distorts the order of events because he is interested in poetic effects. He does not appeal merely to the curiosity or the rational understanding of his reader. He recognizes that in verse sustained sentiment aided by the systematic progression of compressed, rhythmic language can be relied upon to produce a coherence of effect that could be attained in prose only through careful analysis and thorough description.[44]

The detailed points Kroeber is making are of course perfectly valid, but he constantly associates discontinuity, the exploitation of rhythm, compression, and other effects exclusively with poetry, thereby underrating the resilience of the novel genre. Apart from more realistic works like *Tom Jones*, it is revealing that Byron expressed warm admiration for *The Monk*, Schiller's *Ghost-Seer*, *Frankenstein*, and *Vathek*; all novels which in varying degrees use complex narrative structures and heightened scenes, and preternatural effects or unpredictable visual transformations—that is, some of the very strategies which he himself uses in his own verse narratives. According to Kroeber, Byron began his career composing fantastic romances and achieved maturity once he had assimilated realism into his works and thus brought them closer to novels. By the novelistic Kroeber clearly implies a work of social documentation containing description and analysis in an orderly sequence, and it is equally clear that a late narrative like *The Island* would not confirm his thesis. Here, as we have seen, Byron selects narrative detail in order to create a mythic dimension to the action which neither leaves realism behind nor rests on documentation or complete explanation. Similarly, the ghost narratives of Canto XVI of *Don Juan* and the deliberate inclusion of the unearthly Aurora Raby amongst the house guests of Norman Abbey do not suggest a terminus in realism.

Byron repeatedly forces a gap between the sequence of events and his organization of them. *Sujet* is distanced from *fabula*, so that the exact nature of events can be left fluid or so that he can concentrate on their consequences. Temperamentally Byron could scarcely ever introduce a subject without turning it round to examine it from a different perspective, and his verse narratives exemplify this process in magnifying or diminishing their protagonists or in leaving clarified but unresolved the moral nature of the action. The only hint of why Byron abandoned his vampire story has been given by Mary Shelley, who records in her preface to *Frankenstein* that Byron and Shelley, 'annoyed by the platitude of prose, speedily relinquished their uncongenial task'.[45] It may be that Byron found the journal method had locked him into a narrative with a single perspective and thereby debarred him from the rapid shifts of pace and technique which characterize his verse narratives and which anticipate so strikingly the developments to be taken and still pursued by later prose fiction.

NOTES

1. *Three Gothic Novels*, ed. E. F. Bleiler (New York, 1966), pp. xxxi–xl.

2. Mary Shelley, *Frankenstein*, ed. M. K. Joseph (London, 1969), p. 7.

3. *The Works of Lord Byron: Letters and Journals*, ed. Rowland E. Prothero, 6 vols (London, 1898–1901), IV, 287.

4. Henry R. Viets, M.D., 'The London Editions of Polidori's *The Vampyre*', *Publications of the Bibliographical Society of America*, 63 (1969), 83–101.

5. *Byron's Letters and Journals*, ed. Leslie A. Marchand, 12 vols (London, 1973–82), VI, 114, 119 (hereafter, *LJ*).

6. *LJ*, VI, 125.

7. *LJ*, VI, 140.

8. Robert Southey, *Thalaba the Destroyer*, second edition, 2 vols (London, 1809), II, 81.

9. *Medwin's Conversations of Lord Byron*, ed. Ernest J. Lovell, Jr (Princeton, 1966), p. 177.

10. *LJ*, III, 105.

11. 'Lalla Rookh', *Blackwood's Magazine*, 1 (June 1817), 280.

12. *Medwin's Conversations*, p. 258.

13. *LJ*, V, 186.

14. *LJ*, III, 205.

15. *LJ*, VI, 265.

16. *The Poetical Works of Thomas Moore*, ed. Charles Kent, Blackfriars Edition (London, 1883), p. 301.

17. *LJ*, X, 90.

18. The advertisement for *Childe Harold's Pilgrimage* announces Byron's possible intention of developing Harold as a 'poetical Zeluco'.

19. Dr Moore, *Zeluco*, 2 vols (London, 1810), I, 28.

20. *Notes of a Journey from Cornhill to Grand Cairo* (1845), chapter 5; Mark Twain, *The Innocents Abroad or The New Pilgrim's Progress* (1869).

21. Theodore Redpath, *The Young Romantics & Critical Opinion, 1807–1824* (London, 1973), p. 218.

22. *A Voyage into the Levant* was published in an English translation in 1718. The other main authority on vampires, also referred to by Polidori, was Augustin Calmet's *Dissertations sur les apparitions des anges, des démons, et des esprits. Et sur les revenans et vampires*, published in English in 1759.

23. Further possible borrowings might be the comparison between Ianthe and a Kashmir butterfly (from *The Giaour*, l.388), Lord Ruthven's name from Caroline Lamb's *Glenarvon*, and the locket device from *Frankenstein*.

24. Bleiler, p. 267.

25. Bleiler, p. 265.

26. Bleiler, p. 287.

27. Bleiler, p. 288.

28. James B. Twitchell, *The Living Dead: A Study of the Vampire in Romantic Literature* (Durham, N.C., 1981), p. 115.

29. *Quarterly Review*, 18 (1818), 495.

30. Twitchell, p. 114.

31. *The Diary of Dr. John William Polidori, 1816*, ed. William Michael Rossetti (London, 1911), p. 15.

32. *Mary Shelley's Journal*, ed. Frederick L. Jones (Norman, Okla., 1947), p. 57.

33. *Medwin's Conversations*, p. 188.

34. Bleiler, p. 279.

35. Bleiler, p. 274.

36. *The Hour of One: Six Gothic Melodramas*, ed. Stephen Wischhusen (London, 1975); *The Vampire*, p. 26 (each play is paginated separately).

37. *The Letters of Percy Bysshe Shelley*, ed. Frederick L. Jones, 2 vols (Oxford, 1964), I, 421.

38. 'Sketch of a Tradition Related by a Monk in Switzerland', *Blackwood's Magazine*, I (June 1817), 270–73.

39. Leslie A. Marchand, *Byron: A Biography* (London, 1957), pp. 38–39.

40. *LJ*, V, 195.

41. Karl Kroeber, *Romantic Narrative Art* (Madison, 1966), p. 66.

42. Elizabeth French Boyd, *Byron's Don Juan: A Critical Study* (New York, 1958), p. 11.

43. Thomas Moore, *Life of Lord Byron*, 6 vols (London, 1854), V, 234–36.

44. Kroeber, pp. 139–40.

45. *Frankenstein*, p. 8.

Authoring the Self: *Childe Harold* III and IV

VINCENT NEWEY

In a famous stanza of *Childe Harold*, Canto III,[1] Byron celebrates poetic creation as a becoming of the self:

> 'Tis to create, and in creating live
> A being more intense, that we endow
> With form our fancy, gaining as we give
> The life we image, even as I do now.
> What am I? Nothing; but not so art thou,
> Soul of my thought! . . .
>   (III.6)

The 'I', the subject writing, is literally 'nothing': being and life are not so much something 'given' as something 'gained' through imagination, thought and acts of formulation.

Childe Harold III and IV is pervaded by this sense of the self as that which is constantly being brought into existence in the mind and through language—and which is therefore also always provisional and on the point of dissolution. At times, indeed, Byron can see in writing and 'the life we image' only a tissue of empty signs, as when he contemplates 'The furrows of long thought, and dried-up tears, / Which, ebbing, leave a sterile track behind' (III.3), where the energies of body, brain and emotion have, as it were, been shrunk to mere lines and marks, a pointless trace upon the page. The reference here is to the tale of Harold, which Byron takes up once more at the beginning of Canto III, but the effect of denial is apparent, too, in places where he refers to himself:

> Once more upon the waters! yet once more!
> And the waves bound beneath me as a steed
> That knows his rider. Welcome, to their roar!

> Swift be their guidance, wheresoe'er it lead!
> . . . I am as a weed,
> Flung from the rock, on Ocean's foam, to sail
> Where'er the surge may sweep, or tempest's breath
> > prevail.

(III.2)

Here Byron generates at first a wholly positive personal and poetic identity. Less pilgrim than adventurer, he revels in the pure 'bounding' instant, embracing the excitement of being 'all at sea' ('Welcome, to their roar') and goalless ('Swift . . . wheresoe'er it lead'), yet affirming a secure, intimate balance between his own force and that of nature and inspiration—for the 'waves', signifying the rhythms both of the sea and of poetry itself, move like a 'steed' beneath him, autonomous but responsive to the weight and touch of a practised 'rider'/writer. Then, however, this assertion of privilege, power and vigorous expectancy is suddenly displaced by a reverse configuration: Byron declares himself to be 'as a weed'—insignificant, insentient, forever acted upon. What this event shows is not just an inability on Byron's part to sustain a hopeful posture, but how language itself may delete as well as create 'being'. The 'I' slides over into the stasis of a word—a signifier determined above all perhaps by the exigencies of form itself, that is of rhyme ('steed'-'weed'), but in any case dissolving the poet's 'becoming' in its own.[2]

Such moments of affirmation and denial, raising questions of authorial power and powerlessness, are integral to the mental topography of *Childe Harold* III and IV, and we shall meet various examples in the course of our overall discussion of that topography, its nature, dynamics, and philosophical implications. Before moving to the broader view, however, I would like to focus upon another particular stanza, this time from near the end of Canto IV, again involving an act of self-definition:

> And I have loved thee, Ocean! and my joy
> Of youthful sports was on thy breast to be
> Borne, like thy bubbles, onward: from a boy
> I wantoned with thy breakers—they to me
> Were a delight . . .

For I was as it were a child of thee,
And trusted to thy billows far and near,
And laid my hand upon thy mane—as I do here.
(IV.184)

According to Mark Kipperman, an ambitious recent inter-
preter of *Childe Harold*, Byron here asserts 'the creative suprem-
acy of the individual with clarity and strength': the poet is akin
to the vast fathomless source of Creation—the Ocean 'bound-
less, endless, and sublime' (IV.183)—but is in a sense even
greater than the sea he sports with, standing above it and
laying his hand upon its 'mane'.[3] But the stanza is a lot more
complex than that. For one thing, it could be said that the
individual's 'supremacy' seems to consist of no more than the
capacity for creating illusions: that Byron's image of omnipo-
tence, the sea beneath his caressing hand, is so manifestly
strategic that it proclaims the omnipotence as a phantasm of
the mind, a wish rather than any achieved reality. The whole
stanza, moreover, is a site for the play of subjective desire at
another level, as Byron lays claim to a special dispensation, the
birthright of ocean's 'child'; and here we become aware of an
eerie force in the poetry, something rich, strange, and indica-
tive of veiled depths. The terms in which the dispensation is
framed are curiously sensuous, even erotic: the 'mane' he
gently touches merges of course the 'steed' image of III.2 with
reference to the might ('main') of the ocean itself, yet it signifies
at the same time the yielding, submissive plenitude of a lover,
following as it does upon details of being borne upon the
breast, the joys of one who 'wantoned' in delight, experiencing
the 'pleasing fear' of a trespass into the mysterious realm of
Otherness. Peter J. Manning talks of *Childe Harold* as Byron's
'attempt to construct an omni-competent self, glossing over the
stresses it reveals', and locates the source of these stresses in the
residual trauma of an early withdrawal of maternal love, the
incestuous relationship with Augusta, his half-sister, and the
separation from his wife.[4] There is something in this, despite
the notorious shakiness of biographical grounds of interpre-
tation (for we may simply be constructing 'the life' backwards
from the text). Though Byron says he is 'nothing', this does not
mean there are no psychological pressures behind, and at work
in, the poetry—whatever the precise conditions from which

they arose. In the present stanza, his creation of a fantastical secret world of mutuality, ending in an active illusion of mastery ('And laid my hand . . .'), at once projects and vicariously supplies an interior need, fills and concedes an emptiness.

This psychological dimension is something else we shall recurrently encounter—an ingredient in a process inscribed with the message that we live in and by the fictions we create, and that this represents a condition both of limitation and limitless opportunity. But do Cantos III and IV of *Childe Harold*, as the stanzas we have examined may suggest, consist only of odd, fragmentary episodes, lacking any overarching purpose or progressive design? This is apparently so for one major critic of Byron, who calls the poem 'a discontinuous scheme of self-assertion and self-cancellation'.[5] And there are ample places where the poet seems himself to point to the fragmentedness of his vision, notably the much-discussed stanzas on 'the broken mirror', where he speaks of the mind engendering a 'thousand images of one that was, / The same, and still the more, the more it breaks' (III.33),[6] and, more hard-hitting, his thoughts at the tomb of Metalla on building himself a 'little bark of hope' from the ruins of a shattered existence:

> But could I gather from the wave-worn store
> Enough for my rude boat, where should I steer?
> There woos no home, nor hope, nor life, save what is here.
>
> (IV.105)

This implies the inevitability, for Byron, of living in the present moment, whether intense or hollow; his only abode is immediate and passing time, the sphere of restless reflection and making where the individual and the world he inhabits, self and truth, are not stable entities but are constituted here and now. Yet these lines are also an instance of the expression of a wish—this time for that which is lamented as absent. No one writing (either a long poem or a critical article) can do without teleological assumptions, some principle of order or some centre of value. Patterns of quest and aspiration *are* present in *Childe Harold*: Byron wants (that is, lacks *and* desires) somewhere to steer, a locus of higher truth and a state of higher being. In Canto III he steers towards Nature, in Canto IV towards Art.[7]

Canto III

Mark Kipperman sees in the later stages of *Childe Harold* the coming of the 'first existentialist hero in English literature', for 'though the movement is slow and hesitant, the poem concludes with an assertion of life and endless *possibility* raised within a desert of stultifying illusions and death'.[8] And Kipperman's reading is an offshoot from Jerome McGann's wide-ranging and influential account of the poem, which stresses the emergence in Canto IV of an 'unreluctant consciousness' of '[life's] contraries which so madden and exhaust the spirit'.[9]

We have already seen something of the limitations of Kipperman's view of the poem's conclusion, and shall see more. What I wish to point out here is that there is already strong evidence of his 'existentialist' Byron, and of McGann's 'unreluctant consciousness', at the beginning of Canto III. Indeed, the progenitor of existentialism, Kierkegaard, has a statement that would make a good epigraph for the Canto: 'There ought to be, in every human being a longing for a higher and more perfect. But this longing must not hollow out actuality'.[10]

The early stanzas, in both references to Harold and reflections of the poet *in propria persona*, delineate a whole series of ontological states in which the mind has become divorced from 'actuality'; and these states are described largely in negative terms, as impasse, arrestment, failure, delusion. There is, for example, the poet's 'crush'd feeling's dearth' (6), and his memory of the boiling eddy of his own wild thoughts, a 'whirling gulf of phantasy and flame' (7). Even steadfastness represents less a capacity to take the shocks of life than a withdrawal to the margins and to the ambit of submission— the 'strength to bear what time can not abate, / And feed on bitter fruits without accusing Fate' (7). When Harold appears, he but doubles and extends these impressions. In society, he is caught 'within the vortex, roll'd / On with the giddy circle, chasing Time' (11)—trapped in a life that is itself a hollowness, going nowhere, consuming the space of his existence in an impossible pursuit of the phantoms of 'beauty' and 'Fame'. In solitude, he drifts, with 'nought of hope left', into an undynamic resignation that 'made Despair a smilingness assume' (16).

Where Byron does, among these passages, upvalue solitary contemplation, it is to throw the shadow of the greatest 'actuality' of all, our mortality, across the spirit's flights of fire. Harold could people the stars with 'beings bright', forgetting 'earth-born jars' and 'human frailties', but thus falls victim to an inevitable reversal:

> Could he have kept his spirit to that flight
> He had been happy; but this clay will sink
> Its spark immortal, envying it the light
> To which it mounts, as if to break the link
> That keeps us from yon heaven which woos us to its brink.
>
> (III.14)

Though respecting transcendental aspiration, Byron stresses the irreducible power of our earthly nature, a temporal and spatial reality which will, when challenged or ignored, intensify its weight, binding us down.

This is not the self-indulgence of a smiling despair, nor any stoical or oneiric retreat from life. Byron's awareness is always greater than that of his eponymous hero, who functions in this part of the poem to define by contrast an unfolding consciousness which, though bred in isolation, is wide-awake, active, alert to the contraries of the human condition, above all the mismatch of desire and possibility, the promptings of the spirit and the frailty and enchainment of mortal substance. When Byron then turns to Waterloo—'Stop!—for thy tread is on an Empire's dust!'—that consciousness rises to embrace the corporate affairs of men. Not only does mankind inhabit a cosmos not in harmony with his spiritual gifts and needs, he creates a socio-political microcosm at variance with his own best interests. Chronicler of the age's great mistake, the poet laments, not the futility of war itself, but the victors' reinstatement of the 'thraldom' of monarchical power:

> How that red rain hath made the harvest grow!
> And is this all the world has gained by thee,

> Thou first and last of fields! king-making Victory?
> (III.17)

This is Byron's acclaimed 'European' voice, monumental, passionate in Freedom's cause yet elegiac and mounting soon to a proverbial register unrivalled, except by the Johnsonian 'grandeur of generality', in pointing such truths as the vanity of human wishes or the experience of loss:[11]

> Ambition's life and labours all were vain;
> He wears the shattered links of the world's broken chain.
> (III.18)

> They mourn, but smile at length; and, smiling, mourn:
> The tree will wither long before it fall . . .
> The day drags through, though storms keep out the sun;
> And thus the heart will break, yet brokenly live on: . . .
> (III.32)

In the sphere neither of history nor of being is there, as Byron sees it, any fit between what is and what ought to be. But this unaccountable irony is not felt in any 'reluctant' way, and on the contrary leads to the recognition that there is 'a very life in our despair' (34). As the 'fever of vain longing' for the dead brings forth such 'life' out of vacancy, so Waterloo, the 'place of skulls', is for Byron no site of silence or blank disquietude but one to be richly mined by the archaeology of the mythopoeic imagination.

That imagination works with most energy and persistence upon the figure of Napoleon, where the ancient theme of *quantum mutatus ab illo* is resurrected in an emblematization of fallen pride, the fickleness of Fortune, and yet, at last, also the unvanquishable mind. The 'conqueror' of the earth is now its 'captive'; he who was once 'A god unto [him]self' is 'nothing, save the jest of Fame' (37): but still

> When the whole host of hatred stood hard by,
> To watch and mock thee shrinking, thou has smiled
> With a sedate and all-enduring eye;—
> When Fortune fled her spoil'd and favourite child,
> He stood unbowed beneath the ills upon him piled.
> (III.39)

The emphasis finally falls, however, somewhere else—upon
the daemon within. Faint Johnsonian accents give way to a
definite recall of Dryden's Achitophel, as Byron recasts the
satanic myth in modern form:[12]

> But quiet to quick bosoms is a hell,
> And *there* hath been thy bane; there is a fire
> And motion of the soul which will not dwell
> In its own narrow being, but aspire
> Beyond the fitting medium of desire:
> > . . . a fever at the core,
> Fatal to him who bears, to all who ever bore.
> > > (III.42)

It is at this point that we become forcibly aware of the
process of 'doubling' in the text which is Byron's characteristic
artistic signature in *Childe Harold*. The account of Napoleon is
manifestly an elaboration of aspects of the earlier presentation
of Harold, the driven outsider 'Proud though in desolation' and
untaught to 'yield dominion of his mind' (12), the 'restless'
spirit in whom the 'heat' of an 'impeded soul would through
[the] bosom eat' (15). 'Sophists' and 'Bards', as well as
'Statesmen', are for Byron among the 'unquiet things' subject
to daemonic impulse (43), and in a later doubling he discourses
on the fate of 'the self-torturing sophist, wild Rousseau', whose
consuming passion was ideal beauty

> > which became
> In him existence, and o'erwhelming teems
> Along his burning page, distempered though it seems.
> > > (III.78)

Most of Byron's figures are, like Napoleon, examples of the
'spirit antithetically mixt' (36); the author of *La Nouvelle Héloise*
is the abiding spectacle, at once inspiring and cautionary, of
the paradox of imagination, the 'etherial flame' that 'kindle[s]'
and 'blast[s]' (78). One of Byron's greatest insights into
creativity is a sense of the links between the image and erotic
fascination: Rousseau fell in love, not with living dame, but
with an Idea of his own making. Unlike the poet, who sees all
this, his longing for a 'higher and more perfect' hollowed out
actuality until it ceased to exist. He went mad.

Now, this doubling is of course fundamental to the becoming

of Byron's text, which proliferates—at once unfolds and
fractures—in a series of inequations. This seems to me a more
accurate way of putting it than to talk, as one might be tempted
to do, of Byron's weaving of variations around a theme, for that
would be to suggest a conscious orchestration that is on the
whole lacking. Roland Barthes defines narrative as an emanci-
patory logic, a transcending of 'the first *form* given man,
namely repetition';[13] but *Childe Harold* III, reflective rather
than narratological, bears witness to the persistence of 'the
first form' itself, though also confirming the inevitability in
language and mental life (except in special situations) of
divergence, of a sameness that is never an equality. Repetition
is always a meaningful event, demanding explanation. How do
we interpret it in *Childe Harold?*

On one level, certainly, in terms of a *Romantic* preoccupation.
The poem's repeated configurations of the daemonic reflect
and feed that obsession with the shadow side of interior being
which surfaces as early as, for example, the 'craz'd' bard of
Gray's *Elegy*, persists in such figures as the poet of 'Resolution
and Independence' who is trapped in a vicious cycle of 'fears
and fancies', and emerges with particular force in the maniac of
Shelley's 'Julian and Maddalo' (a poem owing much to Byron
himself), whose hell, like Rousseau's, is the torment of compul-
sive encounter with a phantom 'spirit's mate'.[14] Yet these
configurations are also ineluctably 'personal', in that they are
themselves projected from within. Mythopoeic energies are no
more apparent in *Childe Harold* than their 'psychopoeic'
counterpart—energies whose source and centre are the self.
The embrace of actuality does not preclude subjective determi-
nants and goals.

The figures Byron creates are thus doublings of himself, and
involve all the motivations and yield customarily associated
with the phenomenon of the 'double'. For Freud, the ultimate
function of the double was as a mechanism for self-observation
and self-criticism, a special agency able to 'stand over against
the rest of the ego . . . which we become aware of as our
conscience'.[15] Something of this effect is, of course, apparent in
Byron. His doubles are not the guilt-stained emanations
identified by Freud in 'the pathological case of delusions of
observation':[16] it is Rousseau, 'phrensied' and with a mind that

was 'suspicion's sanctuary' (80), who suffered from persecution
mania. They are, rather, products of the mature 'ego' in the act
of exteriorizing and transcending the darker possibilities of
imaginative existence: Byron's accounts of those who bear 'a
fever at the core'—Harold, Napoleon, Rousseau, his own
unworthy self whirled in the maelstrom of 'phantasy and
flame'—are both an *idée fixe* and a denial of its tyranny, a
recurrent surfacing and censoring of psychological danger. Yet
there are other impulses at work, approachable through the
emphasis of Freud and Rank upon the split aspect of the
double, which is at once 'an assurance of immortality' and an
'uncanny harbinger of death'.[17] Indeed, the whole text of *Childe
Harold* is in a simple way an 'energetic denial of the power of
death',[18] for, as Byron implies when predicting the survival of
the 'voice' when the 'heart . . . is cold' (III.140), it will persist
so long as there is a single reader to receive it. More
specifically, however, Byron appropriates to himself the nature
and status of the driven outsider, one 'not fit with [mankind] to
stir and toil'—what Shelley called 'the Pilgrim of Eternity':

> But there are wanderers o'er Eternity
> Whose bark drives on and on, and anchored ne'er shall be.
> (III.70)

Critics have regularly pointed to the events of 1816 as the
shaping influence behind Canto III—Byron's fall from grace
and struggle to rise again, 'separation from Lady Byron . . .
bitter charge and countercharge . . . national ignominy, isola-
tion from Augusta, and final exile from England'.[19] But what
matters is not that 'the poetry' reflects 'the life' but that Byron
writes his life into a destiny, situating himself in a typological
relationship to the fated hero, or the eternal wanderer. If
Napoleon or Rousseau are in a sense parasitic upon his
imagination, which nourishes their greatness, so does he find
in them the image of his own 'being more intense', the
'antithetical' mixture of his spirit.

'I live not in myself' (III.72). Byron commits himself
progressively to the extinction of any self prior to the word and
the image, and chooses the freedom—and the instability—of
living through others and in constantly changing guises. In the
later parts of Canto III, he makes trial of the role of worshipper

of Nature, taking the poem in a new direction, dissolving all
concern with 'the actual' in favour of a pursuit of the 'higher'
and 'more perfect'. Though, as we have seen, he has recognized
the limits of aspiration and desire, and though he has cast
himself as one who 'anchored ne'er shall be', he now bids for
both a philosophy of transcendence and a safe harbour for his
spirit—a shrine, a home. He tries to turn the tables on his own
dynamic pessimism.

The attempt is launched via another 'doubling' in the text,
for Byron picks up and transfers directly to himself a model of
well-being earlier apportioned, in passing, to Harold, for
whom desert, forest, breaker's foam

>   spake
> A mutual language, clearer than the tome
> Of his land's tongue, which he would oft forsake
> For Nature's pages glass'd by sunbeams on the lake.
>   (III.13)

There is, however, an interesting contradiction here, in the
shift from 'spake / A mutual language', which suggests reci-
procity or communion between the forces of mind and nature,
to the idea of 'Nature's page', which reduces nature to a
constellation of signs and passes the initiative all to the
interpreting mind. And in the landscapes themselves nature is
very much a text to be read—to be squeezed for every ounce of
emotional advantage:

> Clear, placid Leman! thy contrasted lake,
> With the wild world I dwelt in, is a thing
> Which warns me, with its stillness, to forsake
> Earth's troubled waters for a purer spring.
> This quiet sail is as a noiseless wing
> To waft me from distraction; once I loved
> Torn ocean's roar, but thy soft murmuring
> Sounds sweet as if a sister's voice reproved,
> That I with stern delights should e'er have been so moved.
>   (III.85)

Kipperman complains that this is too much a created ideal,
rather than nature as it really is.[20] But that of course is the
point: the stanza is not primarily a record of an extra-linguistic

reality, but a topography of mental process, a straining of the subjective spirit for a site of ontological repose. The activity of the mind is inscribed at every point: in the opening imperative (nature *ordered*), in 'contrasted' (nature *situated* in relation to the quest for sanctuary from previous turmoil), in 'warns' (nature *read* as a signpost towards a purer state of being), in the sibilant consonants and hushed vowels which *compose* nature's voice as a 'soft murmuring', and in the concluding metaphoric connection—'as if'—which concedes a psychological leap determined by sexual, or desexualized, impulse. And from this activity, a sort of autodidactic induction, then springs, in a series of memorable stanzas, an understated yet buoyant epiphanic mood, culminating in a sense of universal harmony. A living fragrance 'breathes' from 'the shore / Of flowers yet fresh with childhood', and some bird 'Starts into voice a moment, then is still'; the starlit dews silently 'infuse / Deep into Nature's breast the spirit of her hues': all is 'concentered in a life intense' and shares in 'that which is Creator and defence' (86–89). Then

> stirs the feeling infinite, so felt
> In solitude, where we are *least* alone;
> A truth, which through our being then doth melt
> And purifies from self: it is a tone . . .
> . . . which makes known
> Eternal harmony . . .
>
> (III.90)

This seems to me a lot more impressive than several critics have been willing to allow, including Michael Cooke, who refers to Byron's 'transcendentalism manqué', and Philip W. Martin, who (much less interestingly) downgrades Byron at every opportunity to the level of an inept pickpurse of conventional Romantic ideas.[21] We have only to compare the above-quoted stanzas with something from the most obvious precursor text, Rousseau's *Rêveries*—'The more sensible the soul of a contemplative man is, the more he abandons it to the extasies this harmony excites. A reverie soft and deep invades all his senses; he sinks with delightful enebriety into the immensity of that beautiful system'—[22] to appreciate how vividly Byron realizes the experiential content and gains of solitary contemplation. Apart from his purchase on areas of unselfconscious feeling, moreover, there is a remarkable audacity, a pushing at limits, in the broader effort to look beyond the confines of self, mortality, and a fallen world which runs through this latter half of the poem. For Byron, absorption in nature is nothing less than a personal salvation, an escape from the state of Original Sin in which he sees himself implicated, an Adam unparadised, or an outcast Cain:

> And thus I am absorb'd, and this is life:
> I look upon the peopled desert past,
> As on a place of agony and strife,
> Where, for some sin, to Sorrow I was cast,
> To act and suffer, but remount at last . . .
>   (III.73)

His engagement with nature is not just a means of self-justification, though it certainly involves this—the explanation, on the model of Rousseau ('I had rather shun than hate them'),[23] of exile and isolation as an advantageous retreat from a 'contentious world' (69). It is, also, a testing of redemptive possibilities, of imagination as a means of grace. When he considers Clarens, the setting of Rousseau's *La Nouvelle Héloise*, he perceives it as the earthly paradise itself, a *locus amoenus* where the fertile harmonies of nature—'gush of springs', 'bend of stirring branches', 'bud which brings / The swiftest thought of beauty'—combine with Love 'unto one mighty end', giving earnest of 'a still higher and more comprehensive order' (103).[24] 'Spurning the clay-cold bonds which round our being cling' (73), he envisions a perfect world in which the spirit may rest, and be free.

Yet there *is* an element of the manqué in all of this, if by that word we understand something which might have been but is not, which has missed being. Nowhere does Byron's poetry more clearly undo or set limits to its own affirmations than in these sections of *Childe Harold* III, where achievement is consistently shadowed by non-achieving, potentiality by its circumscription, plenitude by lack, completion by incompleteness. This happens on occasion sequentially, for after celebrating 'absorption' Byron then immediately defers that state to a future, and ironic, context—death:

When elements to elements conform,
And dust is as it should be, shall I not
Feel all I see, less dazzling, but more warm?
The bodiless thought?

(III.74)

Self cannot truly be lost this side of the ultimate dissolution. Certainly, it cannot be absorbed in nature or 'eternal harmony', because, as we have seen, these exist as a construct of the creating mind, either as perceptual process (Leman) or envisioning (Clarens). Self in *Childe Harold* is always an ambiguous essence, both enabling and disabling. Byron may talk of 'that which is Creator and defence', but these are marginalized concepts, and the whole drift of the poetry is towards signifying an anthropocentric universe in which man is, for better or worse, his own 'Creator' and 'defence': for better, because we may create according to our gifts and needs; for worse, because whatever we create can have the status only of a passing show or provisional fulfilment, and because we remain vulnerable always to the influx of dark imagining, conflict, dissatisfaction.

Canto III of *Childe Harold* draws to a close in further foregroundings of the power and limits of creation, and their connection with desire and its irresolution. Kipperman sees the tempest sequence that follows the stanzas on peaceful Leman as a crucial point of maturation, Byron's renunciation of created ideals in favour of confrontation with the 'energies of the real experienced world'.[25] To my mind, however, this reading involves a false distinction between what is 'created' and what is 'real'; for the storm landscape is as much of the mind's making as the benign Nature of Leman had been. The sequence is an orgasmic fantasy, tinged with dreams of revenge. Whereas the poet had previously heard a sister's mild reproof, he now sees a presence beckoning him to mysterious stern delights: night, storm, and darkness are 'wondrous strong, / Yet lovely in your strength, as is the light / Of a dark eye in woman' (92). Byron again wishes for absorption, but this time into the dionysiac rhythms of unrestrained and explosive exaltation, as he begs to be a 'sharer in thy fierce and far delight', and the 'glee / Of the loud hills shakes with its mountain-mirth, / As if they did rejoice o'er a young earthquake's birth' (93). The landscape seems at once a dynamic otherness and the chimera of his own passion, a phantasm with which he desires an impossible union. There then emerge, however, different images, where the heights on either side of the chasm formed by the swift Rhône become 'lovers who have parted / In hate', left 'war within themselves to wage', and the poet reads in the action of the lightning a purgative penetration of the secret place of desolate apartness:

> as if he did understand,
> That in such gaps as desolation work'd,
> There the hot shaft should blast whatever therein lurk'd.
> (III.95)

For Kipperman, Byron's awareness of the conflicting energies in nature brings him, by a sort of Fichtean 'interdetermination' whereby self is defined by response to not-self, to a sharper sense of the restlessness within himself.[26] This is true:

> the far roll
> Of your departing voices, is the knoll
> Of what in me is sleepless,—if I rest.
> But where of ye, oh tempests! is the goal?
> Are ye like those within the human breast?
> Or do ye find, at length, like eagles, some high nest?
> (III.96)

But what matters is not so much Byron's recognition of the autonomous and ceaselessly active forces at work within the self as a longing to give them absolute realization. Having projected into the lightning's force the image of a consummation involving the application of power—the 'hot shaft'—and its satisfaction in the cleansing of desolation, he finally proclaims the wish for some single moment of total self-expression and self-fulfilment:

> Could I embody and unbosom now
> That which is most within me,—could I wreak
> My thoughts upon expression, and thus throw
> Soul, heart, mind, passions, feelings, strong or weak,
> All that I would have sought, and all I seek,
> Bear, know, feel, and yet breathe into *one* word,

And that one word were Lightning, I would speak;
But as it is, I live and die unheard,
With a most voiceless thought, sheathing it as a sword.
                    (III.97)

Inscribed here of course is Byron's urge to wreak vengeance upon—strike down—those who have wronged him, and the inadequacy of words to achieve that end. But there is a profounder drive, and deeper impotence, at issue. The self can never be fully embodied or fully lost ('unbosomed') through language, though we may devoutly wish it: as in the act of love, the release of energy is also its evacuation, leading on to powerlessness and a sense of incompleteness. Byron glimpses in this stanza a moment of self-assertion, a becoming, so great that the self—soul, heart and all—would be obliterated; lightning, after all, simultaneously makes its mark and burns itself out. That glimpse, however, is full of irony, for it is a glimpse of death. Byron may say, with regret, 'I live and die unheard', but in so doing he points the eternal paradox of living and being heard: incompleteness, the wanting that is both aspiration and not-having, is the inescapable condition of being and the essential grounds of creation and the text.

In a journal entry clearly associated with this stanza, and particularly with the desire to utter the self *out of* existence, Byron refers to persistent 'recollections of bitterness—& especially of recent and more home desolation' which dogged him during composition of the poem, wrecking all efforts to 'lose my own wretched identity'.[27] The burden of 'wretched identity', signally increased by the collapse of his marriage in the early months of 1816, cannot simply be dissolved in a word, or even a whole canto. For no one can the past be lost, but for Byron the problem is the greater in that he feels it as a constant weight upon the present—not a Wordsworthian joy in the glowing embers but pain that they still live. For all his testing of redemptive possibilities in Canto III, and for all his expense of energy, he can finally summarize his position only in terms that he had seemingly stood beyond at the beginning: steadfast resignation—a capacity 'to steel / The heart against itself' (111)—and the knowledge that poetry may at least 'beguile / My breast, or that of others, for a while' (112), where we are returned to the introductory stanzas on the 'strength to bear' and imagination as a veil of 'forgetfulness' (7, 4). The most he can claim is that same proud independence he had 'read into' the figure of Napoleon, shot through with that strain of self-justifying retreat from the 'world' put forth as a prelude to the verses on Leman:

> I stood and stand alone,—remember'd or forgot.
> . . . .
> I have not loved the world, nor the world me,—
> But let us part fair foes; I do believe,
> Though I have found them not, that there may be
> Words which are things,—hopes which will not deceive . . .
> (III.112, 114)

Thus Byron traces a circle, getting nowhere, consuming all idea of advance, intellectual, psychological, experiential, in an accretion of the self into a fixed state of being. *Childe Harold* III is no drama of maturation, but a holding operation; its *telos* is not of transcendence or absorption, but of standing alone and standing fast.

This is confirmed by Byron's closing address to his daughter, Ada. Here he does lay claim to a future, and to a place in *someone*'s affections: his voice will blend with Ada's visions, 'reach into thy heart,—when mine is cold' (115); and if 'dull Hate' should try to drain his blood out of her being 'Still thou would'st love me, still that more than life retain' (117). But this is clearly a strategic bid for consolation (owing something to Wordsworth's address to his sister at the end of 'Tintern Abbey')[28]—an act of will and faith which declares the mind's resilience but also its dependence on fictions, on words that are not things, on hopes that may well deceive. Significantly, the Canto ends with an affirmation that concedes impotence, changes nothing. Remembering this time Coleridge's prayer for his child in 'Frost at Midnight',[29] Byron resigns the future all to Ada herself, wishing her a 'fire . . . more tempered', a 'hope far higher' (118); but even this blessing tells of want, separation, and a sense of 'wretched identity'—'Fain *would I* waft such blessing upon thee, / As, with a sigh, I deem thou *might'st have been* to me!' (italics mine).

Yet irresolution and standing fast are not impasse. They leave the future open, and the relevant future is of course Canto

IV of *Childe Harold*. There is something else in Canto III,
however, which in the event spurs Byron on. Several critics,
and not least McGann, have stressed the importance of
aspiration in Byron, and his interest in images of climbing.[30]
Napoleon's ascent to the 'loftiest peaks' of ambition brings
down tempests on his 'naked head' (45), but the artist-poet's
mountings of the mind are less dangerous and more pro-
ductive: Byron celebrates the experience of sublimity that
'expands the spirit' (62) and later, on the white Alps, envisions
how he 'must pierce' to the 'great and growing region, where /
The earth to her embrace compels the powers of air' (109). In
Canto IV expansion of the spirit replaces absorption as the
essence of the Byronic epiphanies. That these will be sought
more in the palaces of Art and Religion than of Nature is
signalled by the sight of the promised Land of Italy spread out
below the poet as he stands aloft on the Alps—'Italia' and her
'consecrated pages', the 'fount at which the panting mind
assuages / Her thirst of knowledge' (110). The reference to
Italia's 'pages' is interesting, and follows hard upon references
to those of man's Maker and those of the poet himself:

> But let me quit man's works, again to read
> His Maker's spread around me, and suspend
> This page, which from my reveries I feed . . .
>   (III.109)

The aims and ambitions of Canto IV become increasingly and
explicitly tied up with the processes of making and reading
texts—world as text and self as text. This fact Byron's critics
have not, to my knowledge, fully recognized.

Canto IV

'A palace and a prison on each hand' (1). Whatever the actual
topography of Venice, the grammatical error is revealing, for
whichever way Byron turns in *Childe Harold* IV he discovers
configurations of both glory and confinement, the aspiring
height and the abysmal dungeon-depth. This composite per-
ception—not an 'either . . . or' but an 'and . . . and'—had of
course regularly emerged in Canto III, as in the account of the
great but fallen Napoleon; but in Canto IV it is the constant

term in a swirling concatenation of creative and interpretative acts, a sort of heterogeneous chain of events. It is not that Byron cannot make up his mind, but that he sees everything in essentially the same two ways.

Venice, for example, is a monument to 'withered power', a place of absence with its 'crumbling palaces' and 'empty halls', a 'spectred city', but it is also a holy spot whose spirit comes uncalled to the receptive mind:

> I saw from out the wave her structures rise
> As from the stroke of an enchanter's wand:
> A thousand years their cloudy wings expand
> Around me, and a dying Glory smiles
> O'er the far times . . .
>
> (IV.1)

Places are for Byron always both something in themselves and a testing-ground for the imagination: here his own imagination moves confidently, finding plenitude in vacancy itself, being touched by the glory of a decayed past.

Interwoven with, and developing out of, Byron's response to Venice, however, is a strong theoretical grasp of the dual nature of the creating mind, its inexhaustible energy and its infinite vulnerability. Expanding the less rounded insights of Canto III, to the 'beings' through which we may live an intenser and 'more beloved' existence, escaping 'mortal bondage' (5), he opposes, variously, a sense of our 'over-weening phantasies' (7), the 'electric chain' along which some shadowy image of past time transmits bitterness sharp as 'a scorpion's sting' (23), or the inevitable fading of epiphanic joy—'The last still lovelier—till—'tis gone—and all is gray' (29). Tasso's fire could not be quenched by the malice of tyranny or the 'hell' of a dungeon-cell (36), but the mind itself can be a greater hell, beset with 'demons', transforming the world in the image of its own despair, making 'the sun like blood', the earth 'a tomb' (34). This is self-torturing wild Rousseau again; and the cautionary side of his history is picked up once more later, in the remarkable stanzas on the spring of Egeria (115ff.), the nymph beloved of Numa. Here the legend of the votary-king's infatuation—his 'nympholepsy'—is read by Byron as a paradigm of man's pursuit of 'holy Love', a union blending 'a

celestial with a human heart' and imparting 'the purity of
heaven to earthly joys', but then suggests the entrapment of
'desiring phantasy', our vain yearning for some 'fruit forbidden
to our wants'. Byron sees very clearly the links between
imaginative creation, the religious impulse, and erotic fascina-
tion but if Egeria and her Elysian spring are a 'sweet creation'
bearing witness to the mind's capacity for conceiving and
bodying forth the Ideal, that capacity may also be a fatal spell
that binds us to an endless quest for phantoms of our own
making and hence to constant disappointment: 'The stubborn
heart, its alchemy begun, / Seems ever near the prize,—
wealthiest when most undone' (123). Art itself Byron finally
perceives as a form of narcissistic desire—the projection and
tyranny of an impossible dream:

> Of its own beauty is the mind diseased,
> And fevers into false creation:—where,
> Where are the forms the sculptor's soul hath seized?
> In him alone . . .
> The unreach'd Paradise of our despair,
> Which o'er-informs the pencil and the pen,
> And overpowers the page where it would bloom again?
> (IV.122)

Byron characteristically wanders into truth in Canto IV:
here a psychological truth that deconstructs the claims of Art
to be a reflection or mirroring of some extra-personal spiritual
Truth, just as Canto III had raised questions about its claims
to be the record of any fixed, extra-linguistic reality. The poem
proceeds by association of ideas, moving on, circling back, and
at this point Byron places the fever of illusion within the
broader context of the human condition as a whole, declaring,
not for the first time nor the last, but with peculiar and
rounded intensity, the disharmony between man and the
cosmic order. There is a powerful orthodox consciousness of
the Fall in Byron, blended here with a hard philosophical
intoning that brings to mind Kierkegaard's and Heidegger's
studied rejection of Idealism—where individual actions can be
explained as necessary elements in the total scheme of things—
in favour of a view of existence as unendowed with goals or
predetermined purpose, a journey drawn on by 'phantom

lures' whose only certain end is Death, 'the sable smoke, where vanishes the flame'. We wither from our youth—'Sick—sick; unfound the boon—unslaked the thirst'—in a world ruled by the unspiritual god, Circumstance, whose 'crutch-like rod . . . turns Hope to dust' (124–25):

> Our life is a false nature—'tis not in
> The harmony of things,—this hard decree,
> This uneradicable taint of sin,
> This boundless upas, this all-blasting tree,
> Whose root is earth, whose leaves and branches be
> The skies which rain their plagues on men like dew—
> Disease, death, bondage—all the woes we see—
> And worse, the woes we see not—which throb through
> The immedicable soul, with heart-aches ever new.
> (IV.126)

Yet Byron then immediately rises to the challenge of this potentially terminal vision of helplessness and pain by affirming, again with a deliberateness that reminds us of the Existentialist position, the individual's 'right of thought', his 'last and only place / Of refuge':

> this, at least, shall still be mine:
> Though from our birth the faculty divine
> Is chain'd and tortured—cabin'd, cribb'd, confined,
> And bred in darkness, lest the truth should shine
> Too brightly on the unprepared mind,
> The beam pours in, for time and skill will couch the blind.
> (IV.127)

The 'faculty divine' is thought itself, the capacity for creation and self-creation, for reflection and acts of decision, of knowing and understanding; though in part something 'given', a beam pouring in, it is also something 'effected', learned and worked at with skill. It is a possible basis for action, and for growth.

This marks a turning point, a moment of forward impetus, in *Childe Harold*, after which, as various critics have pointed out,[31] Byron moves into a deeper, richer, and in some ways more positive register as he explores the 'exhaustless mine / Of contemplation' (128) that is Rome. It is as if, having categorically confronted the darkness and bitterness of life, emblematized in the image of the poisonous upas tree, he can fully release the regenerative force and solidity of his own mind, previously imaged in the tannen tree, loftiest on the least-sheltered rocks and 'rooted in barrenness'—'the mind may grow the same' (20). Earlier passages on the Italian landscape had signalled the lures to which the poetic consciousness is always vulnerable—arrestment and fragmentation, the mind collapsed back into itself or pointlessly meandering through a wilderness of vacant forms, solipsism or seeming madness:

> But my soul wanders; I demand it back
> To meditate amongst decay, and stand
> A ruin amidst ruins . . .
>
> (IV.25)

Rome had been like Niobe, 'childless', 'voiceless', 'empty' (80), and in this had been a mirroring of the poet, too, in his negative aspect—immobile, bereft of his child, wordless in his woe. Meditation itself had been seen as a route to error and illusion, for 'we but feel our way to err', and Rome is as 'the desart, where we steer / Stumbling o'er recollections; now we clap / Our hands, and cry "Eureka!" it is clear— / When but some false mirage of ruin rises near' (81). But these lures, these phantoms, and these fantastical mis-takings, though they cannot be eradicated, may be countered by a rooted and mobile determination to redeem meaning from the wreck of the past, both corporate and personal.

What Byron first discovers in the mine of contemplation, as, approaching the Coliseum, he applies the 'right of thought' with renewed vigour, is a way of casting off the burden of 'wretched identity' which had so manifestly troubled him at the end of Canto III and had been carried over into Canto IV as a bitter sense of self-mutilation on the 'thorns' of some unspecified wrongdoing or false move. In the 'lightning' episode of Canto III he had fallen mute before the recognition that there can be no equivalence between emotion and expression, sheathing like a 'sword' (words sealed off) his 'voiceless thought' of condemnation against those who had given him offence. Now he takes the opposite tack, replacing feeling with words whose force, whose effect, will be supplied from the hearts and minds of those who read his text. Instead of the single act of self-assertion he had desired before, which would have meant his own obliteration, we have the self-preservation of the written record and the integrity of forgiveness:

> But in this page a record will I seek.
> Not in the air shall these my words disperse,
> Though I be ashes; a far hour shall wreak
> The deep prophetic fulness of this verse . . .

> That curse shall be Forgiveness.—Have I not—
> Hear me, my mother Earth! behold it, Heaven!—
> Have I not had to wrestle with my lot?
> Have I not suffered things to be forgiven?
> Have I not had my brain seared, my heart riven,
> Hopes sapp'd, name blighted, Life's life lied away?
>   (IV.134–35)

In a reversal of the earlier episode, Byron makes himself the 'seared', 'riven' victim of the lightning-stroke, and not its perpetrator; catharsis comes for him, not through any unleashing of passion, but from translating the wounds inflicted upon him, both 'mighty wrongs' and 'petty perfidy', into memorial inscription, a series of questions which will reach accusingly into the future, persisting like the 'tone of a mute lyre', even moving in 'hearts all rocky now the late remorse of love' (137). He is liberated from 'self' by, in a sense, writing it *out of existence*, deferring the completion of desire until he may 'breathe', something 'unearthly', in the consciousness of others. He does after all reduce his being, if not to *one* word, then to but a few: he is content to leave his mark, committing to Time and Fate the outcome—'I sleep, but thou shalt yet awake' (133).

Reading these passages we become disconcertedly aware, I think, of pose and rhetorical gesture—in the pseudo-Promethean cast and exaggerated terms of the poet's curse, in the evident 'madeness' of the whole project for erasing bitter self-consciousness, in the elaborate ritual of bringing to Time's 'divinely desolate' temple the offering of 'Ruins of years—though few, yet full of fate' (131). But this artifice and overstatement, at times risking parody of the mythic-heroic, is of course a potent ingredient of Byron's 'right of thought' and the message it engenders. One way in which skill has 'couched' his blindness—removed the cataract—is the insight that life is indeed a playing of parts, and what we call reality is after all only what the mind puts forth, a text to be read or mis-read, a signification to be taken this way or that. The point is underlined in the great set-piece on the Coliseum gladiatorial contest, where, overstepping the relatively naive (though impressive) vision of Venice's dark and bright eternities, Byron recapitulates the ironic toning of the Waterloo passages, yet with a sharper edge, more sceptically. Returning to the theme of absorption, he describes himself as being somehow transported to the past, becoming 'a part of what has been', 'all-seeing but unseen' (138); but what he sees is very much his own reconstruction of history's page: the past becomes a theatre of which he is at once director, audience, and reviewer, reviving and commenting on a drama which transforms life into a set of symbolic attitudes ranging from cruelty and pathos to the virtual farce of futile self-esteem. In the death of the gladiator, 'Butcher'd to make a Roman holiday', is inscribed man's inhumanity to man, all the more horrifying a consumption because the sacrifice is but a ritual diversion for crowd and emperor, a rule of the game:

> And here the buzz of eager nations ran,
> In murmured pity, or loud-roared applause,
> As man was slaughtered by his fellow man . . .
> Such were the bloody Circus' genial laws,
> And the imperial pleasure.
>   (IV.139)

The detached, sardonic bite of the puns on 'holiday', 'genial' (suggesting 'friendly' as well as 'tutelary spirit') and 'pleasure' ('enjoyment' as well as 'prerogative') introduces a note of intimate cynicism new to *Childe Harold*. It leads on immediately to a broader scepticism, as the scene, though placed very precisely in history, yields for Byron an eternal pattern of futility and death:

>   . . . Wherefore not?
> What matters where we fall to fill the maws
> Of worms—on battle-plains or listed spot?
> Both are but theatres where the chief actors rot.
>   (IV.139)

Men play their parts—and rot. Byron's rootedness consists at this point of a self-possessed and active disenchantment.

History is perceived as a drama against which it is pointless to complain, not simply because the plot always ends in death, but because it *is* a drama, a pageant without purpose beyond that of its own self-sufficient spectacle. At the same time, however, spectacle does solicit response, whether it is staged in the Coliseum as it was or in the 'arena void' that the Coliseum has become, where Byron perceives the 'garland-forest' of weeds as 'laurels on the bald first Caesar's head' (144), a sharp satirical surprise that images the very figurehead of imperial might, the demi-god who had life and death literally under his thumb, as himself a puppet in Time's own overarching plot, faintly ridiculous, old man or fool bedecked.

Though the past may be theatre, theatre may be rich with human interest and meanings. And at the centre of the Coliseum episode lies the nobility and pathos of the dying gladiator himself—not scepticism but celebration and sober sadness:

> I see before me the gladiator lie:
> He leans upon his hand—his manly brow
> Consents to death, but conquers agony . . .
> The arena swims around him—he is gone,
> Ere ceased the inhuman shout which hail'd the wretch who
>   won.
>
> He heard it, but he heeded not—his eyes
> Were with his heart, and that was far away;
> He reck'd not of the life he lost nor prize,
> But where his rude hut by the Danube lay,
> *There* were his young barbarians all at play,
> *There* was their Dacian mother . . .
>   (IV.140–41)

This of course is based on the statue in the Capitoline Museum. What Byron finds fittest to redeem from the past is its art, from which he fashions an iconography of feeling. Here we are aware of two dramas being played out, the public and the private, and of different levels of response. The crowd itself is blind to the courage and agony of the vanquished, hailing only the victor; the poet's focus, following that of the precursor artist, is all on the dying glory of the victim—just as his sympathy had been all with the bull in the bullfight episode in

Canto I (71ff.). That glory resides, however, not only in the outward show of manliness and dignity, by which the gladiator transcends the role assigned to him by the mob, but in the hidden sphere of emotion, the gladiator's thoughts of home and family. The gladiator sees differently from the crowd; the poet sees comprehensively, penetrating even beyond the sculptor's vision to the interior drama of loyalty, longing, and deprivation—a universal truth of Nature, life in a symbolic attitude.

Though all-seeing, however, Byron is not exactly unseen in these stanzas, especially when we take into account his reference to the barbarians' future vengeance against Rome. He re-creates the historical event in his own image, or rather in the image of his characteristic conception of his destiny as that of the stoical but feeling exile, bereft of family, victim of an inhuman society, cut off from other men in a shroud of thoughts. The gladiator is as it were a miniature double of the poet, and the evocation of a psycho-drama behind surface appearances seems self-reflexively to point one of the ways in which the whole text operates. Experiential determinants and a consequent doubling of the text through repetition persist even in these later reaches of *Childe Harold*. We shall meet them again when considering its subsequent, more formal representation of artefacts. Suffice it to say for the moment, however, that in this passage, though we may recognize the protagonist as a mirroring of the self, the overall effect is solidly objective, as if subjective—psychopoeic—energies had disengaged themselves from the ambit of self-consciousness to enrich, and find stable concentration in, a general, and powerful, configuration of human strength and human vulnerability.

There is, as the poem draws to an end, a strong drive in this direction, towards emblematic—and formidably melodramatic—portrayal of primary ontological states. The stanzas on the legend associated with the cell beneath the Church of St Nicola in Carcare are a particularly good example, involving as they do a translation of the spectacularly odd into the strikingly representative, and an explicit discourse on the mind's capacity to disclose and animate the 'triumphs' of 'sacred Nature'. Contemplating the ruined Coliseum, Byron had pointed to the unreliability of perception, for what seems

from a distance something 'cleared' turns out to be something
'plundered', the skeleton of a decaying fabric (143). But there is
a deeper seeing, beyond error or illusion, and greater than fact,
as the poet makes out in the dark void of the dungeon, no
'insulated phantoms of the brain' but 'full and plain', the
forms of old man and female 'young and fair . . . / With her
unmantled neck, and bosom white and bare':

> here youth offers to old age the food,
> The milk of his own gift:—it is her sire
> To whom she renders back the debt of blood
> Born with her birth. No; he shall not expire
> While in those warm and lovely veins the fire
> Of health and holy feeling can provide
> Great Nature's Nile . . .
>
> (IV.150)

The images and the story are of course in a sense anterior to the
poetic event, but the latter is of first importance—the re-
creative light of imagination and the reading of what it reveals.
In the fable of youth returning the gift of life to age Byron finds
a constellation of truth—the power of love, Nature's triumph—
which outweighs his sense of bitter fruits as he recollects that
Eve's offspring was Cain (149), and which renders insignificant
any sweeter myth of origins like the making of the milky way
from Juno's breast (151). It has for him a 'purity', a 'holiness
appealing to all hearts', which is the more telling because it
requires us to transcend an apprehension of violation and
unnaturalness, a 'reverse of [Nature's] decree' (151); the risk in
Byron's incipiently grotesque rhetoric—'those warm and
lovely veins . . .'—only serves to validate the inspirational
claims of an iconographical text which, abstractly considered,
might repel. The pressure is all towards affirmation, both of
human instinct and of the maker-reader's power to nourish the
spirit: a power allegorized in the action of the daughter's milk
itself, no drop of which 'clear stream its way shall miss . . .
replenishing its source / With life' (151). Byron retraces and
emphatically reverses the characteristic negative strains of his
vision: he looks for consolation not to an impossible heaven but
to the heart; mortal bondage and the dungeon of despair
become the nurturing womb of loveliness and sacred feeling;

imagining becomes, not a subjection to fantasy, but a fountain of superior truth.

This is a highpoint of the poem. Yet Byron appears to crave an affirmation even purer and more sublime, and appears to find it in the art of the Vatican, especially the Apollo Belvedere which attests, not just 'the quasi-immortality that the human spirit achieves when it "bodies forth" the forms of art',[32] but the divine spark in man, a power of conception and creation equivalent to Heaven's:

> if it be Prometheus stole from Heaven
> The fire which we endure, it was repaid
> By him to whom the energy was given
> Which this poetic marble hath array'd
> With an eternal glory—which, if made
> By human hands, is not of human thought . . .
> (IV.163)

The Apollo itself is untainted by nature and untouched by time, an expression of both the energy of the god and ideal beauty:

>   brow
> All radiant from his triumph in the fight;
> The shaft hath just been shot—the arrow bright
> With an immortal's vengeance; in his eye
> And nostril beautiful disdain, and might
> And majesty, flash their full lightnings by . . .
>
> But in his delicate form . . .
>   . . . are exprest
> All that ideal beauty ever bless'd
> The mind with in its most unearthly mood,
> When each conception was a heavenly guest—
> (IV.161–62)

The poem reaches here a point of rest, a sacramental repose before an unearthly perfection witnessing to the numinous and man's sharing in it.

Yet there is something else about Byron's Apollo that captures attention, and ultimately problematizes its status and effect. It is noticeable that the Deity on which the poet gazes reiterates two of his former images of himself, as pugnacious avenger and imaginative idealist, but also that these, more fully than in the Coliseum episode, have passed into pure form, geometric design; while similarly, in the preceding description of the Laocoon—'A father's love and mortal's agony / With an immortal's patience blending', the 'long envenomed chain' of the snake 'Rivet[ing] the living links' (160)—the poem's concern with human dignity and suffering, confinement and struggle, so strong in the iconography of the dying gladiator and the legend of St Nicola, had been transferred to the context of static representation, impression, not life in a symbolic attitude but the symbolic attitude itself. The repose thus involves a loss as well as a gain, for the currents of self-consciousness and consciousness of the world, the energies that have driven the poem, have been stilled, bracketed off, framed in miniature. The greatness of the poem ironically questions the greatness of transcendent Art at the very point where Art's 'eternal glory' is most patently foregrounded.

In a way, moreover, Byron's celebratory response to the Apollo is itself intrinsically insecure and shadowed by darker meanings, by a sort of built-in counter-signification. His valorizations of sublime artefacts in *Childe Harold* always have some element of uncertainty and self-limitation. Earlier, for example, he had described the Venus de Medici in its 'full divinity' as 'the unruffled mirror' of the 'loveliest dream' that ever beamed from heaven on human soul, but at the same time had been able to see in that mirror the veil of heaven only '*half* undrawn' (49, 53); and in delineating the beholder's experience of this ideal image he had slipped into a language more of sensual than spiritual plenitude, making the religion of Beauty a dionysiac whirl rather than any sacred communing, as we grow 'Dazzled and drunk . . . till the heart / Reels with its fulness' (50). Byron's reaction to the beauty of the Apollo Belvedere is more reverent and less ambiguous than this. Yet it cannot altogether escape a similar recognition of the limits to which man is ineluctably chained, of the gulf between nature and Supernature which Art theoretically bridges but cannot delete. Though the Apollo may in theory bear witness to the divine spark, it remains in practice 'wrought', 'made / By human hands'. To say that it expresses the mind 'in its most unearthly mood' is to concede the mind's characteristic earthbound state; to say that it has not caught 'a tinge of years' is to confirm the duress of temporality. In naming the unerring and inviolable perfection of the Apollo, Byron names also the imperfections and constraints of nature itself. That very perfection does not truly exist because it exists as statement, as a reading of a 'poetic marble': is the god then a presence, a heavenly visitant, or a constellation of terms, an imaginary guest? It is interesting that in the Venus de Medici stanzas Byron should attack the connoisseurs who would 'describe the undescribable', applying the 'paltry jargon of the marble mart' to an image of divinity that leaves us speechless, arousing 'blood', 'pulse', and 'breast' (50, 53). He sees that the Supernatural is that which is unspeakable. But though he uses no paltry jargon himself, he is necessarily tied to language as a means of realizing the realm of the Spirit and of the Divine, and in the act of realization is inscribed the impossibility of entering that realm, leaving the earthly and its circumscriptions behind. We are reminded of the stanza near the beginning of Canto III, where Harold's flights of the spirit are compromised by the weight of mortal substance which 'sink[s] / Its spark immortal, envying it the light / To which it mounts' (14). That same duality, the aspiration and the prohibition, the power and the powerlessness, is also the inescapable condition of the author himself, the poet writing. Words, the source of freedom and 'becoming', bring restrictions and betrayals of their own.

   Robert F. Gleckner, talking of *Childe Harold* as an inversion of the standard pilgrimage through darkness to 'a personal salvation', designates its movement a descent into 'the bowels of nothingness and despair'.[33] This influential view must be treated with care. In particular, Byron never does renounce transcendental aspiration, though he knows its ends cannot be achieved except in flashes, at least while life continues. As in Canto III he had situated the self's total 'absorption' in a dimension beyond that of nature, so, visiting St Peter's in Canto IV, he perceives the immediate expansion of the mind amidst the grandeur of God's Holy of Holies as an intimation—a promise *and* a falling short—of an otherworldly event:

> thy mind,
> Expanded by the genius of the spot,
> Has grown colossal, and can only find
> A fit abode wherein appear enshrined
> Thy hopes of immortality; and thou
> Shalt one day, if found worthy, so defined,
> See thy God face to face, as thou dost now
> His Holy of Holies, nor be blasted by his brow.
>   (IV.155)

This keeps faith with the capacity and the reachings of the spirit, but the ultimate goal of spiritual advance is of course located in a meeting of which no man may be assured ('if found worthy'), and which is so configurated as to suggest an encounter, face to face, whose outcome cannot be known for sure. Existence is grounded in hope, not certainty. McGann has encouraged a whole generation of readers to consider that at St Peter's 'the perception of the union of Nature and Supernature, which he sought and partially achieved on the Alp, is finally given [Byron]'.[34] No such perception ever really emerges, however, as McGann himself then indicates when stressing Byron's 'further understanding' that the actual destination of the desire for plenitude is 'not satisfaction, but creation, and the conditions of its being is constant movement, increase, growth'.[35] That is to say, *Childe Harold* ironizes, while remaining dependent upon, never relinquishing, a teleology of fulfilment for the poem, for pilgrimage, and for the life of man as well.

As McGann's brilliant reading shows, the famous stanzas on 'piecemeal' apprehension amount to an analysis of 'what pilgrimage means, but also what the method of *Childe Harold* has entailed':

> Thou seest not all; but piecemeal thou must break,
> To separate contemplation, the great whole
>   . . . so here condense thy soul
> To more immediate objects, and control
> Thy thoughts until thy mind hath got by heart
> Its eloquent proportions, and unroll
> In mighty graduations, part by part,
> The glory which at once upon thee did not dart,

Not by its fault—but thine: Our outward sense
Is but of gradual grasp—and as it is
That what we have of feeling most intense
Outstrips our faint expression; even so this
Outshining and o'erwhelming edifice
Fools our fond gaze, and greatest of the great
Defies at first our Nature's littleness,
Till, growing with its growth, we thus dilate
Our spirits to the size of what they contemplate.
(IV.157–58).

Making, being, and reading are all brought together and allegorized here as processes that involve us in constant passage and possibility. To adapt McGann's words, they are processes of 'gaining anew, of becoming and going somewhere else', an 'endless activity of self-discovery and renewed self-development'; not something that can be concluded or fulfilled, but a series of 'consecutive vital particularities'; 'comprehension is achieved only in successive, and relatively ignorant, perceptions . . . partial acts of perception'.[36] Yet can we use McGann's words with complete confidence? Do they not have ingredients of self-contradiction and misreading? He seems to want it both ways when talking of 'endless activity' and 'comprehension . . . achieved', and to get *Childe Harold* wrong when implying a wholly positive movement of 'gain', of 'increase, growth', and a structure of sequential, incrementally 'consecutive', parts. What Byron outlines in these stanzas is a gradual recognition of 'glory' and a gradual 'dilation' under the special conditions of sublime influence, and the process of comprehension and increase can be applied to his own poem, and the mental life it expresses, only if we recognize that process as simultaneously involving repetition and circling, bewilderment and loss, the dilemmas of consciousness and the dissolution of gains. There is a notable dilemma registered in the above-quoted stanzas, where our 'Nature's littleness' is only provisionally left behind, and the fundamental split remains between that littleness and the capacity of 'our spirits'; nature may be 'fooled' but it cannot be cancelled; feeling can outstrip 'faint expression', but cannot make it essentially less faint. And the episode ends then in a strange and telling anticlimax. 'The fountain of sublimity displays / Its depth, and thence may draw the mind of man / Its golden sands, and learn what great conceptions can': Byron's experience of sublimity peters out into the hanging silence of 'can', bearing witness not to any possession of flowing 'golden sands' but to his faintness of expression, the inadequacy of words, the fading of language and the moment itself. He must go somewhere else, and that somewhere is the equally circumscribed affirmation of the stanzas on the Apollo Belvedere.

But McGann does give us overall a Byron who is 'existential, trying', 'deeply pathetic, not triumphant'.[37] Mark Kipperman, on the other hand, wants desperately to present the poet as possessor of a victorious heroic consciousness, and to this end takes the apostrophe to the Ocean as an assertion of the 'dynamic and creative supremacy of the individual', so that the sea is an objective correlative of the self, 'creating living forms even as the mind of man creates its forms'.[38] Such a parallel is certainly proclaimed in Wordsworth's spousal verse on Snowdon, where the mighty breathing place of Nature's power, the infinite source of creation, becomes a 'genuine Counterpart / And Brother of the glorious faculty / Which higher minds bear with them as their own';[39] but there is nothing of the kind in *Childe Harold*, and Byron, on the contrary, establishes the vast infinite deep as the 'glorious mirror', not of man, but of Other, the Almighty. Empires have decayed but

> not so thou,
> Unchangeable save to thy wild waves' play—
> Time writes no wrinkle on thine azure brow—
> Such as creation's dawn beheld, thou rollest now.
>
> Thou glorious mirror, where the Almighty's form
> Glasses itself in tempests . . .
> Dark-heaving;—boundless, endless, and sublime—
> The image of Eternity—the throne
> Of the Invisible; even from out thy slime
> The monsters of the deep are made; each zone
> Obeys thee; thou goest forth, dread, fathomless, alone.
>
> (IV.182–83)

Byron steadfastly refuses (as Wordsworth does not)[40] to internalize or humanize the attributes of divine authority, freedom, and creative might. He insistently draws distinctions between these attributes—the 'unchangeable', the 'boundless', the 'endless'—and man on whom time *does* write a 'wrinkle', whose 'control / Stops with the shore', who sinks 'unknown' into the watery plain, whose creations bring 'earth's destruction' but melt like the 'snowy flake' into the waves (179–82). Any attempt, like Kipperman's, to make Byron the celebrant of a human capacity equivalent to and even 'greater than the vast power of unconscious being'[41] is bound to fail before this explicit contrast and the ironic separations that emerge in the text at points where we feel the *possibility* of a conflation of self and ocean in terms of mutual might and liberty. In a sense Byron too is 'unchangeable', the same now as at 'creation's dawn', but only inasmuch as he has gained little in the course of this life and, by implication, the poem he has created, and has not altered essentially from the suffering yet resilient self that began the childe's pilgrimage:

> some suffering, and some tears
> Have left us nearly where we had begun:
> Yet not in vain our mortal race hath run,
> We have had our reward—and it is here;
> That we can yet feel gladden'd by the sun,
> And reap from earth, sea, joy almost as dear
> As if there were no man to trouble what is clear.
>   (IV.176)

Byron feels time as a weight upon him—'long years . . . *have* done / Their work'—and knows how scant is the progress that may be clutched from its continuum. Yet, with characteristic ambivalence, he makes some claim for the yield of life and writing—modest reward, but something. In Canto IV Art and Life have supplied a nourishment for the spirit. Without denying this, however, he chooses at last to reiterate and privilege the pleasures of aloneness and unselfconscious being in the presence of nature, which he had explored in Canto III but now extends back beyond the poem, to youth and childhood itself:

> I love not Man the less, but Nature more,
> From these our interviews, in which I steal
> From all I may be, or have been before,
> To mingle with the Universe, and feel
> What I can ne'er express, yet can not all conceal.
>   (IV.178)

The recollection of his own text (and behind that again of Rousseau)[42] allows the poet finally that consoling image of paradisal and youthful fulfilment on Ocean's breast, and of mastery, in the 'child of Ocean' stanza which I discussed at length at the beginning of this essay. But this stanza, which Kipperman takes straightforwardly as proof that Byron is 'more powerful' in his reflective freedom than the sea he sports with,[43] in fact returns us to a strong sense of the radically equivocal nature and precariousness of Byron's mental and creative acts. As we have seen, it is half therapeutic memory and half regressive fantasy, less a lived 'interview' or stealing from the self than an imaginative theft driven by subjective desire. 'From a boy / I wantoned with thy breakers . . . / And laid my hand upon thy mane—as I do here': to be the same as before, to perceive a continuity between past and present, may (as in Wordsworth's application of the Puritan quest for evidences of election) autodidactically stabilize and secure identity, but in Byron that continuity is as it were a pleasing illusion snatched from the conjurer's box, a spell of words signifying an instantaneously woven rather than authentically rooted assertion of wholeness and privilege. And is this assertion in earnest or in play? It is as if in placing the ocean beneath his 'hand' he impossibly reduces it to a toy, and thus infers, with something of a knowing smile, the blind audacity, the self-delusions and strategic manipulations as well as the majestic authority, of writerly power. Is the Poet wise man, knave, or fool? All three, in truth—all three.

Radically equivocal. That's how *Childe Harold* is: like its constituent parts, it ends, and issues, in resolute irresolution, the characteristic nexus of affirmation and denial, freedom and confinement. The closing strains recapitulate the three abiding themes—corporate life, individual being, and writing. The first of these resurfaces in the interpolated stanzas on the national tragedy of the death of Princess Charlotte in childbirth. As in the Waterloo section of Canto III, Byron responds with distinctive force to the spectacle of history, in a manner that proves it to be parasitic on his creativity as well as, in a two-way process, food for his imagination and artistic fame. He becomes myth-maker and sharer in a myth, sympathetically elaborating the nation's collective hopes for the dawning of a

new age, the 'promised joy' which 'fill'd the imperial isles so full
it seem'd to cloy' (168), but much more its mourning, the
'electric chain of. . . despair' that bound men together and also
bound them down, 'opprest / The land which loved thee'
(172). This final emphasis on the chain of despair, of course,
sharply distinguishes Byron's vision from the ameliorist phil-
osophy of Shelley, who, at least in the period 1816–20, clung to
the belief that the myth-making mind could create symbols of
love and relatedness prophesying the limitless capacity for
ideas to persist amidst the wreckage of human hopes, and to
provide moral and political salvation:

> To love, and bear; to hope till Hope creates
> From its own wreck the thing it contemplates . . .
> This, like thy glory, Titan, is to be
> Good, great and joyous, beautiful and free;
> This is alone Life, Joy, Empire, and Victory.[44]

For Byron, human hopes and human creations, man, society,
civilization, are always subject to an overarching tragic
destiny, and, though they may rise and fall, move ultimately
towards oblivion, chaos, and death—what he calls 'Destruc-
tion's mass', the 'abyss' into which Charlotte, 'hope of many
nations', has sunk. Significantly, he includes his own creation,
Harold, in the general fate, seeing him pass away into the same
abyss:

> He is no more—these breathings are his last;
> His wanderings done, his visions ebbing fast,
> And he himself as nothing:—if he was
> Aught but phantasy, and could be class'd
> With forms which live and suffer—let that pass—
> His shadow fades away into Destruction's mass,
>
> Which gathers shadow, substance, life, and all
> That we inherit in its mortal shroud . . .
> (IV.164–65)

And finally the poem itself fades away, under the cloud of its
own littleness, inconsequentiality, and illusory nature: it dies
into an echo, and has been but 'a protracted dream':

> The torch shall be extinguish'd which hath lit
> My midnight lamp—and what is writ, is writ,—
> Would it were worthier! . . .
>
> (IV.185)

The shadow of negation and cancellation falls at last over Byron's making and what he has made—his *Pilgrimage.*

Yet the poem is never more ambiguous in its workings than at the point of its extinction, where its 'glow . . . is fluttering, faint, and low' (185). Though all things pass into the gulf of dissolution, they have, as we have seen throughout Canto IV, the habit of rising again, reconstituted by the interaction of mind and matter, whether the 'sea Cybele' of ancient civilization emerging proud from the ocean (2), or the dying gladiator raised from the dust of the magic circle and the vacancy of the loops of time, or Nature's sacred triumph redeemed from the dungeon of St Nicola, or even the figure of Princess Charlotte emblematizing a nation's aspirations and their bereavement, a 'deep and immedicable' wound that repeats the gladiator's but affects the whole of Freedom's heart (169). Earth's own wound, the abyss of Death and Chaos, is not only a terminus but a place of origins, the house of phantom forms ready to be imagined and written into existence. So, too, is *Childe Harold's Pilgrimage* a terminus and starting-point, a site for re-creation. It is not political liberty that matters most to Byron, but personal freedom, the mobility to go on creating in a fallen world—and that mobility is in the end bequeathed to us, his readers:

> . . . if in your memories dwell
> A thought that once was his, if on ye swell
> A single recollection, not in vain
> He wore his sandal-shoon, and scallop-shell;
> Farewell! with *him* alone may rest the pain,
> If such there were—with *you*, the moral of his strain!
>
> (IV.186)

It is up to us to make something of what has become nothing, to make the faded 'dream' a new reality in our minds, to relight the torch and revivify the glow, to turn 'what is writ'—words—into meaning.

This freedom, however, brings with it both burdens and obstacles—and is itself a freedom to discover as much as to cope with or transcend limits. Byron offers to us the responsibility of making him immortal—neither Childe Harold nor he will die so long as a single reader of his text remains—but also of interpreting and perpetuating the truth of his 'strain'. We may ignore or refuse the task, but if we accept we submit to the sorcerer's riddle, an enigma that cannot be solved, and to a process that can never be completed. As it draws to a close, the text actually props open the jaws of a dilemma that prompts engagement but disables certainty. '*If such there were*': did the Childe exist at all, what precisely was his 'pain', and what, if any, is the relation between Byron and the Pilgrim whose journeyings we have traced?

> . . . if he was
> Aught but phantasy, and could be class'd
> With forms which live and suffer—let that pass—
> (IV.164)

This consolidates, even as it apparently denies ('let that pass'), a central puzzle of the poem to which generations of readers have set their minds: is that Pilgrim a fiction, or is he the author's real, living and suffering, self? There is, of course, no answer, for the real Byron is, like the Author of the ocean, invisible and fathomless, shrouded as well as expressed by his creation. The question traps us, drives us on to thought, yet resists solution—just as Byron's mention of the 'fardels of the heart—the heart whose sweat was gore', which he would happily consign to the abyss of Destruction (166), sustains in us a desire to penetrate his private desert places, though these may be but a mirage spun to ensure that we make trial of *his mind*'s 'gulf of phantasy and flame' and substantiate his 'dream of fame' (166), taking up the burden of endlessly re-creating the 'shadow, substance, life, and all' of the mass of his poem. 'Signs are small measurable things, but interpretations are illimitable . . . every sign is apt to conjure up wonder, hope, belief, vast as a sky':[45] we read texts under the assumption that they are knowable, graspable, but reading is itself an adventure with no end; it is fuelled by a grand illusion of mastery; its greatest limitation is that the quest for meaning is limitless, yet therein lies also its greatest glory. If Byron's text 'Fools our fond gaze', it is that we may 'dilate / Our spirits'.

Byron's commitment to personal heroism has often been celebrated: his commitment, that is, to the capacity of the individual to act meaningfully in a tragic world of 'flow and change, in which all things . . . are swept forward by their own pressure into new conditions of being and ultimately to chaos'.[46] Such heroism, present in *Childe Harold*, is repeated, some would say in a finer tone, in *Don Juan*, which is in fact the subject of the above citation. It is not, however, a heroism that belongs simply to the sphere of *living*, that outward side of existence which we call life. It lies, rather, on the inside of experience and being-in-the-world—a *dynamis* of consciousness and interior effort made manifest in the interchangeable and indivisible activities of 'making' and 'reading'. Though *Childe Harold* is vividly referential, impressive in its realizations of history, civilization, or nature, the 'world' man inhabits, its pressing actuality is not that of any material realm beyond the text but the actuality of the mental process embodied in it, the blend of idealism and vigorous scepticism that is endlessly reconstructive and an endless dissolution, a knowing and not knowing, perception as insight and perception as ignorance, writing and undoing 'what is writ', finding the signs meaningful or meaningless, being triumphant or defeated. And so it is in the 'flow and change' of our encounter with Byron's work. Acclaiming the 'master over irony', Kierkegaard defined 'actuality', not as a phenomenon exterior to the self, but as a frame of mind, a continual movement of consciousness:

> Actuality in this way acquires its validity—not as a purgatory, for the soul is not to be purified in such a way that it flees blank, bare, and stark naked out of life—but as a history wherein consciousness successively outlives itself, though in such a way that happiness consists not in forgetting all this but becomes present in it.[47]

Whether the process brings happiness or not, such is the movement which is authored in *Childe Harold* and which *Childe Harold* authors in us. ''Tis to create, and in creating live': living is no more and no less than passing mentally beyond the point at which we have arrived—forever generating a future from a deleting of the present. Each moment of consciousness, each giving or receiving of thought, is at once a dying and a birth, *telos* and inception.

NOTES

1. All references to *Childe Harold's Pilgrimage* are from *Lord Byron: Complete Poetical Works*, ed. Jerome J. McGann, volume II (Oxford, 1980). References are to Canto and stanza, with the former omitted for quotations within the text where it is readily identifiable from the surrounding context. Cantos III and IV both belong to the period of Byron's exile from England, being published in 1816 and 1818 respectively. Following the customary approach, I shall treat them as closely interconnected and in separation from the first two Cantos, which appeared together in 1812. For a succinct account of the history of publication and the relation between the four Cantos, see McGann, *Complete Poetical Works*, pp. 265ff., where a relevant bibliography is supplied.

2. To my knowledge, Byron cannot have been acquainted with the induction to Wordsworth's 1805 *Prelude*, which existed only in manuscript. Yet there are uncanny similarities of theme and imagery, a comparison of which reveals in Byron the emergence of a poetic identity distinct from, but complementary to, the temperately jubilant and liberated Wordsworth who casts confidently around for a 'guide', 'a twig or any floating thing'. Wordsworth declares 'I cannot miss my way', and is free to 'quit the tiresome sea and dwell on shore', settled to the prospect of successful trials of the spirit in a world of genial forms; Byron, on the other hand, is a pilgrim without home or faith, for better or for worse 'all at sea'. The 'floating thing' which in Wordsworth is a sign drawing the poet on to some profitable end is in Byron the poet himself—'a weed'. This supports the illuminating comparative view of the two poets broached in M. G. Cooke, *The Blind Man Traces the Circle: On the Patterns and Philosophy of Byron's Poetry* (Princeton, N.J., 1969), chap. 2, *passim*, and developed by the same author in 'Byron and Wordsworth: the Complementarity of a Rock and the Sea', in *Lord Byron and His Contemporaries*, ed. Charles E. Robinson (London and Toronto, 1982), pp. 19–42. Philip W. Martin, *Byron: A Poet Before His Public* (Cambridge, 1982), uses Wordsworth mostly to 'prove' Byron a reductive appropriator of current philosophic attitudes.

3. Mark Kipperman, *Beyond Enchantment: German Idealism and English Romantic Poetry* (Philadelphia, 1986), pp. 196–97. Though Kipperman's chapter on Byron came to hand when this essay was at an advanced stage of preparation, and though I challenge his conclusions in significant respects, I would like to acknowledge my indebtedness to certain of his emphases and perspectives.

4. Peter J. Manning, *Byron and His Fictions* (Detroit, 1978), p. 98.

5. M. G. Cooke, *The Blind Man Traces the Circle*, p. 55.

6. See, for example, the excellent discussion of these stanzas in Robert F. Gleckner, *Byron and the Ruins of Paradise* (Baltimore, 1967), pp. 243ff.

7. For comments on prevalent critical attitudes to the place of teleological structure in *Childe Harold's Pilgrimage*, see pp. 177–80 below.

8. Kipperman, *Beyond Enchantment*, pp. 184–85.

9. Jerome J. McGann, *Fiery Dust: Byron's Poetic Development* (Chicago, 1968), p. 92. Most subsequent comment has been substantially influenced by this study, which remains, in my view, the outstanding book on Byron.

10. Søren Kierkegaard, *The Concept of Irony*, trans. Lee M. Capell (Bloomington, Indiana, 1968), p. 337; quoted in Kipperman, *Beyond Enchantment*, p. 81.

11. The best account of this aspect of *Childe Harold*—now perhaps an underrated feature of the poem—is still that of G. Wilson Knight, in *Poets of Action* (London, 1967; reprinted Washington D.C., 1981), pp. 187–95.

12. The recall of Dryden's portrait of Achitophel—'A fiery soul, which working out its way, / Fretted the Pigmy Body to decay'—is at some points very precise: see *Absalom and Achitophel*, ll.150ff.

13. Roland Barthes, 'Introduction to the Structural Analysis of Narratives', in *Barthes: Image–Music–Text*, essays selected and translated by Stephen Heath (London, 1977), p. 124.

14. See Gray's *Elegy*, ll.101–18 and Wordsworth's 'Resolution and Independence', passim, to which might be added, for example, the 'dreaming thing, / A fever of thyself' of Keats's revised *Hyperion*. I offer relevant detailed analysis of 'Julian and Maddalo' in 'The Shelleyan Psycho-Drama', *Essays on Shelley*, ed. Miriam Allott (Liverpool, 1982), pp. 84–91.

15. Sigmund Freud, 'The Uncanny', *Freud: Art and Literature*, ed. Albert Dickson, The Pelican Freud Library, volume XIV (Harmondsworth, 1985), p. 357.

16. Ibid.

17. Ibid.

18. Otto Rank, quoted by Freud, op. cit., p. 356.

19. The neat summary is by Gleckner, *Ruins of Paradise*, p. 225.

20. Kipperman, *Beyond Enchantment*, p. 187.

21. Cooke, *Blind Man*, p. 40; Martin, *Poet Before His Public*, pp. 64ff., where, however, a convincing range of parallels with Wordsworth, Rousseau, and Edward Young is identified. Byron's relationship to Wordsworth's 'natural religion' is of course a complex affair, covered in different ways by both these critics; but my point is that, though Byron is manifestly more self-conscious about and less authentically rooted in the type of transcendentalism expressed in 'Tintern Abbey' and other poems (the 'blessed mood' in which we are 'laid asleep in body, and become a living soul' and the 'sense sublime' of 'something far more deeply interfused'), we should take his application of that transcendentalism more seriously than to see it simply as a regurgitation of that 'dose' of 'Wordsworth physic' which, according to Thomas Medwin, he remembers getting from Shelley in Switzerland (see Thomas Medwin, *The Life of Percy Bysshe Shelley*, ed. H. B. Forman (Oxford, 1913), pp. 293–94). One likely source of Byron's concepts of 'absorption' in nature and of retreat from mankind that has not (I believe) been noted is

Cowper: compare, for example, *Childe Harold* III.69 and 89–90 with Cowper's *Retirement*, ll.45ff. and 93ff. ('Absorbed in that immensity I see . . .').

22. Jean-Jacques Rousseau, *Rêveries d'un Promeneur Solitaire*; quoted in Martin, *Poet Before His Public*, p. 226.

23. Quoted in Martin, op. cit., p. 72.

24. See Byron's prose note to stanza 99.

25. Kipperman, *Beyond Enchantment*, p. 186.

26. Op. cit., p. 188.

27. Journal entry for 29 September 1816, *Byron's Letters and Journals*, ed. Leslie A. Marchand, 12 vols (London, 1973–82), V, 104–05.

28.   If solitude, or fear, or pain, or grief,
        Should be thy portion, with what healing thoughts
        Of tender joy wilt thou remember me,
        And these my exhortations! Nor perchance—
        If I should be where I no more can hear
        Thy voice, nor catch from thy wild eyes these gleams
        Of past existence—wilt thou then forget . . .
                    ('Tintern Abbey', ll.143–49)

29. See Coleridge, 'Frost at Midnight', ll.44–64. It is noticeable that, while Dorothy in 'Tintern Abbey' is conceived as continuing the poet's own former self and his experience, Hartley is the locus of Coleridge's *hopes* for a future different from 'far other scenes' of a desolate past. Byron—in stanzas 115 and 118—combines both ideas, the continuance and the hope for a better future. His language, however, is much less stable in its affirmations than that of either of his two predecessors and at certain points deconstructs its own positive claims as a route to self-redemption: when he says (114) that he 'would deem . . . happiness no dream' he in effect underlines the *wishfulness* and *unreality* of those claims—and, incidentally, casts an ironic light back upon the precursor texts, declaring the constructedness of their consoling affirmations. Again, Byron is conscious of the power and the limits of 'the written'.

30. See, in particular, McGann, *Fiery Dust*, pp. 36–37.

31. For example, M. K. Joseph, *Byron the Poet* (London, 1964), or Harold Bloom's concept of Byron's eventual 'therapeutic aesthetic idealism', *The Visionary Company* (New York, 1961), p. 234.

32. Joseph, *Byron the Poet*, p. 27.

33. *Ruins of Paradise*, p. 230.

34. *Fiery Dust*, p. 37.

35. Ibid.

36. *Fiery Dust*, pp. 38–39.

37. *Fiery Dust*, p. 138.

38. *Beyond Enchantment*, p. 196.

39. *Prelude* (1805), XIII.88–90; ed. Ernest de Selincourt, corrected by Stephen Gill (Oxford, 1970), p. 231.

40. See *Prelude* (1805), III.171ff:

                    Of Genius, Power,
            Creation and Divinity itself

> I have been speaking, for my theme has been
> What pass'd within me . . .

41. *Beyond Enchantment*, p. 197.

42. 'Do all they can, my repugnance can never reach aversion . . . I had rather shun than hate them . . .' (*Rêveries*, quoted in Martin, *Poet Before His Public*, p. 72).

43. *Beyond Enchantment*, p. 197.

44. Shelley, *Prometheus Unbound*, IV.573–77; *Shelley: Poetical Works*, ed. Thomas Hutchinson, revised G. M. Matthews (Oxford, 1970), p. 268.

45. George Eliot, *Middlemarch*, chapter 3; ed. W. J. Harvey (Harmondsworth, 1965), p. 47.

46. Alvin Kernan, *The Plot of Satire* (New Haven, 1965); reprinted in *Romanticism and Consciousness*, ed. Harold Bloom (New York, 1970), p. 363.

47. Kierkegaard, *Concept of Irony*, p. 241.

Byron's Artistry in Deep and Layered Space

GEOFFREY WARD

I

To adapt and develop a term used in passing by Harold
Rosenberg, we might say that the modern artist has been
driven to choose between an exploration of deep, and of
layered, space.[1] Metaphysics, religion and subjectivism will
tend towards an imagery of deep space, as in the landscapes of
Friedrich and Turner, or the more abstract but related
conjurations of their descendants, Jackson Pollock or Mark
Rothko.[2] Any hierarchical ordering of reality will likewise tend
towards an art of deep space. By contrast the work of Cézanne,
say, or Picasso in his Cubist period present an art of layered
space: Picasso's world is post-religious in this sense, and its
component energies are depicted in sequences of shapes and
flats that have no necessarily metaphysical extension. This
distinction between deep and layered space can be seen in the
history of poetry as much as painting. For example, Tenny-
son's narcotic lyricism, his hymning the absorption of con-
sciousness by memory, dream or sensory abandon, make him
very much a poet of inner space, despite the vividness with
which he evokes the things and surfaces of the outer world.
Browning, by contrast, is fundamentally a poet of layered
space, despite the occasional exceptions such as 'Childe
Roland'.[3] Roughly speaking, crucial developments in twen-
tieth-century poetry have tended to demystify and colonize the
deep in the service of a layered-space, humanist credo. This is
true of both the Audens, early and late; his conversion
modified Auden's ethical outlook but never really added a
spiritual dimension to his poems, which were resolutely
sociable, always and only of this world. Turning to the

European continent, the ructions within French poetry of the 1920s and 1930s engineered by the Surrealists had to do with the appropriation of deep spaces of reverie, dream and prophecy in the service of a layered-space, Marxist humanism. During the same period in America, Marxism as such may have made less headway, but the work of William Carlos Williams presents an in many ways analogous attempt to yoke the visionary tradition of Romantic poetry to a pugnacious, layered-space materialism determined to free modern art from the taint of metaphysics. Williams's poems are composed of instants of recorded perception, of sharp and shifting surfaces whose claim on our attention is urged by their *intensity*, rather than by their place in some order. So, it might be said that while poets of the nineteenth century such as Tennyson and Browning were able simply to develop their inclination towards an art of deep or of layered space, an increasing secularization in the society outside the poem was to bring a corresponding aggression to the advances of layered-space art in the modern age. The case of Carlos Williams is particularly helpful in this context because it is so extreme; even in the poetic avant-garde, attempts to rid poetry of its deep space, its metaphysical tendencies, have rarely been so thoroughgoing.[4] Artists have more usually shown a tendency towards deep or layered space, rather than his extreme commitment. Whitman and T. S. Eliot, for example, approached the relationship between European and American poetry with radically opposed sets of ambitions and anxieties, but in the work of both we see a breaking of form, implying an art of layered space, but issuing from a sensibility whose investment in both subjectivity and a cosmological outlook makes of each poet an explorer of the deep.

For our purposes, the antagonism between a deep- and a layered-space *Weltanschauung* can be traced back to the emergence of Romanticism, and its attempts to understand and work through the implications of the French Revolution for both political and artistic practice. The rival claims of a hierarchical world-view and a new, levelled realm in which the present moment dominates perception, with resultant attractions and dangers, have their origin in this period of political upheaval. On the whole, it does seem to have been easier for artists who were close to those events in time to come to an accommodation between the old and the new than it has been for the major writers of our century, who have been driven to more drastic sorts of choice and position-taking. In Wordsworth's case, for example, the reconciliation of a new art of fragmentation and a reverent attitude towards the metaphysics of wholeness was achieved fairly smoothly. Shelley, in his different way, manages to harmonize a progressive, humanist politics of layered space with a celebration of the purposive interrelatedness of all worldly phenomena that is so deep-space as to be virtually mystical at times. Likewise Keats's constant urge towards an intensification of the present moment of experience does not prevent him from suggesting ultimate locations for experience which are absolutely the province of a deep-space metaphysics. Byron is the odd man out. In his poetry the accommodation is not made. Byron was equally alive to the claims of religion, incarnate in *Don Juan*'s Aurora Raby, and to the disorderly, layered-space world that is surveyed in parts of *Childe Harold's Pilgrimage*. He was both torn and brought to maturity as a writer by his inability to honestly go over to either one side or the other, and his use of comedy and satire enabled him to build a bridge of irony between the two worlds only for want of something better: 'that I may not weep', as it were. In this essay I will argue that Byron was always driven to choose, but was never able to choose, between the alternative views of deep and layered space, and that this vertigo is more instructive than the relatively smooth accommodations to which Wordsworth or Whitman were able to come.

Pressures of space and my own fecklessness have conspired to make this introduction shuttle between the art of the nineteenth and the twentieth centuries with more haste than would ideally be desirable. However, there are advantages to be gained from jamming things together in this way. For one thing, no harm can be done by stressing Byron's modernity: the picture of an émigré Dandy, cursing the decline in English verse-writing from a gondola on the way to some amatory escapade, is entertaining, but it does disservice to Byron as the poet of our current dilemmas, which I would argue originated in his time.

Despite Modernist injunctions to, in Pound's phrase, 'make it new', twentieth-century art has in its central traditions been exploring questions that were broached first in the previous century. It would be easy but misleading to be seduced either by the excitement or the sense of order promoted through an avant-gardeist view of literary history, whereby each vanguard movement draws from, repudiates and finally cancels out its predecessors, only to be superseded in its turn. Of course it is not merely neat but actually true in certain instances; in this particular area the supplanting of Dada by Surrealism, Eliot's relationship to the lyricists of the gaslit Nineties, Wordsworth's absorption of Cowper have something in common. Naturally, the theory of supersedence is most likely to be substantiated by the case of the strong poet vis-à-vis the weaker, though even there (as with Cowper) supersedence outside the psychological arena is more a perpetuation than an effacement by virtue of the historical importance the major poet can confer retrospectively on the minor. The theory of vanguardism mimics unconsciously the advances of industrialism and technology which begin, alongside Romanticism, at the end of the eighteenth century. We are still, I believe, in the Romantic age, living out the political and aesthetic questions posed by the French Revolution and followed by the advent of industrialization. In a sense no poetic revolution has occurred greater than that which separates *Lyrical Ballads* from the verse which preceded it. The alternative possibilities of an art of deep or layered space, of a radically inward or of a post-metaphysical view, are indirect consequences of the French Revolution. The taste for ruins, for example, is contemporary with the emergence of republicanism, a connexion drawn at the time by the Marquis de Sade, who saw in the tale of terror an indirect reaction to political upheaval. It is improbably probable, therefore, that the Gothic ruin has become the most continuously attractive and popular icon of the last two hundred years, because it unites in a vivid way the power of the old and the newly interesting condition of fragmentation. Once Bastille and Palace had fallen, the smashed architecture of feudalism and the aristocratic order (the kind of buildings to which Byron removed at the age of ten, in the condition he would have found some of them) began through broken windows to emit mysterious and multiple significations, being charmingly picturesque in decay, a focus for nostalgia and conservative resentment, hauntings, but also new order and the promise of material change. Inseparable from the levelling of political hierarchies, an assault on theology in general and Original Sin in particular finds its oneiric, architectural analogue in Gothic eroticism. The Gothic is, we might hazard, a dream-version of power relations, in which the cannon's roar is silenced and replaced by the cry of nocturnal visitation, which may be sexual or may be ghostly, may deny or grant power to the past. Here the garish image of the 'Satanic' Byron was to exercise an enduring influence. I want to pause briefly with that image, if only to look into some of the real contradictions which its unreality tries to veil.

In this infernal circle of Byron studies biography and fiction chase each other at speed and catch each other constantly. Towards the end of the eighteenth century, literary echoes of Milton's Satan seem to have blended with the sideways influence of Schiller's *Die Räuber*, to strike a new chord amplified by Mrs Radcliffe in novels such as *The Mysteries of Udolpho* (1794) and *The Italian* (1797), and by Matthew Gregory Lewis in *The Monk* (1796). A set of traits emerge—pallor, damaged glamour, burning eyes, some secret guilt—which were certainly absorbed by Byron as a young man as part of his self-presentation. It is also fair to say that Byron was like that anyway. The image of the *homme fatal* was perpetuated by the poet in the oblique self-portraits that stalk such separate works as *Manfred* and *Lara*, grist to a legend confirmed by Lady Caroline Lamb's autobiographical fantasia *Glenarvon* (1816), Polidori's macabre tale *The Vampyre* (1819)—which was mistakenly attributed to Byron on its first appearance—and by the phenomenal scores racked up by Byron during his stint as the most celebrated fornicator in Venice. The traits have affected, more than they emanate from, the three or four poems that make up *Childe Harold's Pilgrimage*. Thereafter, the image of the Fatal Man seems to split into its originary parts. Following Byron's activities in Greece, an elevated version of the noble brigand, the idealistic outlaw, begins to represent Byron's posthumous influence on the various nationalist struggles emergent in Europe.[5] The Satanic remnant, relished by the French in particular, drifts away from the realities of either Byron's life or the experience of reading his poems, and becomes a creative misinterpretation important in later nineteenth-century Decadence. Sainte-Beuve chose to link Byron with de

Sade ('les deux plus grands inspirateurs de nos modernes') and Flaubert asserted with uncharacteristic carelessness that 'Il ne croyait à rien, si ce n'est à tous les vices'.[6] Baudelaire, in the section of his *Le peintre de la vie moderne* (1863) concerning the Dandy, links Byron with Brummel and Sheridan, a grouping to which the poet would not have objected. It is understandable also that in some late Notes Baudelaire should have written 'Byron, loquacité, redondance'.[7] Even when as apparently languid as 'Harmonie du Soir' or as limpid as 'Le Balcon', Baudelaire's own materials are ferociously heated and compressed. Essentially a lyric poet, his pathbreaking energies were directed towards opening the lyric to take in anti-lyrical material, a kind of reversed alchemy which forms his bequest to poets as disparate as Eliot and the Surrealists. By contrast, the experience of reading Byron entails mulling over the ideas, feelings, pictures and tones generated by quite large stretches of text, allowing connexions to emerge eventually and not at once. Although he can indeed 'rattle on exactly as I'd talk / With anybody in a ride or walk', travelling with Byron requires at least one change of gear, a considered after-reading as well as the immediate pleasures of the journey. 'Redondance' and 'loquacité' were functional as well as temperamental necessities to Byron. A characteristically strong line from Baudelaire,

> Je ne vois qu'infini par toutes les fenêtres[8]

is a touch Byronic in its baleful grandeur, but differs in basing its method in compression and immediacy. And of course it is Baudelaire who is more representative of the poetic mainstream. The kinds of attention one brings to 'Le Gouffre' are essentially the same as those that need to be applied to 'A slumber did my spirit seal' or 'Because I could not stop for Death'. It is often said, and rightly so, that Byron exercised an influence on European culture more widespread than that of any other English writer of his century. It is also the case that that influence was based in the main on parodic reductions of parts of his work—always, itself, involved in processes of change and doubt—into a static image. So Baudelaire dressed him for the wax museum, alongside Maturin and Poe: 'ils ont projeté des rayons splendides, éblouissants, sur le Lucifer latent qui est installé dans tout coeur humain. Je veux dire que

l'art moderne a une tendance essentiellement démoniaque.'⁹
Yet the inclination towards perversity on principle is far less
marked in Byron than in Poe. Baudelaire, the most acutely
self-aware of poets, evidently had to remain blind to the artistic
possibilities of 'loquacité' in order to become fully himself.

The stereotype of the *homme fatal* being, precisely, an *image*,
fixes what is in truth unfixed, solves for a passing moment
insupportable contradictions with an obliquity resembling at a
cultural level the operations Freud detected in an individual's
Dream-work.

> He stood a stranger in this breathing world,
> An erring spirit from another hurled;
> A thing of dark imaginings . . .
> <div align="center">(<i>Lara</i>, I.315–17)</div>

Ostensibly announcing disjunction and contradiction, such
phrases actually celebrate by making resonantly singular what
would otherwise prove to be irreconcilably plural. To return to
the postulates with which this essay began, echoes of Milton's
Satan and the Gothic anti-hero are given new life so as to
negotiate the contradictory tendencies of a 'deep-space' philo-
sophy (multiple worlds, alienated subjectivity) and the post-
Revolutionary layered space, in which order and traditional
morality may be abolished and the 'stranger' who does the
abolishing suffer no retribution from on high. Similarly, the
Gothic ruin is perched so as to command a view of both deep
and layered space; the first is associated with the powers of
darkness, of the past, and of religion, and yet the ruin is also
outmoded, its broken ramparts a reminder that the course of
history may not run smoothly but that progress is possible. In a
sense, therefore, the Byronic castle embodies on a massive
scale the ambiguities of the Romantic fragment. The fragment
implies *par excellence* the new aesthetics of layered space, for a
broken part-object escapes any certain fixture in a hierarchy of
genres. It attacks the integrity of Classical form. Conversely,
however, the fragment, by manifesting its own miniature life
(Blake's squibs, Coleridge's Notes, a vignette by Thomas
Bewick), is seen to be microcosmic, a promise of deep space
and an ultimately organic and harmonious universe.¹⁰

This ambiguity in the art of the fragment, which speaks at

once of the torn and the whole, has kept its vitality throughout twentieth-century art. Eliot's 'heap of broken images', his shored fragments, were aggressively new—an attack on certain sorts of Classicism—and yet productive of an organic whole, *The Waste Land*. Whether the modern collage be massive, as in Joyce's *Ulysses* and Pound's *Cantos*, or a miniature and whimsical set of juxtaposed bits and bobs by Schwitters or Ernst, it reiterates the appealing ambiguity of the Romantic art of fragmentation, which tries to hold in equilibrium the torn edges and part-objects of layered space, and the promise of ultimate harmony which had always been the preserve of deep-space aesthetics, signs of an organic art and universe. The Gothic ruin is a massive fragment, related to the brooding anti-heroes in some of Byron's poems, and to the literary image of Byron himself which the author fostered and which Baudelaire was pleased to dig up *post mortem* and put back into Decadent circulation. All these images—animate or inanimate, the Gothic ruin or the Satanist—hold the conflicting imperatives of a deep- and a layered-space view in momentary balance, as images in a dream can resolve for a moment tensions which are irreconcilable by day. But Byron was adept at and fascinated by the use of such images precisely because he felt the pressures of the irreconcilability of the old and new worlds more painfully than the other Romantic poets. I want to turn now to the third Canto of *Childe Harold's Pilgrimage*, to see the tensions and contradictions that animated Byron's thought no longer subsumed under a reductive and stereotyped image, but thoroughly explored while remaining (instructively) unresolved.

II

Childe Harold's Pilgrimage may be read as a single work. However, a number of factors including the lapse of years between the composition of the first and last parts, and Byron's changing views about the character of Harold, mean that the text can be taken as a collage of related poems. Either way, Canto III is the most troubled and questioning section of the *Pilgrimage*.

> Oh! who is more brave than a dark Suliote,
> In his snowy camese and his shaggy capote?[11]

Although there may be some archness in Byron's naiveté here, it is still the case that these relatively awful lines (653–54) from Canto II could simply not have occurred in the third Canto. In the intervening years Byron's technical skills as a poet had improved, but inseparable from the weakness of that couplet is a certain blitheness of mind that had also disappeared by 1816. The third Canto articulates the turmoil of a self searching for assurances of authenticity—through paternity, initially; through the stored but necessarily partial experiences of a broken heart; in Nature; through the employment as displaced self-images of figures of power from the external world, such as Napoleon and Jean-Jacques Rousseau, figures however whose powers are broken and whose relation to Byron is at last only fitful: and through the revival of a poetic creation, Harold. Canto III is more closely related to the final Canto than to those that precede it, as the fourth movement of the poem attempts in a sense to answer questions that the third cannot settle. I would suggest, however, that the undeniable, colossal grandeur of that final Canto is rooted in the identification of strong rhetoric with an act of will, in ways that dignify but also weaken Byron's efforts to assuage the turmoil of the previous section. The *genius loci* embodied by St Peter's, a contrasting recognition of that 'unspiritual god' Circumstance, the possibility of faith in a God of deep space and a simultaneous, layered-space suspicion that Reason may be 'our last and only place / Of refuge' (IV.127) are so powerfully orchestrated as to transcend, both in expression and by evasion, the radical uncertainty of Canto III. There the rival claims of a deep- and a layered-space understanding of the world draw from Byron a poetic indeterminacy that is as exciting to encounter on the page as its articulations are painful. Such dilemmas would never be resolved but only superseded, by the eventual development of a comic mode in *Don Juan*.

The opening stanzas of Canto III are marked by several blurrings of the sense that could easily be put down to carelessness, given what we know about Byron's habits of writing. Nevertheless it is curiously the case that these 'errors' incorporate in miniature form the major dilemmas of the poem. In stanza I,

> Awaking with a start,
> The waters heave around me; and on high
> The winds lift up their voices: I depart . . .

Of course it is a textual first-person who awakes, and not the waters, except in so far as any act of human perception may be said to legitimize the grammar of pathetic fallacy by calling the external world to life. A similar effect in the fifth stanza may well have been more consciously intended:

> He, who grown aged in this world of woe,
> In deeds, not years, piercing the depths of life,
> So that no wonder waits him; nor below
> Can love or sorrow, fame, ambition, strife,
> Cut to his heart again with the keen knife
> Of silent, sharp endurance:

In the first two lines it is he who has pierced the depths of life, but in the succeeding lines it is past experience that is said to have cut him, an extended chiasmus whose strangeness is compounded by the grammatical ascription of 'endurance' to the inanimate 'knife', rather than the animate 'heart'. But then the knife is a metaphor for animate energies (love, sorrow, ambition, strife) which no matter how deeply internalized could hardly be held to exist without some kind of effect on, or attachment to, the external world. In consequence these lines exemplify to a degree the Romantic practice of dissolving the distinctions between the internal and the external, as when Wordsworth speaks of sensations

> Felt in the blood, and felt along the heart[12]

implying that the heart has its own geography, or coastline. There is however an added element of uncertainty in Byron's lines, as if the text were signalling, consciously or otherwise, that relations between the inner and outer worlds were to be regarded as especially imperilled or skewed at this stage. A further example arises with an odd change of metaphorical tack in stanza 2:

> Once more upon the waters! yet once more!
> And the waves bound beneath me as a steed
> That knows his rider. Welcome to their roar!
> Swift be their guidance, wheresoe'er it lead!

> Though the strain'd mast should quiver as a reed,
> And the rent canvas fluttering strew the gale,
> Still must I on; for I am as a weed,
> Flung from the rock, on Ocean's foam to sail
> Where'er the surge may sweep, the tempest's breath prevail.

The opening images are typical of Byron in their masculine rhetoric, equestrian precursor to some of the more spiritualized attitudes Shelley would adopt in his 'Ode to the West Wind' of 1819. It is curious that such assertiveness should so rapidly turn passive: unless 'weed' is introduced simply to rhyme with 'steed' and 'lead' then there is once again a marked element of disjunction snarling the poem's attempts to have its narrative proceed straightforwardly.

The harmony and balance in the relations between the internal and external worlds which these examples of Byron's 'carelessness' throw into question are given expression in stanza 13:

> Where rose the mountains, there to him were friends;
> Where roll'd the ocean, thereon was his home;
> Where a blue sky, and glowing clime, extends,
> He had the passion and the power to roam;
> The desert, forest, cavern, breaker's foam,
> Were unto him companionship; they spake
> A mutual language, clearer than the tome
> Of his land's tongue, which he would oft forsake
> For Nature's pages glass'd by sunbeams on the lake.

This is basically (as Wordsworth indignantly complained) a Wordsworthian position. Indeed it is absolutely a *position*, the lines standing slightly outside what they describe, rather than articulating what such a sense of self would feel like from the inside, as Wordsworth's own poetry more usually does. (This is unsurprising, given the attitudes to Wordsworth that Byron expresses elsewhere.) In 'Lines written a few miles above Tintern Abbey', from which I quoted earlier, Wordsworth declares himself attached not to some purely external realm of Nature but to

> . . . all the mighty world
> Of eye and ear, both what they half-create,
> And what perceive;
>   (ll.106–08)

In sum, Wordsworth approached instinctively from the inside, Byron more tentatively from the outside, an at times similar aspiration towards what Byron calls a 'mutual language' of reciprocal identification by the inner and outer worlds. The outer world is given meaning only by the 'half-creation' of the perceiving mind, which is itself only one more roaming offspring of that world. This balanced circularity is always, however, under threat, being situated in time, and so Romantic paradises turn out as a rule not to be perdurable: childhood, young love, the first flush of revolution, opiated visions. Once expelled from those gardens, the broken self must choose between rival explanations of its pain, which I have termed the contrasting matrices of deep and layered space. In the first case, with its potential for a metaphysical or hierarchical world-view, the expelled self is naturally fallen, and can think to regain paradise only through the ambiguous medium of an isolated consciousness, both pride and prison. This is the situation of De Quincey as Opium-Eater, Blake's lovers in 'The Crystal Cabinet', Coleridge's poet in 'Kubla Khan'. In the layered-space world nothing can be regained because there is no metaphysical extension to the succession of moments that make up the real. There are, however, the consolations of movement and the ever-present possibilities of change: I suppose Shelley's *Epipsychidion* incorporates the most strenuous working-out of the implications of this position in the Romantic period. It is noticeable that the stanza from *Childe Harold* quoted above tries to hold the vertical and lateral, the deep- and the layered-space view, in balanced harmony. The mountains rise, vertically, with their metaphysical connotations of higher realities and struggling ascent, but 'there to him were friends'. Harold enjoys for a moment the 'mutual language' of what Shelley in a poem of that same year, 'Mont Blanc', termed the 'unremitting interchange' held by the mind with the 'universe of things'.[13] Both Shelley and Byron may be said to absorb a Wordsworthian interpretation of subject-object relations which their divergent energies and kinds of scepticism lead them to modify in different ways. But at this moment Harold resembles a number of non-Byronic Romantic figures: the ocean is his home, the forest his companion, Nature his book. Yet this is not the mystical immersion of a subjectivity in deep space: Harold has 'the passion and the power to roam', is himself one discrete energy in the world, wandering in layered space.

Wordsworth had drawn some intellectual sustenance from German philosophy, but I want to suggest tentatively that a closer philosophical analogue for English Romantic poetry may be found in the writing of the twentieth-century phenomenologist, Maurice Merleau-Ponty. The 'mutual language' I have highlighted resembles closely the equilibrium of phrases such as these, drawn from his work:

> The world is inseparable from the subject, but from a subject who is nothing but a project of the world, and the subject is inseparable from the world, but from a world which it projects itself.[14]

> His body and the distances participate in one same corporeity or visibility in general, which reigns between them and it, and even beyond the horizon, beneath his skin, unto the depths of being.[15]

We choose our world and the world chooses us.[16]

Merleau-Ponty's phenomenology is closer to Byron and Wordsworth than to other schools of philosophy because, like poetry, it constantly seeks the validation of theoretical enquiry in actual human experience. 'Philosophy', Merleau-Ponty argued, 'is indeed, and always, a break with objectivism and a return from *constructa* to lived experience . . .'.[17] Throughout *Don Juan* it is Byron's presiding intuition that the elaborate intellectual constructions that the mysteries of being in the world lead us to postulate do very rapidly become mere questions against whose undecidability we bump our heads, tumbling back into the fray of 'lived experience', our natural, albeit piecemeal habitat. The later Byron depicts a layered-space world, haunted by question-marks suggestive of the deep: some are incarnate (Aurora Raby), most speculative ('Whence came we?'). Such questions refuse either to resolve themselves or to go away. *Childe Harold's Pilgrimage* is, as its name implies, both more deferential to the possibilities of deep-space explanation, and yet more uncertain, more of a quest. The kind of equilibrium theorized by Merleau-Ponty and embodied in stanza 13 of the third Canto is something

Harold cannot hold onto for very long. Perhaps this Canto is really a series of perceptual events and psychological fixes which upset in their different ways that longed-for equilibrium, which Merleau-Pontyan phenomenology presents as our normal state (did we but know it), but to which Harold, like many estranged Romantic wanderers, obtains access only in flashes.

The lyrical interlude (ll.496ff.) beginning 'The castled crag of Drachenfels' becomes by this reading a false paradise, a ghostly parody of that 'mutual language' whereby the world would choose us and we the world. Here everything in the too-enclosed garden is lovely, a wistful circularity that can only mimic the 'unremitting interchange' of self and other from which Harold's consciousness is at this stage cast out.

> And peasant girls, with deep blue eyes,
> And hands which offer early flowers,
> Walk smiling o'er this paradise;
> Above, the frequent feudal towers
> Through green leaves lift their walls of gray,
> And many a rock which steeply lours,
> And noble arch in proud decay,
> Look o'er this vale of vintage-bowers;
> But one thing want these banks of Rhine,—
> Thy gentle hand to clasp in mine!

Denied the necessary interchange of love ('Thy gentle hand'), the lone consciousness retreats into a negative version of deep space, whose symbols of authority ('frequent feudal towers') are antiquated and oneiric, like the Gothic ruin. The 'proud decay' of selfhood in this plight spells solipsism, and it is not surprising that poems of the later nineteenth century which show the influence of this lyric in cadence or imagery— Swinburne's 'The Garden of Proserpine', Tennyson's 'The Lotos-Eaters'—tend also to set evocations of budding and fading life, exiled and self-centred feelings in a tense relationship.

To dive deeper into exiled feeling, hoping at last to touch bottom, only makes matters worse, for the broken heart will live on

> Even as a broken mirror, which the glass
> In every fragment multiplies; and makes

A thousand images of one that was,
The same, and still the more, the more it breaks;

(III.33)

These lines contain a sceptical, Maddalo-like criticism, *avant la lettre*, of the sort of beliefs expressed in Shelley's most Julian-like poem, *Epipsychidion*, with its more blithely optimistic assertions regarding love:

True Love in this differs from gold and clay,
That to divide is not to take away.
Love is like understanding, that grows bright,
Gazing on many truths; 'tis like thy light,
Imagination! which from earth and sky,
And from the depths of human fantasy,
As from a thousand prisms and mirrors, fills
The Universe with glorious beams, and kills
Error, the worm . . .

(ll. 160–68)[18]

To Byron the broken mirror of the heart can only increase the reflections of what it feels bitter to have lost, whereas Shelley in his attempted legitimization of promiscuity wants to believe that multiplicity is a good, *per se*. Shelley's intense commitment to the acceleration and multiplication of human experience begins as an attempt to put into a linear and progressive form the essentially circular nature of Wordsworth's position vis-à-vis Nature. To put it another way, Shelley wants to turn Wordsworth's deep-space metaphysics into a layered-space insurrection. Byron is sceptical about both the mysticism of the first and the utopian ardour of the second. His commitment to the Wordsworthian circularity of stanza 13 is fleeting, both because Byron does not feel that such paradises endure, and because he is not entirely sure that they ought to. A deep-space world-view is ultimately religious and ahistorical; Byron was troubled by the layered spaces of History, from a first-hand knowledge of politics and armed struggle with which Words-worth had only ever been distantly in touch. 'Stop!—for thy tread is on an Empire's dust!'. Stanza 17 'stops' Harold's solipsistic exile and the smooth Wordsworthian interchange of self and world in their circular tracks. The portrayal of Napoleon which follows is that of a figure who is the antithesis of Harold, and whose proud separateness from the rest of mankind and the world—'A god unto thyself'—is likewise radically opposed to the Wordsworthian position. However, if subjectivity's hall of broken mirrors serves only to multiply pain, and a grander metaphysics of deep space seems compromised by the realities of history, the extraverted self that Napoleon represents, always active and never passive, is also condemned for its egotism, both massive and petty. What then can we conclude concerning the final relationship of these clashing positions, representative alternatively of world-views that might be reconciled or repositioned in triangular format by other writers of his time, but which to Byron in *Childe Harold's Pilgrimage* spell only paradox, pain and impasses?

Of all the Romantic poets, Byron is keenest to preserve the integrity of the self, its coherence, independence and difference from the world that is not it. That world may (however provisionally) show its paradisal aspect, as in Juan and Haidée's idyll or Torquil and Neuha's more protracted escape from judgement in *The Island*; still it is the case that those figures exist both in relation to and in separation from their environment. There is not that fluidity of phenomenological interchange between the self and the world which was so essential to Wordsworth's credo or to Keats's interest in metamorphoses. Instead, we generally find in the foreground of a Byron poem a rhetoric of strong, but (ostensibly, at least) controlled, presence; the language of Byron's insistent masculinity, his bluffness and Britishness, verbal analogues for a clear voice and a firm handshake, 'things' which are in truth signs, all bespeak at the sexual, national or psychological level a control over the self, which controls things in its turn. Of course 'Byron' is a series of works of art, brought to life by the act of reading. To the fore in these works of poetic artifice there is always a complex rhetoric conjuring metaphysical presence. Consequently those readers such as Karl Kroeber who have praised Byron's sincerity and those who, since Carlyle, have complained about the opposite, are in truth moving over the same shifting ground. Those rhetorics through which Byron's poetry is now composed by our act of reading, both go to make up and come to undo his strong fiction of presence. Paradoxically, the articulation of a complete selfhood, a full presence, both dominates *Childe Harold* and yet remains a chimaera that it seeks but cannot find. This Canto begins 'Is thy face like thy mother's, my fair child! / Ada! sole daughter of my house and heart?'. Surely this is both the rhetoric of presence at its most forceful, asking us to feel that we are overhearing 'the real Byron', and an undoing of that very aim, for any authentication of identity is immediately undermined by question-marks. Our attention will be bounced rapidly from Byron as father, to voyages, to fictionalizing, to history, and so on and on, in a dramatic but actually interminable attempt to express a coherent selfhood. That personality with which Byron's text commences, in which it is grounded, and which distinguishes it from the work of the other Romantic poets is also a mirage receding constantly before the poem's advance. Therefore, that phenomenological circularity whereby, to return to Merleau-Ponty, the world chooses us and we the world, the self creating by acts of perception the world which brought it into being, operates in this poem with a comparable ambivalence. It is a circularity both devoutly to be wished, as in stanza 13's 'Where rose the mountains, there to him were friends', and absolutely to be repudiated as a threat to that integrity of separate selfhood which is the rhetoric's dream. The odd 'errors' in the text are small indications of a larger necessity, that we put in suspension any conclusive ascription of any line in *Childe Harold's Pilgrimage* to authorial intention, to error, or to a textual unconscious. The poem's meanings are finally indeterminate. Indeed the poem is unreadable, if readability were taken to spell the end of interpretation, its conclusive termination in a satisfactory reading. Such a chimaera is of course a mirror-image to that proposed by the poem's rhetoric of presence—one real, true reading of the real, true Lord Byron.[19]

These are illusions. The poem generates an indeterminacy of meaning, and that is in part what makes it a poem and not some other kind of document. But I am not suggesting that indeterminacy spells the absolute free play of meaning, with some correspondent loosening of tenure on the powerful articulations of grief, of frustration, of passion that ought to hit and move a reader of this poem. The band of semantic indeterminacy is in one sense exceedingly broad and subject to ceaseless variation between readers and across time: it is also in another sense operative between limits: there are certain things the poem is definitely not concerned with (though we cannot know what it may be seen to be concerned with in the future). The whole peculiar distinction of this third Canto of *Childe Harold's Pilgrimage* is that we never lose our stake in the stoicism, or the pathos or the unexpected kindness to which the poem gives life, at the same time as we witness the merely provisional and phantom nature of those supposedly firm subject-positions from which the text argues such emotions can only issue. That consistency of a governing personality from which the poem would like to believe that it emanates is certainly an identifying feature of the text, but only as a craving, a lack. Thus the text looks for aid from inside its own realm of language, but finds none:

> Could I embody and unbosom now
> That which is most within me,—could I wreak
> My thoughts upon expression, and thus throw
> Soul, heart, mind, passions, feelings, strong or weak,
> All that I would have sought, and all I seek,
> Bear, know, feel, and yet breathe—into *one* word,
> And that one word were Lightning, I would speak;
> But as it is, I live and die unheard,
> With a most voiceless thought, sheathing it as a sword.
>
> (III.97)

'Lightning' is a word much used by Shelley, and this is in an important sense the most Shelleyan moment in Byron's poetry, a moment where the poem reaches for a word that would end the need for words and their endless play of substitutions, a word that would cut through to the real, depicted but never made incarnate by language. The attempt fails, just as Shelley's attempt in *Epipsychidion* to cancel our belatedness in the world, our self-consciousness and the gap between knowing and being, the gap that exists between separate conscious-nesses, would also fail:

> Woe is me!
> The wingèd words on which my soul would pierce
> Into the height of Love's rare Universe,

Are chains of lead around its flight of fire—
I pant, I sink, I tremble, I expire!
                    (ll.587–91)[20]

Readers of this, the climactic moment in *Epipsychidion*, have rarely felt content, chiefly because the poem seems to be talking about something it would somehow have to *do* if it were to convince: to talk in such unimpeded metrical eloquence about expiry is not to expire at all. Yet that is precisely the discrepancy, the Fall, the shadow between expression and reality over which Shelley protests, and which has turned his would-be Icarus-like melting into Oneness into that catastrophic failure a verbal success, the dualism of a well-made Daedalian honeycomb, rather than the all-dissolving, desired blaze. As J. Hillis Miller has said about these lines, and as might be said about Byron's,

> The language which tries to efface itself as language to give way to an unmediated union beyond language is itself the barrier which always remains as the woe of an ineffaceable trace. Words are always there as remnant, 'chains of lead' which forbid the flight to fiery union they invoke.[21]

If Shelley could have achieved his 'one life, one death, / One Heaven' and most importantly 'one annihilation', if Byron could call down lightning in one magic word, then the endless displacements of language would make way for the reality they always chase and for which they are always too late. But there never is such a word, and the botched remnant or sheathed frustration becomes a kind of genetic trace that will start the cycle of 'Soul, heart, mind, passions, feelings' up again. The more that Byron itemizes those energies that would be supplanted by his one word, the more he reaffirms their resistance to any such termination. His actual communicating medium depends on proliferation, in itself a barrier to the conclusive singularity he craves. As with the '*one* word', so with the *one* self, the *one* Lord Byron, the *one* conclusive reading of a poem. It is a chimaera, the fruitless search for which generates the poetic pack whose unruly forward movement is the poem's true and irredeemably multiple, unstoppably mobile, reality. Poems and persons must 'advance or die' (103), and though there may be 'Words which are things, hopes which will not deceive' (114), they exist alongside the magical lightning-word inside our capacity to imagine, rather than our experience, and 'I have found them not'. Rather, words slip away from things into their own proliferation which generates other things: the boldest position to adopt in this world entails an acknowledgement of its ceaselessly Protean play of displacement and substitution instead of the one truth, the consistent self, the vindication of the Johannine Word that would make everything, at last, be all right. The celebrated formulation of stanza 70 tries to keep a purchase on both this layered-space world of displacement, and the deep-space promise of an ultimate answer:

> But there are wanderers o'er Eternity
> Whose bark drives on and on, and anchored ne'er shall be.

To wander, to be driven, to resist anchorage is to concede the layering of our human space, its non-hierarchical and godless organization; yet to place the wandering in the context of 'Eternity' is to keep a hold, however painful, on religious, deep-space possibilities. That double perspective was far less problematic for Wordsworth or Shelley in their different ways than it was for Byron.

The third Canto of *Childe Harold's Pilgrimage* is less of a narrative than any episode in *Don Juan*. Indeed it is so only in the Coleridgean sense of striving to make a whole out of a series, and there are in fact very few serial events in the poem. It seems to me that Byron could easily have begun with Napoleon, or placed the lines about his daughter somewhere else, or perhaps omitted Harold altogether. I do not mean that the poem is flawed, or loose: even more than Eliot's *Waste Land* it is kaleidoscopic in form, and there is therefore no absolute need for a reader's remembrance of the text to preserve the sequential order that one encounters at the time of reading. All the sections and pseudo-characters are intended to comment on each other, but in so doing only disclose their phantom nature, a hollowness in Byron's sense of identity which, as with *The Waste Land*, does nothing to de-realize the pain and fear and vertigo generated by the text. Of course *Childe Harold* does not at all feel like Eliot's poem: but both are concentrated, centreless epics whose lack of a stable centre for experience is their true subject.

III

No more—no more—Oh! never more, my heart,
Canst thou be my sole world, my universe!
(*Don Juan*, I.215)

As we have seen, any unitary summation of the heart's activities in Byron's earlier masterpiece in fact covers a disunity, a 'universe' of shooting and dead stars, of collision and implosion as well as deep space. Byron, having not so much resolved as given up trying to solve his dilemmas from the self-centred yet centreless viewpoint of *Childe Harold* III, moves in *Don Juan* to a more social and extraverted coign of vantage. Professor McGann catches the underlying relationship between the two texts: 'The point of *Don Juan*'s "piecemeal" (*Childe Harold* IV, 157) method is to prolong the experience, and the activity, of learning in the human world'.[22] Larger than *Childe Harold* in so many respects, *Don Juan* is more modest in the limits set on the theme of self-analysis. In reading the poem we are constantly aware of tones and habits of speech which form by their accumulation, and never release us from, an authorial self-portrait, but the clarity of definition present in the new picture of Lord Byron exists precisely because increasing age and experience have now fixed what was once in more tortured motion. The particular pleasure that most readers of *Don Juan* encounter, a feeling that, more perhaps than any other poem, this work is uncannily and marvellously lifelike, is a sensation caused in part by Byron's having turned his attention outwards, so as to let more of the world in. The phenomenological see-saw of self and the world is more level in this later text. Or so at least it must seem, for *Don Juan* to work and enjoy its own distinctive existence. I will want to argue that those qualities of fixture and clarity are exactly those of a mask; not, it must be said, in any flirtatious or deceptive way, or to conceal cleverly one determinate meaning: but this is a text that has not forgotten the radical indeterminacy of the earlier poem of Childe Harold.

That said, Don Juan's is more of a layered-space world on the face of it. Despite Byron's avowed refusal of Horace's 'heroic turnpike road', the poem does begin 'in medias res', and the relatively two-dimensional hero will be bounced from escapade to escapade with a bravura that is anecdotal virtually to the point of amnesia. The 'piecemeal method' is not simply a way of proceeding on the page, but the tracing in verse of a world-view. Reality, however darkly it may be punctuated by questions as to its ultimate significance, is first and foremost a succession of lived instants. 'Human life is not something that can be "gained" or "concluded" or "fulfilled", but must simply be "kept" in our experience of consecutive vital particularities.'[23] Of course 'keeping' may not be a simple operation, and *Don Juan* is on the whole moved more by vitality in the present than by fidelity to the past.

In consequence the temporal and secular particularities of a layered-space world are frequently used to deflate pretensions to the deep.

> He thought about himself, and the whole earth,
>   Of man the wonderful, and of the stars,
> And how the deuce they ever could have birth;
>   And then he thought of earthquakes, and of wars,
> How many miles the moon might have in girth,
>   Of air-balloons, and of the many bars
> To perfect knowledge of the boundless skies;
> And then he thought of Donna Julia's eyes.
>   (I.92)

And so these longings sublime and aspirations high (or deep) are the effect of a distinctively earthly cause:

> If *you* think 'twas philosophy that this did,
> I can't help thinking puberty assisted.
>   (I.93)

It would be easy to accumulate a hundred such instances of skiey aspiration being grounded with a comic jolt. And the element of comedy is of course absolutely vital: the poem's effects would be completely different were it aiming simply to pull aspiration to earth in a dour or merely worldly way:

Perfect she was, but as perfection is
Insipid in this naughty world of ours,
Where our first parents never learn'd to kiss
Till they were exiled from their earlier bowers,
Where all was peace, and innocence, and bliss
(I wonder how they got through the twelve hours) . . .
                              (I.18)

The point is that layered, linear space is kinetic, is now *interesting* to Byron, no longer the series of threats it seemed to pose in *Childe Harold*. Human beings are cherished here for their aspirations, even as the divinities and legends that give those aspirations ghostly life are duly punctured: an irresolute Donna Julia 'pray'd the Virgin Mary for her grace, / As being the best judge of a lady's case' (I.75), a choice of addressee that only a few lines later will appear to have been somewhat inappropriate, and earlier in the same Canto pre-Christian deities are shrunk down to the size of 'garden gods' (45). But if the gods are brought to earth, so are humanist ideals and complacencies; the incidents of cannibalism and brutality in the shipwreck episode of Canto II also embody in their way the revenge of layered-space realities on deep-space illusion. It is much easier to be charitable on a full rather than an empty stomach: Byron actually comes down much harder, more unambiguously, on the complacencies of secular humanism than he does on religion, blasphemous jokes notwithstanding. It is worth considering that the objects of satire must be thought worthy of attack in order to be brought in at all. Byron need not have included reference to the Virgin Mother or 'our first parents' had he felt a complete lack of interest in such figures, and their presence in his tapestry shows an element of provocation and mystery that the poem's satire does not entirely weaken and to which the poem's comedy lends support in rather odd and unexpected ways.[24] It is worth noting also that, although he too is starving in the boat, Juan refuses to eat his fellow-voyagers. In other words, the assaults of a layered-space, secular outlook on pretensions to and rituals of the deep have a little curve in their barbed point that is readily turned back into a question mark.

Byron's complementary habit of disrupting a too-neatly layered representation of human space by hinting at the deep, tends therefore to be encoded in literal questions. 'The goal is gain'd, we die, you know—and then— / What then?—I do not know, no more do you—' (I.133–34); 'What are we? and whence came we? what shall be / Our *ultimate* existence?' (VI.63).

> I gazed (as oft I have gazed the same)
> To try if I could wrench aught out of death
> Which should confirm, or shake, or make a faith;
>
> But it was all a mystery. Here we are,
> And there we go?—but *where*?
>
> (V.38–39)

Such demands both reassert the claims of a deep-space, religious view, and deny it by remaining questions without answers. This doubleness operates in exact and ironic counter-point to the poem's insistence on consecutive, vital particularities. A question must be barbed with doubt when the questioner expects no answer. The writing becomes so fluent in these complementary modes and so pre-emptively aware of the potential of each to undermine the other that it will hover, content to imply lightly the contrary claims of the two world-views. A sighting of the castled crag of Drachenfels, catalyst in *Childe Harold* to the morbidly beautiful song discussed earlier, is here a case in point:

> And thence through Berlin, Dresden, and the like,
>   Until he reach'd the castellated Rhine:—
> Ye glorious Gothic scenes! how much ye strike
>   All phantasies, not even excepting mine!
> A grey wall, a green ruin, rusty pike,
>   Make my soul pass the equinoctial line
> Between the present and past worlds, and hover
> Upon their airy confine, half-seas-over.
>
> But Juan posted on through Mannheim, Bonn,
>   Which Drachenfels frowns over like a spectre
> Of the good feudal times for ever gone,
>   On which I have not time just now to lecture.
>
> (X.61–62)

To say that you 'hover . . . half-seas-over' is to dismiss as drunkenness the vertigo and mystery and metaphysical drama of deep space, the claims of which are nonetheless conceded in phrases such as 'glorious Gothic scenes' and the telling juxtaposition in the same pericope of 'phantasies' and 'soul'. I argued earlier that the Gothic castle is the most enduring icon of the last two hundred years because it holds in an attractive suspension two warring symbological orders, the one to do with religion, hierarchies, the past and the other to do with the secular, with political upheaval and the dominance of the present moment. Byron's first stanza confirms this explicitly; the sight of a Gothic castle moves the perceiver to a twilight zone 'Between the present and past worlds', hovering. His second stanza expresses the same tension in different terms, calling Drachenfels a '*spectre*' (my italics) of 'the good feudal times for ever gone'. A spectre is ambiguous evidence that what has in one sense departed is in some other sense still here. On the other hand, of course, these lines are rather detached in tone, despite their superficial insistence to the contrary, part of a travelogue, and a 'green ruin' is evidence of social change and progress, the primacy of the contemporary. The tension between two different conceptual frameworks, which I suggest have been dominant in Western culture since the late eighteenth century, is present in microcosm in these two stanzas.

A division of the contesting world-views to have emerged since the end of the eighteenth century into picturings of deep and layered space is doubtless as open to charges of over-simplification as any other binary opposition applied to the structure of literary texts. Each major poet has his or her own distinct identity, despite the necessary struggles with precursive writers and poems: likewise each literary work is ultimately the articulation of its own code, no matter how visible might be its subscription to genres or shared rhetorics. In addition, it must be the case that factors helping to make up a deep-space metaphysics in the work of one artist would support a layered-space aesthetic for another. For example, the conceptual and experiential value of the moment in time changes during the nineteenth century in the hands of a theorist such as Walter Pater so as to become for his inheritors in the Nineties and the High Modernist phase—Arthur Symons and Virginia Woolf, say—a sign of deep space. The moment is reverenced in their writings, though each abjures

conventional religion. In Byron's work by contrast it is the
intensity of the separate moment which is most a threat to his
deep-space intuitions. To take another problematic example,
subjectivity in English and American writing can mark an
affiliation to a deep- or a layered-space perception in part
because of the ambiguous foundations of the Protestant con-
sciousness (from which Romanticism had developed) in dis-
sent and new orthodoxy. The opposition between deep and
layered space is therefore a model that at once generates
exceptions. However, those exceptions can themselves be
peculiarly instructive in clarifying the relationship between
what art claims and what it does. And where the model does
not work neatly it may help all the more, and for that practical
reason alone I apply it to the texts in hand. As it happens, the
oppositional model can quite rapidly clarify our understanding
of the basic structure of Byron's *Don Juan*.

A dialectical recourse to the mutual interrogation of deep-
and layered-space intuitions at a local level forms what one
might think of as the motor of this poem. The question
'Whence came we?', by pointing to the concept of origin,
disrupts the layered-space tendency to dwell only in the
present instant. However, the question cannot be answered,
and origin remains present only at a conjectural level: the
consequent seed of doubt becomes the genetic trace that will
start up the cycle of interrogation once again. In a like way,
comic subversions of deities and deep-space dreaminess bring
the attention down to earth with a jolt which again leaves a
spore of doubt, never quite erasing the haunting possibility of
genuine authority in the symbols that have been overturned.
The motor will sometimes idle, as when Byron cruises down
'the castellated Rhine' with views of both deep and layered
space made available by the gently guided movements of his
craft. At times, however, these rival views coincide in a
stereoscopic image that will come to dominate a whole section
or Canto of *Don Juan*. These are the major dramatic images of
the poem, which seem to both epitomize the characteristics of a
deep- and a layered-space philosophy while bringing the
necessity to choose between them up to crisis point. The
shipwreck in Canto II is such an image. Byron itemizes the
details of disaster with a laconic exactitude, implying a

materialist world-view whereby various gory and upsetting effects follow naturally from certain meteorological and other causes: 'Again the weather threaten'd,—again blew / A gale, and in the fore and after hold / Water appear'd' (42), 'The ship was evidently settling now / Fast by the head' (44), 'At half-past eight o'clock, booms, hencoops, spars, / And all things, for a chance, had been cast loose / That still could keep afloat the struggling tars' (51) and so on. This is a world of physical energies, and of things; its current state of tumult may spell catastrophe for the humans on the scene, but Byron's dry tone and unflinching realism present this as a savage corner of a world that nevertheless remains comprehensible. The deep-space pieties of Catholicism get given a cold shower:

> All the rest perish'd; near two hundred souls
>   Had left their bodies; and what's worse, alas!
> When over Catholics the ocean rolls,
>   They must wait several weeks before a mass
> Takes off one peck of purgatorial coals,
>   Because, till people know what's come to pass,
> They won't lay out their money on the dead—
> It costs three francs for every mass that's said.
>
>   (55)

But the ocean is itself a very deep space, and even the lexicon of realism on which Byron chooses to draw at this stage in his poem cannot exclude words whose connotations bring metaphysics to bear on the disaster. 'And the sea yawn'd around her like a hell' (52), 'And first one universal shriek there rush'd, / Louder than the loud ocean' (53), 'Their preservation would have been a miracle' (50), '. . . and there was one / That begg'd Pedrillo for an absolution, / Who told him to be damn'd—in his confusion' (44). And in the stanza quoted above, Byron's main object of censure is not religion, but those who claim deep-space awareness only to travesty it by their own bargaining materialism. This is not the only stretch of Byron's writing to seem a touch Conradian *avant la lettre*, not merely because of its setting but for the insistence on locating the metaphysical *in* the physical, and vice versa. Consider the use of rain and drought in *The Shadow Line*: the climactic break in the weather in that tale is both a literal fact and an almost supernatural intervention. It can be concluded that in the major images of *Don Juan*, those dominant pictures with which Byron chooses to spend some time as distinct from its local effects, we most clearly see the germination of layered-space scepticism not alongside but within metaphysics, just as the question-marks of hell, of miracle, of universality arise from within Byron's most determinedly realist lines.

The narrative of the shipwreck is therefore in a textual though not an emotional sense a point of anchorage. And just as that disaster epitomizes both crass happenstance, a collision of purely earthly energies as well as more metaphysical questions to do with chance and destiny, so the later siege of Ismail is both a flat tapestry of violence and a 'hell' of 'All that the devil would do if run stark mad' (VII.123). Interpretations of the world in terms of either metaphysics or what is effectively nihilism are opposed in Byron's work, and painfully so, and yet it does seem to be the case that the germ of each is always already contained in the other. Ultimately, this seeming paradox stems from the nature of language itself. Words in one sense are doomed always to be late, able only to chase, haunt, shadow, describe a reality they can never *be*. Yet those processes of chasing and describing do in themselves generate another sort of life in the mouth or on the page. When Byron writes 'All that the devil would do if run stark mad', he means to give an added depth to his depiction of military violence, but the phrase he uses is, as we say, a figure of speech, and the wished-for metaphysical depth is therefore flattened in the same instant in which it is asserted. However, language, in its very discrepancy from the reality it supposedly shadows, can set going a multiplicity of meaning, in excess of requirements, which it is the nature of poetry and Romantic poetry in particular to raise to its highest pitch. In a Romantic lyric such as the one by Wordsworth beginning 'A slumber did my spirit seal, / I had no human fears' indeterminacy, based in a slippage of words away from a referential function and into their own semantic proliferation, is immediately dense and to the fore: who am 'I'? Is the 'slumber' anaesthetic or dream-vision? What does 'seal' mean here? Is it good or dangerous to lose one's 'human fears'? In *Don Juan* it is also the case that, again to lean for support on Jerome McGann, 'no amount of critical extrapolation could exhaust the meaning of the poetry—not because the meanings are mysterious (they are not), but because they are multiple'.[25] Wordsworth's lyric is both multiple *and* mysterious, whereas Byron shifts the locus of multiplicity away from the writer's material and onto the reader's response. It is our reactions that sheer away from each other, or remain consecutive as they might with a novel, and are prevented by shifts of perspective and context from gelling into a comprehensive or dominant reading. In one sense, therefore, the function of each Canto in *Don Juan* is to make the next one possible, and the poem is interminable. The seeds of a nihilist or metaphysical scepticism are always at work, germinating in the heart of their opposite so as to take us onward.

IV

Essays such as this like to propose models for reading and interpretation which, because they are made up of words, are fated never to meet the reality (in this case, certain other texts) which they shadow. That is not to say that criticism and its subject are disconnected, or only loosely related: the essay depends on, perpetuates and even modifies the poem in ways that may be parasitic, helpful, or both. Nevertheless, I suspect that these models for reading will always speak of something more clear-cut and defined than the actual experience of reading the poem. Reading involves subtle fluctuations of attention of which the essay is a résumé, forever late. It would be hard to imagine a model for interpretation that could both convince and have built into it the feelings of puzzlement or surprise, say, that may have been fundamental to the reading experience. That was certainly true of my own sense of the speed with which Byron can alternate metaphysical and seemingly anti-metaphysical implication in his writing, which this present effort has not succeeded in incorporating. My difficulties are tied to what is, in a different sense, Byron's difficulty. Once again I shall try to get at this in a sidelong way through a comparison with Shelley.

On the face of it Shelley is a much more 'difficult' poet than Byron, because in a text such as *Epipsychidion* complex metaphysical issues will be named as such, placed squarely in the foreground of the poem, then worked strenuously and at speed. In practice, though, that difficulty is not hard to deal with because as readers we can see at once the kinds of mental operation we are being asked to engage. And so in this sense there are no impediments to reading Shelley, despite his nervy manner and breathless delivery, not to speak of more positive qualities such as the sheer intellectual range of his poetry.[26] Indeed that very breathlessness—conducive to a feeling that at the most basic psycho-motor level a text such as 'Mont Blanc' is in truth unpunctuated—together with Shelley's relative lack of interest in onomatopoeia, are signs that he wants no impediment or resistance whatsoever, between poet and poem, poet and reader, men and women. Onomatopoeia involves a pause, writing's headlong speed retarded so that some thing can be evoked in its separate reality; punctuation, likewise, spells delay. The drive of Shelley's layered-space insurrection tends towards an ideal Oneness that would, ironically, engulf the rebellious singularity that strained to achieve it. Things, in this dualistic world, get in Shelley's way. He wants all barriers down.

I imagine that it would be generally agreed that Byron pays more cautionary attention than Shelley to limits, human and other. In fact that scepticism (which, as we have seen, can debunk materialist as much as metaphysical pretension) actually wants to set limits, wants to generate resistance and impediment, as aids to art and argument. Thus far, it is bound up with the rhetoric of masculinity, the genial and bluff sides of Byron to which anyone who liked his work would probably be responsive. But, as I tried to show earlier in my comments on *Childe Harold*, those qualities turn out on closer inspection to imply a coherence of personality which the poem may conjure and desire, but from which it does not issue. We can go further: coherence of selfhood is a mirage, evading the advance of the text while keeping in our sight. Apparently more earthbound and easier than Shelley, Byron is in truth less straightforward, more mercurial and perhaps (I'm not sure) more *deeply* sceptical than either his powers of mimesis or the rhetoric of personality would lead us at first to believe. Certainly his poems now seem to express both more scepticism and indeterminacy than his other forms of self-presentation did in life.

Therefore, rather than conclude by reiterating my own model of interpretation, a model which by its very nature will already have curtailed prematurely a reading of the poems, I end semi-inconclusively with an aside or coda, which touches on both Byron's indeterminacy and his interest in limits for meaning.

In his Venetian and later phases, Byron's work develops an interest in images of masks, and veiling. A mask both diminishes and multiplies significations. It is a piece of solid fabric, shielding the face from its own vulnerability, curtailing that variety of expression which it cannot always control. It is also a promise, a mystery, perhaps a work of art, and an echo of religious ritual as in the carnival at Venice, which fascinated Byron and which persists to this day. The mask suggests more than it reveals, and yet says less than what it hides would do. Like the carnival, it is both the recurrence of sacred ritual and the excuse for nihilism, a deep-space doorway and a flat leer. At one level it operates in *Don Juan* as part of an appearance-and-reality theme that there is hardly need to catalogue: Juan is 'masked' at various stages by Donna Julia's bedclothes, by the petticoats of the opposite sex, by Haidée and from her father, and so on. The text is replete with figures of speech involving masquerade: 'And, after all, what is a lie? 'Tis but / The truth in masquerade' (XI.37), 'For both commodities dwell by the Thames, / The painting and the painted' (48), 'Be hypocritical, be cautious, be / Not what you *seem*, but always what you *see*' (86). A rapid survey conducted by thumb rather than computer finds these examples everywhere, but most often in the English Cantos. Of 'matters which are out of sight' (XV.2) Byron has this to say:

> But all are better than the sigh supprest,
>   Corroding in the cavern of the heart,
> Making the countenance a masque of rest,
>   And turning human nature to an art.
>
> (XV.3)

Of course this description of the veiling of true feeling sounds very close to the processes whereby other kinds of 'art' get made, and to that extent the stanza is itself a mask. *Don Juan* is unfinished, yet interminable; the ending, in one sense made arbitrary by the author's death, is simultaneously apt. The poem closes with an unmasking (of 'her frolic Grace—Fitz-Fulke', dressed in a monk's 'sable frock and dreary cowl' (XVI.123)) which is itself a surprise, masking further events and explanations which will forever be concealed from us. A mask, like the dream-image of the Gothic castle, holds deep- and layered-space meanings in an alluring and mysterious balance, causing disparate energies that might otherwise snarl the poem to move it harmoniously on. But if a mask may conceal identity or tensions, it can also project them, as in the theatre. Possibly the main reason for Byron's increasing use of the imagery of masquerade can be traced to his having lived in Venice. He may have become so familiar with the plays of Goldoni and the tradition of the *Commedia dell'Arte* that their implied philosophy, which perfuses Venetian culture, became a part of Byron's habitual ways of thinking about the world. The *Commedia dell'Arte all'improvviso*, professional improvised comedy, had its origins in an art of deep space, the sacred representations of the church in the middle ages.[27] However, the actors' development of mime, masquerade and tumbling, with an increasing reliance on bawdy humour and comic violence—Mr Punch was born here—led it in an ever more layered-space, secular direction. Particular actors would become linked in the public mind to a stock role for which they would build up a repertoire of learned speeches, the *zibaldone*, that could be deployed across a number of plays. However, the actors also lived on their wits, and had to be adept at extemporized clowning. This combination of an artistic repertoire refined over time, and an improvisation that went purely off its nerve, would obviously have appealed to the Byron of *Don Juan*. The *Commedia* had already blossomed in the second half of the sixteenth century; by introducing full texts that edged out the art of the improvisers, Carlo Goldoni both raised the *Commedia* to a new pitch of excellence, and destroyed it. He retained the masks—Harlequin, Columbine, Brighella and the rest—but replaced uncomplicated farce by a more sophisticated comedy and attention to character. Again, an art which is textual but wants to retain some purchase on its non-textual origins is common to both Byron and Goldoni. Actors make oral what was initially written down for them; Byron wants an air of conversation or spoken monologue to hang around his written, metrical construction. So there are things in common between Byron and the Italian stage which are not to be found in the Italian poetry that Byron read, in Pulci ('sire of the half-serious rhyme' (IV.6)) or for that matter Whistlecraft.[28] The latter makes no use of digression whereas Byron, notoriously, has 'nothing plann'd' (IV.5) but bases his text on a 'conversational facility' equally interested in material 'new or hoary, / Just as I feel the "Improvvisatore" ' (XV.20), rather as the skilled extemporizer would have done on stage. There are similarities also between the two-dimensional charm of Don Juan and, say, Harlequin. I do not want to draw strict parallels between Byron's characters and those of the *Commedia*, even though it could perhaps be done with Pedrillo, Donna Julia and a few others. Rather I want to suggest that the Venetian comedy implied a certain world-view with which Byron would have been minded to agree in certain moods, and which is woven into the more complicated fabric of *Don Juan*. Both can imply that although we experience our lives as individuals, there are as it were only a dozen or so people in the world—the starstruck youth, the clown, the unattainable beauty, the corpulent merchant—who we truly are. Our experience is unique to us, but of a recognizable type to the outside world, the spectator. It is a comic but a deeply conservative view. It holds in abeyance the intensities of a deep-space view—in particular, the claims of religious faith and a cosmological extension to human affairs—while retaining the deep-space intuition that time moves in cycles and that human nature does not change. It refuses indeed to contemplate a layered-space prompting to insurrection or even the improvement of social conditions, but it retains the scepticism of a layered-space outlook, the suspicion that only what is here, now, is real.

Inglese italianato, diavolo incarnato? I would suggest that Byron's Italianization did not make of him the devil incarnate (a part he had already played in London), but rather introduced to his poetry a repertoire of images which held in attractive suspension and promised a comic redemption to contesting world-views. The mask brought levity and mystery to a contest between metaphysics and nihilism which the poet probably felt more painfully. The mask, associated in Byron's mind with Southern Europe, joined those images from the

North—the Gothic ruin, wild landscape, the alienated hero—
which Byron had both deployed and come to be associated
with in the public mind. The *image*, as such, plays a more
crucial role in Byron's poetry than the work of any of his
contemporaries apart from Keats, whose commitment is of an
altogether different kind. The image masked, temporarily,
tensions that were otherwise insupportable, but which reading
Byron must once again disclose.

NOTES

1. See Harold Rosenberg, *The Anxious Object* (Chicago, 1982), p. 114. I
have expanded for my own purposes terms used by Rosenberg solely to
clarify a point relating to the work of Willem de Kooning.

2. For a fully developed argument linking Abstract Expressionism to the
Romantic landscape tradition, see Robert Rosenblum, *Modern Painting and the
Northern Romantic Tradition: Friedrich to Rothko* (London, 1975).

3. 'Childe Roland to the Dark Tower Came' wells up from areas of deep-
space fear that Browning generally suppressed, much as Henry James's *The
Turn of the Screw* intervenes in its author's commitment to humanism and an
art of layered space. These exceptions that prove the rule are not uncommon
in Victorian writing.

4. Williams's persisting influence on poets as separate as John Ashbery
and Robert Creeley brings him ever nearer the centre of the American poetic
tradition in this century. His closest descendant in the drive against
metaphysics is probably the New York poet Frank O'Hara, whose layered-
space poetry is so resolutely post-metaphysical as to constitute a perimeter
marker for the argument that follows.

5. A comprehensive account of Byron's influence on the nationalist
struggles of nineteenth-century Europe may be found in *Byron's Political and
Cultural Influence in Nineteenth-Century Europe: A Symposium*, ed. Paul Graham
Trueblood (London, 1981).

6. As given by Mario Praz, *The Romantic Agony* (1933; revised edn.,
London, 1951), pp. 82–83.

7. *Baudelaire: Oeuvres Complètes*, ed. Marcel Ruff, Éditions de Seuil (Paris,
1968), p. 652.

8. 'Le Gouffre', *Baudelaire: Oeuvres Complètes*, p. 88.

9. From 'Réflexions sur quelques-uns de mes contemporains', *Oeuvres
Complètes*, p. 483.

10. This argument on the importance of the Romantic fragment was
suggested by Charles Rosen and Henri Zerner, *Romanticism and Realism: The
Mythology of Nineteenth Century Art* (London, 1984), esp. Chapter 1.

11. The best account of the composition of the separate Cantos of *Childe
Harold's Pilgrimage*, and the implications of those circumstances for our
reading of the text may be found in Jerome J. McGann, *Fiery Dust* (Chicago,

1968). The quotation is from Stanza 2 of the 'song' in Canto II of *Childe Harold's Pilgrimage* (ll.649ff.).

12. 'Lines written a few miles above Tintern Abbey', l.29; *Wordsworth and Coleridge: Lyrical Ballads 1798*, ed. W. J. B. Owen (Oxford, 1969), p. 112.

13. *Shelley: Poetical Works*, ed. Thomas Hutchinson, corrected by G. M. Matthews (Oxford, 1970), p. 533. All further quotations from the poetry of Shelley are taken from this edition.

14. Maurice Merleau-Ponty, *Phenomenology of Perception*, trans. Colin Smith (London, 1962), p. 430. (As Baudelaire's French is relatively straightforward and Merleau-Ponty's is not, I have gone for clarity rather than consistency and left quotations from the latter in translation.)

15. Merleau-Ponty, *The Visible and the Invisible*, trans. Alphonso Lingis (Evanston, Ill., 1968), p. 149.

16. *Phenomenology of Perception*, p. 454.

17. Merleau-Ponty, *Signs*, trans. Richard C. McCleary (Evanston, Ill., 1964), p. 112.

18. *Shelley: Poetical Works*, p. 415.

19. My contention that an indeterminacy of meaning is fundamental to our reading of Byron's major poems was encouraged by a reading of Shelley's 'The Triumph of Life' by J. Hillis Miller, in 'The Critic As Host', *Deconstruction and Criticism*, ed. H. Bloom (London, 1979).

20. *Shelley: Poetical Works*, p. 424.

21. *Deconstruction and Criticism*, pp. 245–46.

22. Jerome J. McGann, *Don Juan in Context* (London, 1976), p. 111.

23. McGann, *Fiery Dust*, p. 38.

24. A full and provocative development of the arguable connexions between Byron's comedy and Christian redemption is to be found in Bernard Beatty, *Byron's Don Juan* (London and Sydney, 1985).

25. McGann, *Don Juan in Context*, p. 107.

26. I am assuming that those who think Shelley is some kind of ineffectual angel are all themselves in heaven or some other distant place by now.

27. My information concerning the *Commedia dell'Arte* has been drawn in the main from H. C. Chatfield-Taylor, *Goldoni: A Biography* (London, 1914) and Timothy Holme, *A Servant of Many Masters: The Life and Times of Carlo Goldoni* (London, 1976).

28. Peter Vassallo's *Byron: The Italian Literary Influence* (London, 1984), the fullest account so far of its subject, still pays no attention to the influence of Italian theatre.

Byron and the Sense of the Dramatic

F. M. DOHERTY

Most readers of Byron will now accept the plays into the canon of what is read in anything more than an anthologized way. Critics have seen to it that over the last twenty years what was once a neglected area of Byron studies has had its share of academic treatment.[1] But, apart from special pleading for the excellence of the plays themselves as plays, all readers of Byron are aware that his best work has a distinct and recognizable sense of drama, and sometimes of theatre, whether the works are officially dramatic or not. We can all agree about that, but in what this sense of drama or theatre consists is not quite so clear or agreed. This essay will try to suggest, in some part, how we might look at the dramatic character of Byron's major fictions.

Perhaps to start with the end, it is manifest that in *Don Juan* Byron delighted in a number of set scenes which he exploited brilliantly for their special kinds of theatrical possibilities. A good example of this is presented by the speech which Donna Julia delivers to her suspicious husband while her lover, Don Juan, is hiding in her bed in Canto I. Here Byron quite obviously enjoys the manipulation of this scene for its close similarity to a scene that the theatre would make into a bedroom farce, or, more accurately, a near bedroom tragedy (almost as though Desdemona were to assert herself and round upon Othello). Donna Julia concludes her impassioned and yet, we feel, prepared and practised speech thus:

> 'And now, sir, I have done, and say no more;
> The little I have said may serve to show
> The guileless heart in silence may grieve o'er
> The wrongs to whose exposure it is slow:—

I leave you to your conscience as before,
　'Twill one day ask you *why* you used me so?
God grant you feel not then the bitterest grief!
Antonia! where's my pocket-handkerchief?'
(I.157)

We are meant to rise to her *chutzpah* in so coolly performing the part of the wronged lady, and in doing it so convincingly, but at the same time the reader will be on very familiar ground. We recognize the ways in which Byron's special imagination so constantly draws on a sense of the tragic in life, even at moments of the highest comedy—an imagination, we could say, which was attuned to tragedy.[2] Of course, Donna Julia directs her husband into a possible future when, like a tragic protagonist, he will be eaten away with remorse, and, ironically and comically travestying *Othello*, she asks her maid where her unfound handkerchief is. Byron's comedy is, we find, so often poised over tragedy: farce, Byron's instrument here, is tragedy with a safety net, but with the tragic potentialities especially highlighted.

Leaving her husband to conscience is leaving him where Byron thought all tragic heroes lived their lives—their lives of guilt, as he said often enough in his letters. So, for example, on 12 May 1821 he wrote from Ravenna to Francis Hodgson: 'Who is the hero of "Paradise Lost"? Why Satan,—and *Macbeth*, and *Richard* & *Othello* and *Pierre*, and *Lothario*, & *Zanga*'.[3] And, as he remarks of his drama *Marino Faliero*, 'the devil himself could not have a finer subject, and he is your only tragic dramatist',[4] because acting with knowledge, even when there is no hope of your actions having a happy outcome, no salvation possible, is what makes you a tragic protagonist for Byron. The figure at the centre of this belief is either Satan or Macbeth, and all which either figure represents of defiance and self. This view is clear very early in Byron's career. When, for instance, he wrote to Lady Melbourne on 13 January 1814 about Napoleon, he showed what the stoic attitude meant to him:

By the bye—don't you pity poor Napoleon—and are these your heroes?—Commend me to the Romans—or Macbeth—or Richard 3d.—this man's spirit seems broken—it is but a bastard

devil at last—and a sad whining example to your future
Conquerors—it will work a moral revolution—he must feel
doubtless—if he did not there would be little merit in insensibi-
lity—but why shew it to the world—a thorough mind would
either rise from the rebound or at least go out 'with harness on
it's back' . . .[5]

To move this belief away from the Shakespearean towards
Byron himself is to move from literary tragedy to what seems
increasingly to have become one of Byron's central beliefs
about man. He appears to share with Schopenhauer, and
through that gloomy philosopher with Beckett, the belief that
man's suffering in this world is only explicable as a punishment
for who knows what sin, perhaps the sin of having been born.
Francis Foscari, in *The Two Foscari*, thinks that

> we must have sinned in some old world
> And *this* is Hell: the best is, that it is not
> Eternal.
> (II.i.364–66)

But for the moment in *Don Juan* we are still in the region of
the comic and the farcical, though aware of tragic possibilities.
And characteristically for *Don Juan* the next stanza shifts the
dramatic ground completely. From speech splendidly deli-
vered (and as convincing as only theatrical speech can be when
compared with the hesitant muttering and emotion-choked
spluttering of real life) we move with the narrator to contem-
plation of the speaker herself. But this contemplation is not
from the point of view of any audience, not of the husband-
listener's response to what we would now call the speaker's
body-language, but is in effect a grand and mythic enactment
of woman as a kind of sublime mountain range, a wonder of
beauty as beauty for calm contemplation rather than beauty as
desirable and possessable. The departure from the theatrical
mode could hardly be more surprising, all the more so in that
the stanza seems to be about to offer the reader the sentimental
spectacle of a sobbing lovely lady but gives instead something
much more serenely monumental:

> She ceased, and turn'd upon her pillow; pale
>   She lay, her dark eyes flashing through their tears,
> Like skies that rain and lighten; as a veil,

> Waved and o'ershading her wan cheek, appears
> Her streaming hair; the black curls strive, but fail,
>   To hide the glossy shoulder, which uprears
> Its snow through all;—her soft lips lie apart,
> And louder than her breathing beats her heart.
>
> (I.158)

And yet, Byronically, from the goddess-like grandeur of hair
which 'streams' like meteors of heavenly clouds, the reader
moves through the transition of a dash into the last line where
he is more intimately close not to a goddess but to a woman
erotically and invitingly *there*.

If we now turn to the equivalent section twenty stanzas later,
when the husband is allowed to finish his speech (all of which is
reported, hinted at, suggested, commented on, but never
allowed to be given in his own words, so that we are not
ourselves as readers allowed to inhabit his contours, rehearse
his feelings, give body to his psyche), this is what Byron gives
as a balance:

> Alfonso closed his speech, and begg'd her pardon,
>   While Julia half withheld, and then half granted,
> And laid conditions, he thought very hard on,
>   Denying several little things he wanted:
> He stood like Adam lingering near his garden,
>   With useless penitence perplex'd and haunted,
> Beseeching she no further would refuse,
> When, lo! he stumbled o'er a pair of shoes.
>
> (I.180)

The narrator takes pleasure in the power which he has over his
creatures, witnessing the legal comedy of the wronged wife
using *her* power to dictate sexual terms to her partner—a
narrator who enjoys the ambiguity of 'half withheld, and then
half granted', which suggests not the accepting of an apology so
much as the teasingness of an ill-defined sexual yes/no. He also
delights in the elemental tragicomedy of an Adam excluded
from Paradise, but an Adam who is characteristically Byronic,
a being 'haunted' by 'useless penitence'—Byronic Man. Yet
the speaking voice enjoys much more the intercutting of the
tragic with the bathetic; and once again we tumble into farce:
'When, lo! he stumbled o'er a pair of shoes'.

Being Byron, moreover, he cannot resist the helter-skelter of words which all deflect attention from the striking dramatic moment where the husband notices a strange man's shoes! No doubt some of the narrator's words fill in that space which in the theatre would be required for the silent pause in which the actor holds up his hands, melodramatically shocked, full of visible horror and wonder. Yet we can see how Byron delays the recognition just too long for comedy, just long enough to show his overall control, his refusal to surrender the moment to his actors:

> A pair of shoes!—what then? not much, if they
>> Are such as fit with lady's feet, but these
> (No one can tell how much I grieve to say)
>> Were masculine; to see them, and to seize,
> Was but a moment's act.
>
> (I.181)

The theatrical melodrama is allowed to enter the stanza, but only after the narrator has spoilt all surprise, has taken the centre of the stage himself; and Byron gives the melodrama both a position in the stanza and an impossibly grotesque overplaying, an enjoyed moment from the friend of Monk Lewis and reader of Gothick works:

> —Ah! Well-a-day!
> My teeth begin to chatter, my veins freeze—

This is how a novelist, if placed between the Gothick and the Sentimental schools, might respond, presenting not the narrator's reactions, but perhaps those of the bystanders, or even the hero or, more probably, the heroine. The theatrical pose implodes into narrative and mocking comedy. However, this melodrama is cut into (as the shoes in the first place had cut into the almost-tragedy of Adam-Alfonso) by these shoes once again, but now in a comically unexpected way:

> Alfonso first examined well their fashion,
> And then flew out into another passion.

We have an almost too slow-witted Spanish husband intrigued not so much by the masculinity of the shoes as by their style; and line by line Byron jumps from state to state, from mode to mode, from emotion to emotion, from level to level. As the reader heads on he is led to the mingling of the theatrical, narrative, mocking, *double-entendres*. He likes being played with, being mocked for his expectations which are not fulfilled. And we may recognize, too, that Byron's Donna Julia belongs to that tradition of Restoration theatre's vocal ladies able to turn their language into weapons, both offensive and defensive.[6]

Thus Byron skilfully turns a narrative poem into a complexly functioning multiple voice, using theatre as one of the ways of operating within the poem. And this is really where one celebrates Byron's genuine ear for the speaking voice, a facility which, while by no means constant within his poetry, does enliven and ensoul some of his greatest work. A short encomium by Arthur M. Z. Norman foregrounded this real and sometimes unacknowledged dramatic gift:

> His speech is the pithiest; charged with the personality of the speaker; speeding the action; and bringing its point home in lashing sentences. It is usually a natural speech . . .[7]

We cannot but approve this view of Byron's *best* dramatic speech, but there is something more fundamental to be recognized behind all praise of vocal aspects of Byron's theatrical skills, whether displayed in the dramas, in the mysteries, the Oriental Tales, or *Don Juan* itself, one constant and undeniable feature. Byron's sense of drama derives from division.

Different critics give different accounts of division, but we all intuitively grasp this feature of Byron's work, all respond to its effects. Some critics, such as Allen Perry Whitmore, see the division of the individual will in conflict with conscience or duty. So, for instance, this critic sees *The Deformed Transformed* as being Byron's attempt to portray the two natures of man— the subjective and passionate in Arnold, and the objective, dispassionate, coldly sceptical, intellectual nature in The Stranger. This, he suggests, though 'an ambitious experiment', was 'like the other aspects of the drama, not clearly worked out'. Well, clear or not, the critic sees all the main characters in Byron's dramas, all the 'tragic heroes', Manfred, Marino Faliero, Francis Foscari, Sardanapalus, and Cain, as 'impressive studies in mental conflict'.[8]

Looking at the same plays, another recent critic sees the

conflict in slightly different terms. For Kavita Sharma, *The Deformed Transformed* is transitional between the dramas proper and the mock-heroic epic tone of *Don Juan*. The work is strongly autobiographical, with Arnold and Caesar as 'two facets of Byron's personality': Arnold's dreams reflect Byron's own longings, while Caesar's Shavian wit and irreverent attitude point to Byron's capacity to laugh at himself and mankind. This dual personality found its perfect expression in *Don Juan* where all disparate elements were reconciled in laughter, demonstrating a good-humoured acceptance of the short-comings of people and the world.[9]

The reconciliation of elements which tug in different directions is in the laughter of *Don Juan*: this view has much indeed to recommend it. Yet finally, for my own purposes, it is as well to see that this conflict of opposites is apprehended more universally in Byron's work, dramatic and non-dramatic, by, for instance, George Ridenour, who defines the relationship between violence and tranquility as a central opposition:

> as violence and disorder lurk behind the most winning manifes-
> tations of tranquility and harmony, the tranquil and harmo-
> nious are fated inevitably to dissolve again in the violent and
> chaotic. This is an apparently immutable law of Byron's
> world.[10]

Byron's engagement, overtly and covertly, with conflict is what we really mean when we talk of Byron and the sense of the dramatic. When we find a non-ironic or one-directional piece of writing, then we know that this is not going to be the best of Byron. We respond most warmly to him where the work generates an awareness of struggle, contradiction, discord—where it represents what might be termed the *Macbeth* part of the Byronic spectrum. This is when the work shows a man who, like Brutus, Macbeth or any other of Byron's own tragic protagonists, is divided against himself, in inner turmoil, but in the end choosing a way which leads to a kind of integrity. Byron exhibits this in his own life in his understanding of himself, or, rather, in his declaration of how he wants to see himself and be seen by others, as is apparent, for instance, from his early letters. Writing to Lady Melbourne in February 1814, he says:

—You tell me not to be 'violent' & not to 'answer'—I *have not* & shall *not* answer—and although the consequences may be for aught I know to the contrary exclusion from society—and all sorts of disagreeables—'the Demon whom I still have served— has not yet cowed my better part of Man—' and whatever I may & have or shall feel—I have that within me that bounds against opposition . . .'[11]

Byron's romantic view of Macbeth, a view which emphasizes this tragic hero's lack of free-will, suffuses Byron's whole life and work, is omnipresent and powerful.

We may instance a good and straightforward example of this at work in that section of *Marino Faliero* where the Doge confronts Israel Bertuccio and contrasts his own spiritual state with that of the conspirators:

> When all is over, you'll be free and merry,
> And calmly wash those hands incarnadine;
> But I, outgoing thee and all thy fellows
> In this surpassing massacre, shall be,
> Shall see and feel—oh God! oh God! 'tis true,
> And thou dost well to answer that it was
> 'My own free will and act', and yet you err,
> For I *will* do this! Doubt not—fear not; I
> Will be your most unmerciful accomplice!
> And yet I act no more on my free will,
> Nor my own feelings—both compel me back;
> But there is *hell* within me and around,
> And like the demon who believes and trembles
> Must I abhor and do. Away! away!
> (III.ii.508–21)

One of the striking linguistic features of this speech is that it serves two separate functions, that of the public declaration and that of the private soliloquy. Where Macbeth tries to keep the two parts of himself, the private and insecure imaginative and sensitive part, and the public, open and boldly masculine part, distinct, the inner terrors and fears in the Doge emerge in 'oh God! oh God! 'tis true', and the firm and public leader is caught out by his own imagination's apprehending the horrors of massacre. Again, we could now point to a dramatic irony in 'those hands incarnadine', because of our knowledge of what Macbeth discovered after Duncan's murder when his hands, now dripping with blood, seemed to pluck out his eyes, and from his appalled imagination welled that image of all seas turning to blood:

> Will all great Neptune's oceans wash this blood
> Clean from my hand? No; this my hand will rather
> The multitudinous seas incarnadine,
> Making the green one red.
>
> (II.ii.60–63)

The later audience will, surely, respond negatively to the now charged word 'incarnadine', and it might equally be alerted by the special rhythm of 'abhor and do', an echo of part of the Weird Sisters'

> And, like a rat without a tail,
> I'll do, I'll do, and I'll do.
>
> (I.iii.9–10)

But this latter, submerged and distorted echo seems not to come so much from the Doge's imagination as from Byron's, a Byronic echo stimulated by the word and idea of *demon*, but overall a demon who, like Macbeth, and like the Doge himself, is caught in a dilemma, unlike the Weird Sisters who are inhuman, without feeling, without the possibility of salvation or damnation.

What the speech from the Doge shows, I think, is that Byron sometimes comes too ventriloquially close to his central figure, making too close a connection between author and character, without that necessary distance for the fully independent *dramatis persona* (as we remember Aristotle had proclaimed in the *Poetics*).[12] But Byron faced other temptations as a dramatist too, both rhetorical and psychological.

The rhetorical temptation is to fashion a voice which is too public and histrionic for the purposes of personal revelation or self-discovery, something which Byron is aware of in himself and something which he mocks superbly in Don Juan's farewell to Spain in Canto II, stanzas 8–10 of *Don Juan*. Here the eloquence of a prepared and melodramatic speech is impaired both by the ship's lurching and by Juan's queasy stomach, a combination which leaves him more in need of a stiff brandy and less of stiff sentiments.[13] On occasion, the soap-box in Byron might be said to get the upper hand, allowing the histrionic takeover in places when the grand or the grandiloquent seemed needed. There are the times, we could say, when Byron's heroic speeches ring too loudly with echoes from speeches of Brutus or Macbeth, when the uniqueness of a speaking voice is clouded and distorted by the generic voices of Shakespeare's tragic heroes.

So, we could instance again the Doge in *Marino Faliero*:

> 'Tis true, these sullen walls should yield no echo:
> But walls have ears—nay, more, they have tongues; and if
> There were no other way for truth to o'er-leap them,
> You who condemn me, you who fear and slay me,
> Yet could not bear in silence to your graves
> What you would hear from me of good or evil;
> The secret were too mighty for your souls:
> Then let it sleep in mine, unless you court
> A danger which would double that you escape.
> Such my defence would be, had I full scope
> To make it famous; for true *words* are *things*,
> And dying men's are things which long outlive,
> And oftentimes avenge them; bury mine,
> If ye would fain survive me: take this counsel,
> And though too oft ye made me live in wrath,
> Let me die calmly;[14]
>
> (V.i.273–93)

The *Macbeth* 'o'erleap' and 'oftentimes' appear in their own right, and the *Julius Caesar* 'The evil that men do lives after them; / The good is oft interred with their bones' comes in via

> Yet could not bear in silence to your graves
> What you would hear from me of good or evil;
> . . .
> Then let it sleep in mine . . .

All critics feel very strongly if they feel at all the Byronic drift towards the Shakespearean archetype, commonly Macbeth, often Brutus, and occasionally King Lear, a pattern which can be paralleled by the allusions in Byron's letters.[15] Occasionally the critic may write at length on Byron and Shakespeare, as Wilson Knight has done,[16] but more usually they content themselves with noting such allusions, kinships, echoes and contrasts as either suit or strike them.[17]

The second temptation for Byron as dramatist is the too-close identification of his own speaking voice and that of the dramatic figure. Such temptations succumbed to might be represented by the kind of revulsion against sexual instinct and activity which Lucifer expresses in *Cain: A Mystery*, an expression of the expansiveness of the soul limited by the horrors of the body, a Romantic *Weltschmerz*:

> But if that high thought were
> Linked to a servile mass of matter—and,
> Knowing such things, aspiring to such things,
> And science still beyond them, were chained down
> To the most gross and petty paltry wants,
> All foul and fulsome—and the very best
> Of thine enjoyments a sweet degradation,
> A most enervating and filthy cheat
> To lure thee on to the renewal of
> Fresh souls and bodies, all foredoomed to be
> As frail, and few so happy . . .
>
> (II.i.50–60)

Take away a little of the bitterness about the cheatingness of sexual desire, sexual surfeit and the cost of it all, and you are not very far from:

> So, we'll go no more a roving
>   So late into the night,
> Though the heart be still as loving,
>   And the moon be still as bright.
>
> For the sword outwears its sheath,
>   And the soul wears out the breast,
> And the heart must pause to breathe,
>   And love itself have rest.

Byron/Lucifer here is like Byron/Stranger or Caesar in *The Deformed Transformed*, like the narrator in *Childe Harold's Pilgrimage*, Canto IV,[18] like the voice which we hear sometimes in *Don Juan* when the narrator seems to take himself very seriously and sees his world as blighted, deceitful and as a type of hell.[19] Indeed, Byron is aware of the temptations which as a writer he faces to be single-minded, mono-voiced. He is much happier

when he allows himself two voices, or a voice which is divided
against itself; and he can certainly be very good at two voices
which are in contrast or opposition in some way, genuine
dramatic dialogue, as Arthur M. Z. Norman quite stoutly and
properly maintains.[20]

When he can avoid the declamatory set speech and the
temptation to write himself out again as Macbeth, and when
he can use the gaps between one voice and another, then Byron
is most successful. So in a narrative poem with a gap between
the narrator's voice and the hero's (as in *Childe Harold's
Pilgrimage* Cantos I and II) we have a work which allows
theatrical fragments and techniques to be controlled, framed
and commented on; the invented narrative voice can interrupt
and can notice or not as it pleases its imagined audience,
speaking directly to the reader when it wants to, but able at will
to retreat into its own world of narrative when it so decides.
The ability to dramatize a voice, unique in itself, containing
complexities, unresolved ambiguities, contradictions, is the
greatest achievement of Byron's poetic genius, and the irony is
that his sense of the dramatic is probably best of all displayed
in some parts of the non-dramatic works, especially *Don Juan*.
Nevertheless, the natural sense of theatre with which he was
gifted certainly operated extremely powerfully in the plays,
each one of which can be shown to be concerned with conflicts
within the dramatic hero. We remember that Byron saw
drama, especially tragic drama, in terms of damnation, the
dramatic hero being doomed to destruction in a world which
demanded that he act, and in acting bring about his own
destruction. His great tragic hero, he said, was Lucifer, and the
great tragic heroes are all doomed men, men of 'guilt'.[21] They
could, from Byron's standpoint, be held both to be compul-
sively self-destructive and yet to affirm the nature of the self
beyond all. The plays proper tend towards the psychological
inner contemplation of conflict or the rhetorical set-piece of
public declamation, from *Cain* at one extreme as a genuinely
deep piece of inner exploration to some of the declamatory
verse of *Manfred* at the other.[22]

One feels that the greatest interest of the plays themselves is
really in the central figure and his dilemmas, his mental and
moral state, and greater issues of politics or philosophy might

be said to be underemphasized, even where we have apparently public figures involved. The interest is in the reality of the private world within the public domain, and here we would think of Sardanapalus, Marino Faliero, the Doge in *The Two Foscari* and Manfred. But in his dramatic development Byron ended with experiments like *The Deformed Transformed*, and we can see that this, beyond all the other plays, belongs to the Byronic world of division: here the interest is divided between the two figures of Arnold and the Stranger, analogous to the narrator and central figure in *Childe Harold's Pilgrimage*, and a division which is central for *Don Juan* and its management of the theatrical. The division comes into its own in the later part of the play and moves the play closer and closer to *Don Juan* both in method and tone. As one recent critic (among others) observes:

> The only noticeable character in the play is that of Caesar who, far more than Idenstein, resembles the narrator of *Don Juan*. As the narrator exposes Don Juan's self-deception, so does he expose Arnold's. Each time Arnold waxes sentimental, grows vain or heroic, Caesar deflates him with a comment designed to illustrate the gap between reality and experience.[23]

But it is at precisely this point that one must hesitate a little. We can too easily now end by making an apology for his dramatic ventures, recognizing that the dramas are a blind alley which he should never have gone down, or at best stages on the way towards the great *Don Juan*. This latter view, as I have suggested, has something to commend it to us, but we must beware of such a view if it contains the critical fallacy of an artist's necessary and consistent progression towards a master-work at the end of his artistic life. In Byron's case some critics have felt this to be so plainly demonstrable that they can provide diagrams, as does M. S. Kushwaha's *Byron and the Dramatic Form*.[24] I pass over the diagram, but the critical account could be quoted. The plays, it is held, provide

> as Donald M. Hassler points out, the positive premises for the satire of *Don Juan*, but show also a gradual and clear shift towards its central vision. The journey from *Manfred* to *The Deformed Transformed* is, in essence, a journey in the direction of this epic satire, showing clearly how Byron moved, step by step,

from the land of romantic hues to a country of stark realism. The plays, as such, provide a significant link between his verse-romances and his later satires, and help us to understand his poetic development.[25]

Such evolutionary neatness and critical flaccidity will not do. The truth is more than this. It is that Byron's best work, early and late, is concerned with conflicts, and the gradual merging of the *personae* of *Childe Harold's Pilgrimage* shows one of the major truths about Byron. He is at his best and happiest when there is multiplicity within the central figure, a multiplicity which will contain contradictions, and he is always ready to exploit a conflict within a set scene between opposed characters, especially when one of these figures is himself the Byronically divided man.

We should see the dramas therefore not as a bridge between one kind of fiction ('romance') and another ('epic satire') but as a central clue to the distinctive structures and characterization of all Byron's poems, from his early 'Elegy on Newstead Abbey' to Juan's final escapades in Norman Abbey.

NOTES

1. After the pioneer work of Samuel C. Chew Jr, whose *The Dramas of Lord Byron* (Baltimore, 1915) was reissued in 1964, there have been, among the many other works: Bonamy Dobrée, *Byron's Drama* (Nottingham, 1962); Paulino M. Lim Jr, *The Style of Lord Byron's Plays* (Salzburg, 1973); Allen P. Whitmore, *The Major Characters of Lord Byron's Dramas* (Salzburg, 1974); B. G. Tandon, *The Imagery of Lord Byron's Plays* (Salzburg, 1976); *New Light on Byron*, ed. James Hogg (Salzburg, 1976).

2. There is no space here to investigate the multitudinous ways in which Byron, writing *improvisatore* at full stretch, without care or preparation, in his letters and journals, runs for incidental illustration and emphasis to Shakespearean tragedy, and especially *Macbeth*. Without doing more than roughly count occurrences, now readily available in the index to Marchand's superb edition, we can say that there are so many different ready quotations from *Macbeth* that Byron almost had the play by heart.

An author who has done the counting of Byron's references to all plays, Shakespeare's included, is M. S. Kushwaha in his *Byron and the Dramatic Form* (Salzburg, 1980), pp. 24–34 (Shakespeare pp. 29–30).

3. *Byron's Letters and Journals*, ed. Leslie A. Marchand (London, 1973–82), VIII, 115 (hereafter cited as *LJ*).

4. *LJ*, V, 203: letter to John Murray, 2 April 1817.

5. *LJ*, IV, 27.

6. Compare George Meredith on Congreve's *The Way of the World*:

> The flow of boudoir Billingsgate in Lady Wishfort is unmatched for the vigour
> and pointedness of the tongue. It spins along with a final ring, like the voice of
> nature in a fury, and is, indeed, racy eloquence of the elevated fish-wife.
> Millamant is an admirable, almost a lovable heroine. It is a piece of genius in a
> writer to make a woman's manner of speech portray her. You feel sensible of her
> presence in every line of her speaking . . .

7. 'Dialogue in Byron's Dramas', *Notes and Queries*, New Series I (1954), 306.

8. See Allen Perry Whitmore, *The Major Characters of Lord Byron's Dramas* (Salzburg, 1974), pp. 7–8:

> His characters are studies of various degrees of spiritual struggle, revolving
> around the rival claims of the individual will and those of conscience or duty.
> These two aspects of the human spirit attracted the poet's interest greatly, and all
> of his great tragic heroes can be shown to be striving to determine which of these
> two rival claims shall rule their lives.

9. Kavita A. Sharma, *Byron's Plays: A Reassessment* (Salzburg, 1982), passim.

10. George M. Ridenour, *The Style of Don Juan* (New Haven, 1960), p. 145.

11. *LJ*, IV, 53.

12. Part II, Section xvii: Everyman Library edn. (London, 1955), p. 33.

13. It might seem invidious to point a finger, but the kind of emotive rhetoric which is *not* a soliloquy but is really a meditation or reflection on 'Man, on Nature and on Human Life' might be exampled by the Doge's speech in *The Two Foscari*, II.i.333–65.

14. There are echoes here which, incidentally, could be added to those many already noted in Appendix III, 'Shakespearean Echoes in *Marino Faliero*', in Samuel C. Chew Jr, *The Dramas of Lord Byron*, pp. 179–81.

15. The first reference to *Macbeth* in the letters is in August 1806 (*LJ*, I, 96) and the latest in October 1823 (*LJ*, XI, 73).

16. *Byron and Shakespeare* (London, 1966).

17. The task still remains of examining all of the allusions and uses made by Byron of Shakespeare, in spite of the work now devoted to Byron the dramatist.

18.   Our life is a false nature—'tis not in
        The harmony of things,—this hard decree,
        This uneradicable taint of sin,
        This boundless upas, this all-blasting tree,
        Whose root is earth, whose leaves and branches be
        The skies which rain their plagues on men like dew—
        Disease, death, bondage—all the woes we see—
        And worse, the woes we see not—which throb through
        The immedicable soul, with heart-aches ever new.

                                                        (126)

19. E.g. Canto VII, 1 and 2.
20. 'Dialogue in Byron's Dramas', *Notes and Queries*, I (1954), 304–06.
21. 'Who is the hero of "Paradise Lost"? Why Satan,—and *Macbeth*, and *Richard* & *Othello* and *Pierre*, and *Lothario*, & Zanga': *LJ*, VIII, 115.
22. E.g. II.ii.164–76:

> We are the fools of time and terror: Days
> Steal on us, and steal from us; yet we live,
> Loathing our life, and dreading still to die.
> In all the days of this detested yoke—
> This vital weight upon the struggling heart,
> Which sinks with sorrow, or beats quick with pain,
> Or joy that ends in agony or faintness—
> In all the days of past and future, for
> In life there is no present, we can number
> How few—how less than few—wherein the soul
> Forbears to pant for death, and yet draws back
> As from a stream in winter, though the chill
> Be but a moment's.

23. M. S. Kushwaha, *Byron and The Dramatic Form*, p. 182.
24. Op. cit., p. 193.
25. Ibid.

'I leave the thing a problem, like all things': On trying to catch up with Byron

PHILIP DAVIS

I *A Night Bird*

A problem: Byron is not difficult to read but he is hard to understand. The meaning in his poetry often seems very present, yet equally very transient. The spirit of his thing isn't going to be caught easily, and so I must start by letting go a few hare-brained thoughts which I shall only try to round up later on.

Here is one thought. When Byron writes

> The night (I sing by night—sometimes an owl
> And now and then a nightingale) . . .
>
> (*Don Juan*, XV.97)

I find myself thinking this: why did Byron so characteristically write *at night?*

Suppose one answer might be: manic-depression.

Imagine a man who previously had lived all his life day into night—driving himself hard at work, ending the day exhausted; but suddenly one morning he finds himself unable to get up for work and for months afterwards sleeps much of the day, or pretends to. As he lies in bed, in some sort of helpless reaction against his own life, everything seems to be turning upside-down:

> Downstairs! Downstairs, a few feet beneath my bed, was enemy territory. People, familiar or unknown, but particularly the familiar ones, threatened me when they sat on my chairs or walked through the living room. Echoes from cupboards and

doors opening and closing heightened my fear. Who was doing that? Why so much noise? Why so much silence?

He is now beginning to live in reverse, only going downstairs 'late at night prowling inquisitively through the house', when the rest of the family is asleep. Just as before, hiding upstairs, 'I wanted to know everything and nothing'; so, on his ghostly re-entry into downstairs life only at night, 'I wanted to see but not to be seen'. This is a living death; the man is in two worlds.[1]

My reader will be wondering why I should quote all this, so lengthily, at the beginning of an essay meant to be about Byron. But it is because the case I am describing is really a modern version of Manfred:

> The lamp must be replenish'd, but even then
> It will not burn so long as I must watch:
> My slumbers—if I slumber—are not sleep,
> But a continuance of enduring thought,
> Which then I can resist not: in my heart
> There is a vigil, and these eyes but close
> To look within; and yet I live, and bear
> The aspect and the form of breathing men.
>
> (*Manfred*, I.i.1–8)

Is the watch really more to look out for something outside than to avoid seeing something (equally vigilant) within? The act of attention here is also an act of hiding. For if the eyes stop looking and close, they will see and open in a deeper sense: it's like a terrible equivalent of those strange movements upstairs and down, night and day—from noise to silence, between wanting to know everything and wanting to know nothing—where one realm still suddenly becomes its opposite and where evasion becomes itself another trap, or confrontation another escape. This is a terrible way of getting stuck, for it is getting stuck restlessly, with every movement. 'We are, I know not how', said Montaigne, 'double in ourselves, which is the cause that what we believe, we disbelieve, and cannot rid ourselves of what we condemn.'[2] This is the Scorpion that Byron depicts in *The Giaour*, writhing within itself.

And yet how different from all this is the tone of what we began with:

> . . . (I sing by night—sometimes an owl
> And now and then a nightingale) . . .

So, let's try a looser response to the question, 'why did Byron write at night?'. After all, the author of *Don Juan* would surely appreciate that it wasn't through writing poetry that Chaucer's young Squire slept 'namoore than dooth a nyghtyngale'. It is in the very nature of *Don Juan* to put the act of thinking up against the act of loving, and then also wonder whether the act of sleeping might not be better than both. 'And yet a third of life is pass'd in sleep' (XIV.3). So, may we not ask: hadn't Byron anything better—or at least more natural—to do at night than write and be wise (belatedly)? For after all, it is not as though Byron himself would resent a cheeky question about Art:

> Think you, if Laura had been Petrarch's wife,
> He would have written sonnets all his life?
>
> (*DJ*, III.8)

Think you the Owl increasingly usurped the Cuckoo as Byron prematurely aged? For, speaking of ageing, Montaigne—one of Byron's favourite authors—gives this warning against assigning *moral* credit to what is an essentially temporal, physical and, above all, saddening process: 'I abominate that incidental repentance which old age brings along with it . . . I can never think myself beholden to impotency, for any good it can do to me . . . Miserable kind of remedy, to owe one's health to one's disease!'.[3] And yet this is precisely the sort of levelling recognition that Byron himself would relish: it is for reasons akin to Montaigne's that Byron calls Time, rather than Age, our 'sole philosopher'.[4] What seems to preside over life—such as Age or Wisdom or Night—is itself in the process of time only a part of life's succession. Hence so many big things in the verse of *Don Juan* pass inside little brackets. Yet this is still Manfred's helplessness in another mode or time-zone or pace—the inability of self to preside over itself, the sense that even as we drive we are driven. The same things can look so different in Byron, as well as different things so confusingly alike. Anyone who tries to patrol the critics' beat will find Byron's movements difficult to trace.

Depression and evasion; the insufficiency of Eros; the ironic belatedness of Wisdom, almost to the point of its own irrelevance. Whether we take it seriously or comically, 'why did Byron write at night?' points in these ways to two almost opposite answers: night is a hiding place, subordinate to one's personal day; night is a sacred place, coming first impersonally before ever day dawns. Let us take them in that order.

First, Byron's writing at night and at odd hours must have to do with his instinctive dislike of being seen to be literary. At Harrow, he recalled, 'I was never *seen* reading—but always idle and in mischief—or at play.—The truth is that I read eating—read in bed—read when no one else read.'[5] Trelawny reports that Byron's conversation was anything but literary; moreover, 'of nothing was he more indignant, than of being treated as a man of letters, instead of as a lord and a man of fashion'.[6] It is typical of Byron's double secretiveness that in his thus hiding his literariness one also cannot distinguish his sense of pride from his sense of shame or quite establish a definite priority between his hiding things from others and his keeping them to himself. With Byron, that is to say, one thing always seems to be borrowing from its opposite, the two together allowed to carry him along between them. It is the same with his riding of the new Pegasus—that new poetry of self-expressive freedom which he found himself both deploring and spurring on:

> I thought . . . *all* of '*us youth*' were on a wrong tack. But I never said that we did not sail well. Our fame will be hurt by *admiration* and *imitation*. When I say *our*, I mean *all* (Lakers included), except the postscript of the Augustans. The next generation (from the quantity and facility of imitation) will tumble and break their necks off our Pegasus, who runs away with us; but we keep the *saddle*, because we broke the rascal and can ride. But though easy to mount, he is the devil to guide; and the next fellows must go back to the riding-school . . .
>
> (*LJ*, VI, 10)

He only harnessed the horse's power to the extent that he might *let* it carry him away. What makes Byron so dangerous an example is the fine divide he allows between control and lack of control—or, more accurately, between lack of control and collusive acquiescence in it.

We could say that Byron would have liked to re-establish an

Augustan sense of decorum by making art secondary by day, primary by night; by trying to see as naturally signalled two separate realms of being. 'As for poesy—mine is the *dream* of my sleeping Passions—when they are awake—I cannot speak their language—only in their Somnambulism' (*LJ*, V, 157). It is fear of those dreams of his sleeping passions that makes Manfred try to keep awake; but in fact they make him *their* waking Somnambulist. Likewise, no sooner does Byron see things as separate than he begins to find them merging into each other again, either against his will or with his collusion, behind his back. Thus:

> To withdraw *myself* from *myself* (oh that cursed selfishness!) has ever been my sole, my entire, my sincere motive in scribbling at all; and publishing is also the continuance of the same object, by the action it affords to the mind, which else recoils upon itself.
>
> (*LJ*, III, 225)

For, as soon as he talks of poetry withdrawing myself from myself, the mind still does recoil upon itself in that bracket: '(oh that cursed selfishness)'. 'To withdraw myself from myself' becomes, in both senses, to let yourself go—to let yourself go with 'our Pegasus, who runs away with us'. In other words, we have the alarming spectacle of a man who, turning to poetry that his mind may not recoil upon itself, constantly finds and makes in that poetry images of that very self-recoil: the Scorpion

> maddening in her ire,
> One sad and sole relief she knows,
> The sting she nourish'd for her foes,
> Whose venom never yet was vain,
> Gives but one pang, and cures all pain,
> And darts into her desperate brain.—
> So do the dark in soul expire . . .
>
> (*The Giaour*, ll.427–33)

To use poetry as a relief to get away from a painful condition, only to reproduce that painful condition in the poetry, is like fleeing madness in a way that is itself still half-mad. The fiction can only free itself from the charge of being a mere relief from reality by being subjected to the thought of that reality again and cancelling its own relief in the process, with almost heightened imagined pain. That is partly what Byron means by sailing well but on the wrong tack.

This confusion between two worlds—

> Between two worlds life hovers like a star,
>   'Twixt night and morn, upon the horizon's verge:
> How little do we know that which we are!
>   How less what we may be!
>
> (*DJ*, XV.99)

—seems to me to have strong kinship with something I have been reading recently in a modern novelist:

> a line from Goethe's West-East Divan: 'Is one man alive when others are alive?' Deep within Goethe's query lies the secret of the writer's creed. By writing books, the individual becomes a universe (we speak of the universe of Balzac, the universe of Chekhov, the universe of Kafka, do we not?). And since the principal quality of a universe is its uniqueness, the existence of another universe constitutes a threat to its very essence . . .
>
> The proliferation of mass graphomania among politicians, cab drivers, women on the delivery table, mistresses, murderers, criminals, prostitutes, police chiefs, doctors, and patients proves to me that every individual without exception bears a potential writer within himself and that all mankind has every right to rush out into the streets with a cry of 'We are all writers!' . . .
>
> Once the writer in every individual comes to life (and that time is not far off), we are in for an age of universal deafness and lack of understanding.[7]

Inside me I think terrible, deadly, isolating thoughts—said Manfred simply to *himself*—'and yet I live, and bear / The aspect and the form of breathing men'. It is the innocent shock not of a boaster but, more vulnerably, of one who finds himself to have been instinctively committed to the Egotistical Sublime without *himself* realizing it. Our novelist here more calmly admits that writing is almost damningly solipsistic, and yet goes on writing as though for common and social purposes, as ever. Somehow a part of himself can still see outside that self which instinctively claims to be everything, with nothing outside it; and there is no reconciliation or even meeting in conflict. 'How little do we know that which we are!' 'We are, I know not how, double in ourselves.'

Clearly, the mood in which Byron exiled writing to that *looser* realm of time-out, amidst the rags of time at the end of the active day, is bound up too with his disgust for 'graphomania':

> I do think the preference of *writers* to *agents*—the mighty stir made about scribbling and scribes, by themselves and others—a sign of effeminacy, degeneracy, and weakness. Who would write, who had any thing better to do? 'Action—action—action'—said Demosthenes: 'Actions—actions,' I say, and not writing,—least of all, rhyme.
>
> (*LJ*, III, 220)

Night is the equivocal time; in the dark the contradictions and confusions get let loose.

What is more, it is the nature of night itself which allows its own transformation from something secondary, at the end of the day as relief, to something primary behind all daily appearances. Typically, at the beginning of Act IV of *Marino Faliero* a minor character leaves the apparently joyous social rout to go out into the Venetian night. In so doing, Lioni takes the play itself into what is a digression or lull—but also into something central though delivered from off-centre. 'All the delusion of the dizzy scene, / Its false and true enchantments', says Lioni on leaving the festivity, 'Are gone':

> . . . Around me are the stars and waters—
> Worlds mirror'd in the ocean, goodlier sight
> Than torches glared back by a gaudy glass;
> And the great element, which is to space
> What ocean is to earth, spreads its blue depths.
>
> (IV.i.68–72)

Lioni's withdrawal from the social throng becomes reminiscent of Plato's warning against mere Appearances in his parable of the Cave, where the cave-dwellers cannot see that the fire which lights them within the cave is as nothing to the sun outside it. 'Worlds mirror'd in the ocean'—the ocean of this Venice world—is that moment of glimpsed Reality which, for Byron, is also the moment of Poetry itself:

> What is Poetry?—The feeling of a Former world and Future.
>
> (*LJ*, VIII, 37)

To Byron the quintessential poetic moment is when something in the content, not only of the play but also of human affairs, seems to transcend the very form in which it is still contained—thus in *The Giaour*:

> Though in Time's record nearly nought,
> It was Eternity to Thought!
>
> (ll.271–72)

The individual in the universal, the eternal in the temporal, what is central found for a second in what is off-centre—as though for that second being on the 'wrong tack' mattered less than sailing well within it.

I can think of two Byronic images which show what it feels like, within the human mind, thus to make poetry in the dark. The first emerges from Byron's imagination of imprisonment in *The Prisoner of Chillon*:

> First came the loss of light, and air,
> And then of darkness too:
> I had no thought, no feeling—none—
> Among the stones I stood a stone . . .
> It was not night—it was not day,
> It was not even the dungeon-light,
> So hateful to my heavy sight,
> But vacancy absorbing space,
> And fixedness—without a place.
>
> (ll.233–44)

It is a feeling of infinite riches in a little room of sense-deprivation; everything as nothing, nothing as everything. Content here dissolves its own form like overflowing music and yet remains swimmingly and invisibly fixed, like blind imaginative thoughts within Manfred's still solid cranium. A second example of this sensation of poetry in the dark comes from another of Byron's thought-experiments—his account of the experience of dying in *Mazeppa*:

> I felt the blackness come and go,
>   And strove to wake; but could not make
> My senses climb up from below:
> I felt as on a plank at sea,
> When all the waves that dash o'er thee,
> At the same time upheave and whelm,

And hurl thee towards a desert realm.
My undulating life was as
The fancied lights that flitting pass
Our shut eyes in deep midnight, when
Fever begins upon the brain.

(ll.550–60)

There the outside world seems contained within an internal one which that external world is nonetheless taking way, even as Mazeppa's horse is driving him on to no place, apparently, but Death. These soul's night-journeys, moving yet static, very much in terms of the physical world yet not quite of it, have a spinning, hallucinatory quality, as night turns time back into space in a sort of re-creative death:

That we become a part of what has been,
And grow unto the spot, all-seeing but unseen.

(*Childe Harold's Pilgrimage*, IV.138)

It is essential to Byron's writing that night should be that equivocal form of death––a way out of one form of life and a way back into another, with knowledge of the route between the two itself left in the dark. For it is not so much the two ideas of night—as secondary or primary—that are important here but, as so often in Byron, the fluidity of *movement* between them, which night itself allows. Imaginatively, night itself seems to blur for Byron the transition between one dimension of being and another—the sort of transition that Byron himself did not want to *know* about if knowledge got in the way of making it. Hence too the rapidity involved in his writing, to fight off consciousness and cross the gaps that a slower consciousness would only serve to widen:

I know not why—I have not continued my journal . . . I know not why I resume it even now except that standing at the window of my apartment in this beautiful village—the calm though cool serenity of a beautiful and transparent Moonlight— showing the Islands—the Mountains—the Sea—with a distinct outline of the Morea traced between the double Azure of the waves and skies—have quieted me enough to be able to write— from [sic] which (however difficult it may seem for one who has written so much publicly—to refrain) is and always has been to me—a task and a painful one—I could summon testimonies

were it necessary—but my handwriting is sufficient—it is that of
one who thinks much, rapidly—perhaps deeply—but rarely
with pleasure.

(*LJ*, XI, 34)

It is just like Byron to borrow from a newly-found calm the
almost opposite capacity for passionate rapidity. It is also like
him to skip knowledge about the gap between not writing and
writing, but calmly see instead within his writing that anal-
ogous bounding of the Morea 'between the double Azure of the
waves and skies'. The very sight of the Morea instinctively had
made him write again, so close in such a case being the relation
of eye and hand. It is Byron's ability to move rapidly from
point to point without our quite seeing how, which is the most
distinctive and disturbing thing about him.

Perhaps the most dangerous too. For Byron is often like
Lioni, going off from the world at a tangent of his own, only to
find a displaced centrality there in an off-centre spot, big
thoughts in passing interludes or brackets; or like Marino
Faliero himself who at the very height of the conspiracy
hesitates in order to become for a moment another person to
one side of the inevitable action, the uncertain double to his
own fatal commitment:

> . . . think not I waver:
> Ah! no; it is the *certainty* of all
> Which I must do doth make me tremble thus.
> (III.ii.485–87)

Always there seems to be a greediness in Byron for those other
possibilities—peripheral in this story, central were it another;
as with the rebels in *The Island*:

> They stood, the three, as the three hundred stood
> Who dyed Thermopylae with holy blood.
> But ah! how different! 'tis the *cause* makes all,
> Degrades or hallows courage in its fall . . .
> However boldly their warm blood was spilt,
> Their Life was shame, their Epitaph was guilt.
> And this they knew and felt . . .
> (IV.259–71)

Sailing strongly, but on the wrong tack. This is the tempera-
ment that Kierkegaard warned against as fictively aesthetic:

For every one can be a good man who wills it, but it always
requires talent to be bad. Hence, many would like to be
philosophers, not Christians, for to be a philosopher talent is
required, to be a Christian humility, and that every one can have
who wills it . . . it requires much ethical courage not to wish to
be distinguished by differences but to be content with the
universal . . . When a man lives aesthetically his mood is always
eccentric because he has his centre in the periphery. Personality
has its centre within itself, and he who has not his self is
eccentric. When a man lives ethically his mood is centralized, he
is not moody.[8]

In such a view the ethical attitude would be that of Bernard
Malamud's *The Natural* where a good woman says to the book's
self-destructive protagonist: 'We have two lives, Roy, the life
we learn with and the life we live with after that'.[9] But Byron
always wanted more than one life, more than two lives. A sort
of half-manic, half-despairing greed also lies behind his desire
to have a full physical life by day and then, as much in revenge
as remorse, a writerly life into the night. 'Action—action', said
Demosthenes, but Byron pluralizes it away from Kierke-
gaard's universal: 'Actions—actions':

'Carpe *diem*' is not enough—I have been obliged to crop even the
seconds—for who can trust to *tomorrow*? *tomorrow* quotha? *to-
hour*—*to-minute*—I can *not* repent me (I try very often) so much of
any thing I have done—as of any thing I have left undone.
(*LJ*, VI, 211)

Byron was always busy mucking up form, putting the life we
live with back into the life we learn with—except for when he
was finding some terribly unbridgeable gap between the two
lives, as between these two stanzas from *Don Juan*:

He who hath proved war, storm, or woman's rage,
Whether his winters be eighteen or eighty,
Hath won the experience which is deemed so weighty.

How far it profits is another matter.—
Our hero . . .
(XII.50–51)

And so, on with the story and away again . . . leaving God
knows what behind.

It is as though Byron led a series of reversible lives, one life mixed up with another until he could quite forget or deny an original:

> I recollect once after an hour in which I had been sincerely and particularly gay—and rather brilliant in company—my wife replying to me when I said (upon her remarking my high spirits) 'and yet Bell—I have been called and mis-called Melancholy— you must have seen how falsely frequently.' 'No—B—(she answered) it is not so—at *heart* you are the most melancholy of mankind, and often when apparently gayest.'
>
> (*LJ*, IX, 38)

Most melancholy when apparently gayest: it is with Byron and melancholy as he said it was with himself and the company of women—he could live neither with nor without it.[10] Indeed, in making melancholy a part of everything he did, he had half stopped it being everything in itself. Instead of being always in it, he always took it, forced it, along with him, in that rapid mobility of his. He had, it would seem, a number of lives in ever-switching layers:

> Changeable too—yet somehow '*idem semper;*'
> Patient—but not enamoured of endurance;
> Cheerful—but sometimes rather apt to whimper:
> Mild—but at times a sort of '*Hercules furens:*'
> So that I almost think that the same skin
> For one without—has two or three within.
>
> (*DJ*, XVII.11)

At any point therefore when in danger of finally being caught, he can slip one skin back over another and internally turn himself back-to-front as it were:

> . . . but who would scorn the month of June,
> Because December, with his breath so hoary,
> Must come? Much rather should he court the ray,
> To hoard up warmth against a wintry day.
>
> (*DJ*, X.9)

That is but the simplest example, another form of reversing day-night into night-day. But to Kierkegaard only a man who had wanted to forget his own centre could be so mobile. 'So now all things are damned, one feels at ease' (*DJ*, VI.23). For another Calvinist poet, the very idea of being most gay when most melancholy was like a foretaste of hell—distraction distracting from distraction:

> I wonder that a sportive thought should ever knock at the door of my intellect, and still more that it should gain admittance. It is as if harlequin should intrude himself into the gloomy chamber where a corpse is deposited in state. His antic gesticulations would be unseasonable at any rate, but more especially so if they should distort the features of the mournful attendants with laughter.[11]

To Cowper, to laugh when innerly crying was at best a temporary distraction and at bottom the sign of somebody who was already a lost man trying to lose himself. For all his evasiveness, Byron could never escape.

Byron himself knew this. There is a stunning image in *Manfred* concerning the protagonist's ambition 'to rise / I knew not whither—it might be to fall':

> But fall, even as the mountain-cataract,
> Which having leapt from its more dazzling height,
> Even in the foaming strength of its abyss,
> (Which casts up misty columns that become
> Clouds raining from the re-ascended skies,)
> Lies low but mighty still.
> (III.i.109–14)

It is not only that the power of his falling is like a semi-revenge upon the fact of his having to fall at all. There is also in that bracket the gentler hope of a second life, again rising only to fall according to the universal law of gravity, yet doing the same thing in a better way only revealed as such, however, by the instigating example of the first. It is an image that Byron repeated again at greater length a few months later when writing the fourth canto of *Childe Harold*. Stanza 69 speaks now of the fall as of 'the hell of waters'; stanza 70 tells how 'the sweat' of these waters rises

> And mounts in spray the skies, and thence again
> Returns in an unceasing shower . . .

Stanza 71 follows the falling waters through the rocks—'like the fountain of an infant sea / Torn from the womb of

mountains by the throes / Of a new world'. This is a Titanic
verse—of fall, rebirth and fall constantly repeated in lighter or
heavier notes: a Beethovenism of poetry ('Muss es sein? Es
muss sein!'). Byron can turn inside-out, upside-down, back-to-
front, slip the noose of any of his own sentences through the
sheer speed of improvising intelligence; but to Kierkegaard
that is precisely how he is trapped, freely trapped.

In stanza 116 of canto V of *Don Juan* the Sultana says, with
flaunting seductiveness, 'Christian, canst thou love?'. And
Don Juan, fresh from Haidée's loss, finds those words, so
casual and off-centre, hit home quite differently, like comedy
reversed: 'So that he spoke not, but burst into tears'. 'No B—it
is not so—at *heart* you are the most melancholy of mankind'.
Where does reading Byron leave us?

II '*I got no good from this reading*'?

The way that Byron can so quickly change his tune in *Don Juan*
is only a foreshortening of something that is going on across his
whole opus—as from *The Giaour* in 1813:

> Then stealing with the muffled oar
> Far shaded by the rocky shore,
> Rush the night-prowlers on the prey,
> And turn to groans his roundelay.
> Strange—that where Nature loved to trace,
> As if for Gods, a dwelling place,
> And every charm and grace hath mixed
> Within the paradise she fixed,
> There man, enamour'd of distress,
> Should mar it into wilderness.
>
> (ll.42–51)

—to *The Island* in 1823:

> The gentle island, and the genial soil,
> The friendly hearts, the feasts without a toil,
> The courteous manners but from nature caught,
> The wealth unhoarded, and the love unbought;
> Could these have charms for rudest sea-boys, driven
> Before the mast by every wind of heaven?
> And now, even now prepared with others' woes
> To earn mild Virtue's vain desire, repose?

> Alas! such is our nature! all but aim
> At the same end by pathways not the same;
> (I.107–16)

There is a paradisal peace, but man like an outlaw ruins it. The paradox works both ways. These men are rough outlaws, yet what are they seeking but gentle peace? If the first passage, 'enamour'd of distress', means 'they ruin the peace which they seek', the second, 'prepared with others' woes / To earn . . . repose', means 'they seek the peace they ruin'. Both fall in the end, like Byron's image of the cataract, but the second is the first temporarily reascending. Byron loved a second go and compulsively needed to re-enter—for reasons confusedly pitched between defiant recidivism and the desperate hope of redemption—the scene of his crimes, as it were. A second natural force hurls its power into the space already broken open by its predecessor:

> . . . of all the band,
> The brightest through these parted hills hath fork'd
> His lightnings,—as if he did understand,
> That in such gaps as desolation work'd,
> There the hot shaft should blast whatever therein lurk'd.
> (*CHP*, III.95)

Byron's love for variations on a theme is a paradoxical mixture of obsession and mobility.

> And it is very characteristic both of my then state, and of the general tone of my mind at this period of my life, that I was seriously tormented by the thought of the exhaustibility of musical combinations. The octave consists only of five tones and two semitones, which can be put together in only a limited number of ways, of which but a small proportion are beautiful: most of these, it seemed to me, must have been already discovered.[12]

This is emphatically not the voice of Byron. Byron had, indeed, his own often exhausted sense of having to live on with what had already gone dead on him. The voice here is different. It is a depressed version of what Kierkegaard might call the Ethical voice. For it says: if it is all going to get nowhere in the end, then there is no point in carrying on repetitively now. Whereas Byron *would* carry on, often in maniacally bitter parody: 'What a strange thing is man, and what a stranger / Is woman'—

> . . . Whatever she has said
> Or done is light to what she'll say or do;—
> The oldest thing on record, and yet new!
>
> (*DJ*, IX.64)

'The changeableness of Woman' is the *form* of this thought, a thought itself so old as barely to have life in it; but the *content* of the thought is itself all change and changing again, a female liveliness that both transcends the dead old saying and charmingly re-establishes it from within. That is itself the very movement between form and content within a *Juan* stanza. Parodying the very parodies of seriousness that the world has left us, the poetry works with just enough difference to make 'the oldest thing' new again while still only making the 'yet new' the old, old story after all. Hence the closeness of this poetry to the prosaic. Yet Byron can get water out of a stone.

Instead of directly asking: what's the use of this in Byron? where does reading Byron get us?—I want to return to our depressive for a moment, the man 'tormented by the thought of the exhaustibility of musical combinations'. Here again I want to put my concerns into a question that would seem too informal for poets other than Byron perhaps; a question that may seem laughably simple- (or literal-) minded. But I must first set the scene for this second question.

In autumn 1826, two years after Byron's death, a young man began to suffer what we now might call a nervous breakdown, though as he himself reported, it was 'the state, I should think, in which converts to Methodism usually are, when smitten by their first "conviction of sin" '. Unable to distract himself with pleasurable diversions, he put to himself a direct moral question: if all your objects in life were now realized, would you be happy? The answer was equally direct. Would you be happy?

> And an irrepressible self-consciousness distinctly answered, 'No!' At this my heart sank within me: the whole foundation

on which my life was constructed fell down . . . I seemed to have
nothing left to live for.

'A night's sleep, the sovereign remedy for the smaller vexations
of life, had no effect.'[13] For this is now a living nightmare—the
nightmare of a man who, finding that he has been led to put the
whole of one life single-mindedly into one central effort, now
also finds it to have been all somehow off-centre. It is of course
the story of John Stuart Mill.

Finding something missing, and finding that what was
missing had to do with an element of human feeling which his
analytic skills had almost dissolved away, Mill tried to add
what was missing to what was already there. He turned to
literature, to the poets, in order to attempt this:

> This state of my thoughts and feelings made the fact of my
> reading Wordsworth for the first time (in the autumn of 1828) an
> important event in my life. I took up the collection of his poems
> from curiosity, with no expectation of mental relief from it,
> though I had before resorted to poetry with that hope. In the
> worst period of my depression I had read through the whole of
> Byron (then new to me) to try whether a poet, whose peculiar
> department was supposed to be that of the intenser feelings,
> could rouse any feeling in me. As might be expected, I got no
> good from this reading, but the reverse. The poet's state of mind
> was too like my own. His was the lament of a man who had worn
> out all pleasures, and who seemed to think that life, to all who
> possess the good things of it, must necessarily be the vapid
> uninteresting thing which I found it. His Harold and Manfred
> had the same burthen on them which I had; and I was not in a
> frame of mind to derive any comfort from the vehement sensual
> passion of his Giaours, or the sullenness of his Laras. But while
> Byron was exactly what did not suit my condition, Wordsworth
> was exactly what did.[14]

This decision, this preference, is almost emblematic of the state
of Byron's standing, relative to Wordsworth, virtually from the
time of his death in 1824 until the present day. But my question
is this: wouldn't it have been better for Mill to have stayed with
Byron rather than to have turned to Wordsworth? To have met
fire with fire?

'The next generation will tumble and break their necks off

our Pegasus', Byron had predicted. And of that next gener-
ation, J. S. Mill knew two contradictory necessities: that he
had aesthetically to cultivate a wider range of sympathies and
sentiments; but that to have the feeling of wanting more
feelings was almost suicidally self-defeating. The older voice of
Montaigne offers a warning here against post-Romantic habits
of reading for psychological identifications:

> I had rather understand myself well in myself than in Cicero.[15]

'We are taught to borrow and to beg, and brought up more to
make use of what is another's than of our own.'[16] For certain,
there is something shameful in the danger of our thus making
ourselves fictitious even in the apparent service of our own real
lives—finding ourselves in Cicero instead. But what do people
do when, like Mill, they find something missing in themselves?
In one mind, clearly Byron was as anti-aesthetic as was old
Montaigne: 'I hate things *all fiction* . . . pure invention is but
the talent of a liar'; 'Nothing can equal my contempt of your
real mere unleavened author', 'the pen peeping from behind the
ear'; and Johnny Keats? 'such writing is a sort of mental
masturbation—he is always f-gg-g his Imagination'.[17] But in
another mind, more driven by immediate needs—in Lara's for
example—then something close to breakdown pushes the man,
who previously had fled his own thoughts in action and in
feeling, to look for them again in books, 'through night's long
hours':

> Books, for his volume heretofore was Man,
> With eye more curious he appear'd to scan,
> And oft, in sudden mood, for many a day
> From all communion he would start away: . . .
> *(Lara,* I.131–34)

We have already seen Byron's swift movements from the land of
the real to the land of the unreal and back again, till at times he
hardly knew one from the other or doubted the difference. The
chaos of dialectical paradox is characteristic of Byron: I mean,
the fact that his comedy should also be so elusively serious; or
that he himself should be—in the words of his future wife—'a
very bad, very good man';[18] or that his anti-aestheticism at one

moment should be in danger of promoting a disauthenticating *over*-directness in art the next.

It is significant, therefore, that Mill came to Wordsworth only after a reading of the whole of Byron made him give up his direct emotional demands upon the poets. 'I took up the collection of his poems with no expectation of mental relief.' For Wordsworth is precisely the poet who makes a second start out of what for others would be an ending disappointment— who finds disappointment, that is to say, to be an essential chastening prelude to a secondary revelation which itself would be unavailable save through this educative realignment of earlier, defeated desires. Thus Mill:

> At the conclusion of the Poems came the famous Ode, falsely called Platonic, 'Intimations of Immortality': in which . . . I found that he too had had similar experience to mine; that he also had felt that the first freshness of youthful enjoyment of life was not lasting; but that he had sought for compensation, and found it, in the way in which he was now teaching me to find it. The result was that I gradually, but completely, emerged from my habitual depression, and was never again subject to it. I long continued to value Wordsworth less according to his intrinsic merits, than by the measure of what he had done for me. Compared with the greatest poets, he may be said to be the poet of unpoetical natures, possessed of quiet and contemplative tastes. But unpoetical natures are precisely those which require poetic cultivation.[19]

The damaging word there is 'compensation', for that is what Mill made of Wordsworth. 'He had sought for compensation, and found it, in the way in which he was now teaching me to find it.' It wasn't that Wordsworth signalled for Mill a secular equivalent of conversion, a radical change in the self; Wordsworth stood rather for therapy, for letting Mill off the hook by letting in a calmer, more indirect, less goal-orientated idea of the self. It was cultural lobotomy. Which of course is preferable to suicide. What Mill had to do in order to survive is understandable; but what survived of him was for ever after compromised and patched up.

None of this, however, could justly be said to be the fault of Wordsworth himself. A more faithful account of what a man such as Mill could have got from reading Wordsworth is given,

in fact, by Ruskin. For, again, Ruskin turns to the great Ode to
consider the shadow line: when adulthood knows it has outrun
those first energies that had seemed to give unceasingly
instinctive guarantees of purpose and being, what then?

> This evil is evidently common to all minds; Wordsworth
> himself mourning over it in the same poem:
>> Custom hangs upon us, with a weight
>> Heavy as frost, and deep almost as life.
> And if we grow impatient under it, and seek to recover the
> mental energy by more quickly repeated and brighter novelty, it
> is all over with our enjoyment. There is no cure for this evil, any
> more than for the weariness of the imagination already des-
> cribed, but in patience and rest: if we try to obtain perpetual
> change, change itself will become monotonous . . .
> . . . There was always more in the world than men could see,
> walked they ever so slowly; they will see it no better for going fast.
> And they will at last, and soon too, find out that their grand
> inventions for conquering (as they think) space and time, do, in
> reality, conquer nothing; for space and time are, in their own
> essence, unconquerable, and besides did not want any sort of
> conquering; they wanted *using*. A fool always wants to shorten
> space and time: a wise man wants to lengthen both . . . We shall
> be obliged at last to confess, what we should long ago have known,
> that the really precious things are thought and sight, not pace. It
> does a bullet no good to go fast; and a man, if he be truly a man, no
> harm to go slow; for his glory is not at all in going, but in being.[20]

Ruskin's *Modern Painters* is in many ways a Wordsworthian
book, and never more so when it speaks so magnificently of
man's glory lying 'not at all in going but in being'. It is also
clearly a Wordsworthian book in what its author fears to be a
post-Wordsworthian age, the urban and industrial age of
'inventions for conquering space and time': 'Your railroad',
says Ruskin in the same section, 'is only a device for making the
world smaller'. Like a microcosm of that predicament, Ruskin
carried on within himself a personal conflict which we would
now call manic-depression. Hence there remains a slight edge
of desperation in that idea of still, puritanically, *'using'* time and
space—a verb that Wordsworth would never have thought of.
Hence too, somewhat like Mill, the appropriation of Words-
worth in the interests of something still close to emotional
economy: how to keep a sense of novelty alive—by going more

slowly over the same sources of nourishment rather than desperately seeking for new ones. Even so, it is tempting to re-defend Mill's preference for Wordsworth over Byron in the very terms which Ruskin here provides.

For, 'a fool always wants to shorten space and time'—like Lara 'in youth all action and all life':

> Burning for pleasure, not averse from strife;
> Woman—the field—the ocean—all that gave
> Promise of gladness, peril of a grave,
> In turn he tried—he ransack'd all below,
> And found his recompense in joy or woe,
> No tame, trite medium; for his feelings sought
> In that intenseness an escape from thought:
> The tempest of his mind in scorn had gazed
> On that the feebler elements hath rais'd;
> The rapture of his heart had look'd on high,
> And ask'd if greater dwelt beyond the sky:
>   (I.116–26)

This looks like life as heroic race and competition, defiantly seeking if there is anything outside to equal the power of that within. But it is also more confusedly helpless than that, for it is already autobiography desperately turned inside-out. The power within cannot be lived with there and has to be dispersed in dissatisfaction outside, 'an escape from thought'. It is that thought which the wise man keeps possession of: 'a fool always wants to shorten space and time: a wise man wants to lengthen both'. Wordsworth doesn't race, but can stop—'the really precious things are thought and sight, not pace':

> . . . and oftentimes,
> When we had given our bodies to the wind,
> And all the shadowy banks on either side
> Came sweeping through the darkness, spinning still
> The rapid line of motion, then at once
> Have I, reclining back upon my heels,
> Stopped short; yet still the solitary cliffs
> Wheeled by me—even as if the earth had rolled
> With visible motion her diurnal round!
>   (The Prelude, 1805, I.478–86)

To stop short isn't the end of the line, with Wordsworth's sense of timing. A sense of something different from ego carries on

sweepingly within it after the ego has made a stop. 'This I feel /
That from thyself it is that thou must give, / Else never can
receive' (XI.332–34). In such realignments within his very
lines, Wordsworth seems to know far more than does Byron's
Lara as to the exact terms of both separation and relation
between himself and the earth. Lara only stops short in a
depressive dead-end that almost physically follows upon his
youthful mania. If similarly Byron's Manfred comes to value a
neo-Wordsworthian stillness at the beginning of act three—
'The golden secret, the sought "Kalon" found, / And seated in
my soul'—it is a valuation arrived at only through a repent-
ance that is consciously too late: 'It will not last, / But it is well
to have known it, though but once: / It hath enlarged my
thoughts with a new sense, / And I within my tablets would
note down / That there is such a feeling' (III.i.13–18). It is as
though for the Lara and the Manfred in Byron such a
recognition only comes when close to death because it *is* a
death. To Wordsworth it was life itself. Doesn't all this prove
Mill basically right in his choice?

Yet the fact is that Ruskin himself would not have put the
comparison between Wordsworth and Byron in the terms
which we have just borrowed from him. Indeed, although
Byron was one of Ruskin's earliest attachments, it seems to be
the case that, after *Modern Painters*, Ruskin increasingly came to
value Byron the more highly, as he aged. He wrote thus in
1880, twenty-four years after writing the passage we have just
been considering:

> The first thing you have got to do, in reading Byron to purpose,
> is to remember his motto, 'Trust Byron'. You always may; and
> the more, that he takes some little pleasure at first in offending
> you. But all he says is true, nevertheless, though what worst of
> himself there is to tell, he insists upon at once; and what good
> there may be, mostly leaves you to find out.[21]

Trust Byron! Why should John Stuart Mill have trusted
Byron? To Mill Byron seemed to offer him no more than the
Spirits offered Manfred:

The Seven Spirits.   What wouldst thou with us, son of mortals
                     —say?
Man.   Forgetfulness—

First Spirit.	Of what—of whom—and why?
Man.	Of that which is within me; read it there— Ye know it, and I cannot utter it.
Spirit.	We can but give thee that which we possess:

(I.i.135–39)

And forgetfulness is not something you 'possess' in consciousness but the opposite—something that dispossesses you of consciousness itself. Only Wordsworth seems to know how properly to gain a loss and find it a gain. Either Byron would lead Mill back into the immobility of the very deadlock from which he started, or—as we have also seen earlier—he would offer him a form of evasive mobility that itself can seem barely trustworthy. Trust Byron? Which Byron? Where is he? He 'mostly leaves you to find out'.

In order to try to find out, let's hold back Mill and Ruskin for a moment and think where Mill might have tried to look for Byron's 'Kalon', his 'golden secret'.

Byron himself won't often help. He said that he turned to his journal as a relief, he didn't know why:

> But I can't read it over;—and God knows what contradictions it may contain. If I am sincere with myself (but I fear one lies more to one's self than to any one else), every page should confute, refute, and utterly abjure its predecessor.
>
> <div align="right">(<i>LJ</i>, III, 233)</div>

The act of reading through the whole of Byron's poetry, as did J. S. Mill, often feels exactly like that too. Say, for example, we put two passages from quite different works next to each other: this from *Lara* (I.337–45)—

> Too high for common selfishness, he could
> At times resign his own for others' good,
> But not in pity, not because he ought,
> But in some strange perversity of thought,
> That swayed him onward with a secret pride
> To do what few or none would do beside;
> And this same impulse would in tempting time

Mislead his spirit equally to crime;
So much he soared beyond, or sunk beneath . . .

with this from *The Two Foscari* (I.i.270–76)—

Mar.   . . . Give me, then, way;
This is the Doge's palace; I am wife
Of the Duke's son, the *innocent* Duke's son,
And they shall hear this!
Mem.   It will only serve
More to exasperate his judges.
Mar.   What
Are *judges* who give way to anger? they
Who do so are assassins. Give me way.

A look at those two passages (the first disguised inside morality, the second demanding it) confirms Byron's obsessive concern with mobility and with its opposite, fixity. But always with Byron the question 'which way round?' is a necessary question:

Pleasure's a sin, and sometimes sin's a pleasure;
(*DJ*, I.133)

Men are the sport of circumstances, when
The circumstances seem the sport of men.
(*DJ*, V.17)

That is to say, Lara's dazzling mobility ('So much he soar'd beyond, or sunk beneath') is really another way of being stuck. At the mercy of his own flight of perversity from common ways, his unpredictability is at another level completely predictable. 'It always requires talent to be bad', 'it requires much ethical courage not to wish to be distinguished by differences but to be content with the universal.' Inevitably Lara's proud secondary use of moral selflessness is equated with what it leads to—crime.

On the other hand, there is the passionate fixity of Marina's ethical courage. Yet when we consider what Marina means by '*judges*'—that judges are *judges* no matter what the human provocations—then that apparently static ideal of what is a judge seems to incorporate far more internal mobility than Lara could ever conceive of. For a judge will not be provoked by provocations but will judge them: he will understand but discount their subjectivity or translate it—on behalf of the helplessly emotional provokers themselves—into such objective claims as it may constitute upon the central case in hand. That is judgement—more like a verb than a noun. Things need not be as fixed as they seem. Marina's own provocatively fixed outrage is now not picked up and interpreted by the authorities but left to its own terms—to work to its own disadvantage. In a more ideal state of affairs, that protest would recognize its own licence to stick and make repeated human appeal as itself borrowed. It is borrowed from a faith that the judges themselves will not stick in turn, with reactive bloodymindedness, but take into account and rise above equally human responses. Dangerously but magnificently Marina's is what Byron would call 'the very *poetry* of politics' (*LJ*, VIII, 47). For Marina's is a complex independence consciously dependent upon recognition from a higher authority which it *wants* to be unequal to it; an authority which Marina is left paradoxically demanding, with inevitable overweeningness, from below. Apparent fixity has had to move and still wants to move far more than it appears to represent. Marina's is forced to be *proud* humility but it is humility too in helpless disguise and appeal. 'And what good there may be, [Byron] mostly leaves you to find out.'

But next put Marina's situation alongside that of Marino Faliero, the insulted and hamstrung Doge of Venice, before his wife:

> Angiolina.   Do not speak thus wildly—
> Heaven will alike forgive you and your foes.
> Doge.   Amen! May Heaven forgive them!
> Angiolina.   And will you?
> Doge.   Yes, when they are in Heaven!
> Angiolina.   And not till then?
> Doge.   What matters my forgiveness? an old man's,
> Worn out, scorn'd, spurn'd, abused; what matters then
> My pardon more than my resentment, both
> Being weak and worthless?
>
> (II.i.262–69)

The Doge's situation is both more and less stuck than Marina's; his being the powerlessness of the powerful, hers the power of the powerless. His refusal to budge is a secondary translation of—a giving of definite personal tangibility to—his sense that he is ineffectually free to feel anything, it doesn't matter what. The Doge of Venice's revolt against Venice is what Byron calls 'the head conspiring against the body' (*LJ*, V, 203): it is as though an individualism, as borrowed as was Marina's, must try to make itself a microcosm of the concealed wrong in that macrocosm within which it has still vulnerably to live. It is the right idea in the wrong place, and doubly so when personal motives, already twisted by the present state of things, cannot help becoming egotistically confused in it all. The Doge feels, almost at the end of his life, as stuck as did Sardanapalus even from the first—'Misplaced upon the throne—misplaced in life':

> If born a peasant, he had been a man
> To have reached an empire: to an empire born,
> He will bequeath none;
>
> (I.i.14–16)

It is dialectical movement of mind—the very thought of an alternative which he cannot have—which itself produces the realization of being contained within effective immobility. Byron's characters so often feel that (in Kierkegaard's phrase) they have their 'centre in the periphery'. And when that is so, even physical movement only serves to *enact* the reality of entrapment, at the least making externally visible the limits of the otherwise mental chain. It only makes a certain amount of difference here that it is sometimes a long lead rather than a short one. For the young mutineer in *The Island* could have been almost anything under other circumstances and more or less had to be this particular something in this story:

> Born in a tent, perhaps a Tamerlane;
> Bred to a throne, perhaps unfit to reign.
> For the same soul that rends its path to sway,
> If reared to such, can find no further prey
> Beyond 'itself, and must retrace its way
> Plunging for pleasure into pain:
>
> (II.185–90)

This takes us back to the situation of Sardanapalus but now via Lara. For though I started this as a demonstration of how in Byron every page will 'confute, refute, and utterly abjure its

predecessor', what has become clear is this: that Byron is
deeply interested not only in the difference between being stuck
and being mobile; not only in the potential movement between
the two and when it is right and when it is wrong to stick; but
also finally in the fact that each incorporates and is only the
other side of the other. We are dealing almost as much in
similarities as in contradictions. And though even if he knew he
would not say it, the existential meaning of Lara's trapped
restlessness lies in an implicit protest that we only lead *one*
life—and never more so than when it seems to have been made
up to include the very possibility of several.

For, finally, put Sardanapalus's stuckness up against some-
thing he himself is amazed to find in his slave-mistress—
sympathy for his estranged wife:

> Myr. I know to feel for her.
> Sar.   That is too much,
> And beyond nature—'tis nor mutual
> Nor possible. You cannot pity her,
> Nor she aught but—
> Myr.   Despise the favourite slave?
> Not more than I have ever scorned myself.
>   (IV.i.456–60)

With that phrase 'beyond nature' it is clear that Sardanapalus
cannot credit this sympathy because *he* can't bear to have wife
and mistress simultaneously in mind. But if Myrrha is freer
and more mobile in herself—such that she can feel the right
thing even inside the wrong place—still, the very freedom is
because she hates and no longer believes in that slavish self of
hers which pre-empts her very gift of love. She shares the wife's
feeling about her—that is where the so-called sympathy
begins! I conclude this: that there are moments in Byron when
a character who now *irrevocably* has to be in this one identity, for
that very reason no longer needs to commit a total responsi-
bility to it, and so paradoxically hardly believes in separate
identity at all. Or to put it another way, so strong is the sense of
something like predestination in Byron that for an instant it
impersonally almost frees the minds of his protagonists in the
very sight of what is still personally determined for and by
them. For that is, for instance, precisely the floating feeling

near the end of *Marino Faliero* when the Doge is caught plotting
against the State:

> What shall I say to ye?
> Since my defence must be your condemnation?
> You are at once offenders and accusers,
> Judges and executioners!—Proceed
> Upon your power.
>
> (V.i.164–68)

This is another part of his realization that, had his coup been a
success, then what now is treason would have been to future
history a triumph; and all this was predictable beforehand,
whichever way it went. We live in such strange time-warps and
perhaps the strangest thing about them is that they are
resolved so easily—in one chance. Yet, for a moment, thoughts
and feelings are freer than the bodies and situations in which
they find themselves. 'What shall I say to ye? / Since my
defence must be your condemnation': free only to know itself
not free, it is a thought which floats in astounding impersona-
lity. And it is that strange end-point that the thinker in *Don
Juan* starts from:

> Don Juan, who was real or ideal,—
>   For both are much the same, since what men think
> Exists when the once thinkers are less real
>   Than what they thought, for mind can never sink,
> And 'gainst the body makes a strong appeal;
>   And yet 'tis very puzzling on the brink
> Of what is called Eternity, to stare,
> And know no more of what is here than there:—
>
> (X.20)

Perhaps now, with this strange material, we have sufficient
for the beginning of an answer to our second question—
wouldn't it have been better for Mill to have stayed with Byron
rather than turn to Wordsworth? I shall try to state that
answer explicitly in a third and final section—but only through
a third question to begin with.

III *Why 'trust Byron'?*

That is my third question. Or, to be more careful and get help:
why did *Ruskin* trust Byron? After all, though Mill called

Wordsworth 'the poet of unpoetical natures', many of the lines
of Byron which we have already quoted seem too hasty and
unfinished, so late into the night, to be quite Poetry with a
capital 'P'. Byron said that the poetry of his plays was to be
read as an 'experiment' in 'mental theatre', an attempt to break
down poetry into an immediate and severe mental simplicity,
like reading Greek tragedy in a rapid translation.[22] It is this
sort of effect in all his poetry that Ruskin not only defends:

> How great work is done, under what burden of sorrow, or with
> what expense of life, has not been told hitherto, nor is likely to
> be; the best of late time has been done recklessly or contemp-
> tuously. Byron would burn a canto if a friend disliked it . . .[23]

but also praises:

> Byron's most careless work is better, by its innate energy, than
> other people's most laboured.[24]

Drudgery—that's what Ruskin felt his own work was, taking
ages to repeat in writing what Turner could think in paint in a
stroke. With the energy preserved innate in his very careless-
ness Byron was the would-be painter's poet: 'Would that I
were a painter! to be grouping / All that a poet drags into
detail!' (*DJ*, VI.109).

Always Ruskin is interested in the necessary but uninten-
tional obscurity of an artist in any medium. Why can't they say
it straighter?—says the puritan in Ruskin. But then he says, as
it were: Trust them, the Truth closes up so fast when you are
near it, they have to go in fast and leave traces of obscurity
behind them in their wake:

> There is wide difference between *indolent* impatience of labour
> and *intellectual* impatience of delay; large difference between
> leaving things unfinished because we have *more to do*, and
> because we are satisfied with what we *have done*.[25]

'I am like the Tiger—' wrote Byron as to his never recasting his
work, 'if I miss the first spring—I go growling back to my
Jungle again—but if I *do hit*—it is crushing' (*LJ*, XI, 54).
Doubtless Byron can be indolent but it is when he is a sort of
intellectual Tiger that Ruskin most admires him. Indeed,
nowhere is Ruskin more Byronically contradictory than when

he writes about 'Finish' as finally both impossible and yet necessary for mere humans.[26] There is something about the truth of *sketchiness*, as appropriate to the human level, which Ruskin respects in Byron as he did in Turner:

> Throughout the sketch, as in all that Turner made, the observing and combining intellect acts in the same manner. Not a line is lost, nor a moment of time; and though the pencil flies, and the whole thing is literally done as fast as a piece of shorthand writing, it is to the full as purposeful and compressed, so that while there are indeed dashes of the pencil which are unintentional, they are only unintentional as the form of a letter is, in fast writing, not from want of intention, but from the accident of haste.[27]

It is with Byron's letter-writing that Ruskin begins his appreciation of the poet in *Praeterita*.[28] But what it should now lead us to is a renewed sense of the extraordinariness of *Don Juan* as vast verse-epistle—its accidentalness and temporariness made *permanently* temporary and *essentially* accidental until, like Byron, we too hardly know whether we are 'here' or 'there'. For Byron is almost transfixed by the thought of boundaries and metamorphoses across them. And just as in Canto IV of *Childe Harold's Pilgrimage*, space—under cover of darkness—goes back into time; or, from another direction, just as a moment of sexual release can become trapped into an eternity of consequence; just so, more lightly in *Don Juan*, a drop of ink and a rag of paper are transformed into, and themselves transform, Literature. With all its sketchy rambling, Byron called *Don Juan* 'Montaigne's Essays with a story for a hinge' (*LJ*, X, 150); and it is this amazing paradox of lasting temporariness in *Don Juan* that Montaigne himself might have seen to be a result of transforming writing back into speaking—into time—into the invisible presence of tone:

> We say of some compositions that they stink of oil and of the lamp, by reason of a certain rough harshness that laborious handling imprints upon those where it has been employed. But besides this, the solicitude of doing well, and a certain striving and contending of a mind too far strained and over bent upon its undertaking, breaks and hinders itself like water, that by force of its own pressing violence and abundance, cannot find a ready

issue through the neck of a bottle or a narrow sluice . . . I am
always worst in my own possession, and when wholly at my own
disposition; accident has more title to anything that comes from
me than I; occasion, company, and even the very rising and
falling of my own voice, extract more from my fancy than I can
find when I sound and employ it by myself. By which means, the
things I say are better than those I write, if either were to be
preferred, where nothing is worth anything. This, also, befalls
me, that I do not find myself where I seek myself, and I light
upon things more by chance than by any inquisition of my own
judgment.[29]

Indeed, such is the relief that Ruskin himself found when no
longer writing as he did in *Modern Painters* but turning to a sense
of presentness and chance in composing *Praeterita*: 'I recollect
that very evening bringing down my big geography book, still
most precious to me (I take it down now, and for the first time
put my own initials under my father's name in it)—'.[30] Thus
too Byron finds himself by no longer seeking himself:

> I think that were I *certain* of success,
>   I hardly could compose another line:
> So long I've battled either more or less,
>   That no defeat can drive me from the Nine.
> This feeling 'tis not easy to express,
>   And yet 'tis not affected, I opine.
> In play, there are two pleasures for your choosing—
> The one is winning, and the other losing.
>   (*DJ*, XIV.12)

This is what we might call unpejoratively the language of
apparent sketch: 'This feeling 'tis not easy to express'—but he
does not have another go at it, except as he goes along. Yet it is
even in that casual way that Byron seems the most directly and
naturally metaphysical of all the poets. For, you feel at such
moments, he baffles you in the same way as he baffles himself.
Why would certainty of success have stopped him writing?
What's the (doubtful) pleasure in losing? Byron needed, if not
risk as in youth, then chance, as Montaigne described. It's
partly the tone of 'So now all things are damned, one feels at
ease': he that is down need fear no fall; no *defeat* can drive me
from the Nine. But it also has something to do with Byron's
stance when he said that, for all his doubts as to an after-life,

'Time must decide; and eternity won't be the less agreeable or
more horrible because one did not expect it' (*LJ*, III, 225).
Feeling free to leave it to the future looks like a way of merely
leaving the present unharassed. But it is also in Byron a way of
genuinely leaving it to the future—bequeathing *it*, the present
itself, not the present taking over the role of its own future and
trying fearfully to disguise itself in anticipating its judgement.
This is trust as much as doubt, the two are one here. 'But all he
says is true, nevertheless, though what worst of himself there is
to tell, he insists upon at once; and what good there may be,
mostly leaves you to find out.' He leaves it:

> And therefore will I leave off metaphysical
> Discussion, which is neither here nor there:
> If I agree that what is, is; then this I call
> Being quite perspicuous and extremely fair.
> (*DJ*, XI.5)

It looks perspicuous but as ever in Byron you can't quite see all
the way through it.

He can only leave a sketch. A modern novelist puts it thus:

> We can never know what to want, because, living only one
> life, we can neither compare it with our previous lives nor perfect
> it in our lives to come . . .
> There is no means of testing which decision is better, because
> there is no basis for comparison. We live everything as it comes,
> without warning, like an actor going on cold. And what can life
> be worth if the first rehearsal for life is life itself? That is why life
> is always like a sketch. No, 'sketch' is not quite the word, because
> a sketch is an outline of something, the ground-work for a
> picture, whereas the sketch that is our life is a sketch for nothing,
> an outline with no picture.[31]

For it is something like this thought—of one life but many
possibilities, leaving that one life at once both finite *and*
unfinished—that can cause Byron to explode in a frustration of
rapid energy:

> . . . could I wreak
> My thoughts upon expression, and thus throw
> Soul, heart, mind, passions, feelings, strong or weak,
> All that I would have sought, and all I seek,
> Bear, know, feel, and yet breathe—into *one* word,

And that one word were Lightning, I would speak;
But as it is . . .

(*CHP*, III.97)

'Would have' as well as do; 'weak' feelings as well as strong; all
the many for once into '*one*'! But 'as it is':

> I can't describe because my first impressions are always strong
> and confused—& my Memory *selects* & reduces them to order—
> like distance in the landscape—& blends them better—although
> they may be less distinct—there must be a sense or two more
> than we have as mortals—which I suppose the Devil has—(or
> t'other) for where there is much to be grasped we are always at a
> loss—and yet feel that we ought to have a higher and more
> extended comprehension.
>
> (*LJ*, V, 221–22)

The landscape picture gives that very order which simulta-
neously loses the sense of chaos; the selection is like decision in
personal life. But it is the prior chaos that reminds us of the
poetic 'former world and future' where more senses could be
employed and be employed together. Byron can only try to
suggest order and disorder at the same time. 'I leave the thing a
problem, like all things' (*DJ*, XVII.13): 'the thing' is typical of
Byron's only sketchily ordered language—it is *precisely vague*,
perspicuously opaque, a language at once casually at ease in its
own terms yet baffled by the referents of its own meaning. For
so often in Byron, the centre of clarity in the language is acutely
conscious of itself as not the centre of control as to the meaning
of things. The fatal truth is, said Manfred, 'The Tree of
Knowledge is not that of Life' (I.i.12). There is always a gap.
    Wordsworth's language often becomes even to himself like
an intimation of immortality: 'My own voice cheered me, and,
far more, the mind's / Internal echo of the imperfect sound'
(*The Prelude*, 1805, I.64–65). When a woman casually asks
Wordsworth whether he is 'stepping westward', the words re-
sound like oracles in the poet's mind:

> The echo of the voice enwrought
> A human sweetness with the thought
> Of travelling through the world that lay
> Before me in my endless way.
>
> ('Stepping Westward')

Where Wordsworth almost hears paradise regained, Byron just seems to leave words as though they won't be picked up again. As Ruskin's doubts about immortality grew stronger, doubtless this affected his choice of poets.[32] There is still mysteriousness in Byron, but it lies (as in the following from *Cain*) in non-self-transcendence:

> Lucifer. Dar'st thou behold?
> Cain.   How know I what
>   I *dare* behold?
>   (II.i.133–34)

How can I know what I dare, 'if the first rehearsal for life is life itself'? Cain's words go into the air of the future and not back into his own mind.

Moreover, it is this issue of transcendence that has to do with the final reason for Ruskin's late championship of Byron against the whole trend of the later nineteenth century. It lies in Ruskin's opposition to the influence of Matthew Arnold. For J. S. Mill's personal choice was, as it were, made impersonally canonical by Arnold's essays on Wordsworth and on Byron which appeared in 1879 and 1881 respectively and were collected together in the second series of *Essays in Criticism*. What attracted Arnold to Wordsworth, I believe, was Wordsworth's moments of calm mastery, when—in the poet's own words in the first book of *The Prelude*—'I / Am worthy of *myself*' (ll.360–61). What Arnold found in Byron, on the contrary, was too much restless self-reference: 'the promiscuous adoption of all the matter offered to the poet by life, just as it was offered, without thought or patience for the mysterious transmutation to be operated on this matter by poetic form'. There are moments of transmutation and transcendence in Byron: 'when he had fairly warmed to his work, then he became another man; then the theatrical personage passed away; then a higher power took possession of him and filled him; then at last came forth into light that true and puissant personality . . . the real Byron'.[33] Yet though Byron was in momentary lyricism 'the greatest natural force, the greatest elementary power, I cannot but think, which has appeared in our literature since Shakespeare', his nature was in substance that 'of the barbarian'.[34] Byron himself said that he had 'something Pagan in me that I cannot shake off' (*LJ*, II, 136). But for Arnold there was a fatal flaw so deep in Byron that though he can at moments shake it off to reveal a deeper self still, nonetheless that transcendence is a magic that cannot long be sustained in him. Arnold thought of this poetic magic as a sort of Celtic indiscipline. For, as he says in his essay 'On the Study of Celtic Literature', though style can recast and heighten what a man has in himself to say, still style only makes Luther, a Philistine at bottom, into a Philistine of Genius, and Byron into a Barbarian of Genius, a flawed Titan.[35] Byron, using other terms, might have agreed: 'he used to declare that he was a fallen angel'.[36] But where Ruskin trusted all this in Byron—the chaotic mixture of bad and good, of strength and weakness—Arnold (like just half of Byron) was only happy when it was transcended, and *not* when we in the world

> Half dust, half deity, alike unfit
> To sink or soar, with our mix'd essence make
> A conflict of its elements.
>   (*Manfred*, I.ii.40–42)

It would have been both better and worse for John Stuart Mill to have gone through that almost microcosmic conflict. For with Ruskin's terms of opposition to Arnold's high classicism, the last piece of our jigsaw seems to fall into place, and we can now turn back to Mill . . .

> In the worst period of my depression I had read through the whole of Byron (then new to me) to try whether a poet, whose peculiar department was supposed to be that of the intenser feelings, could rouse any feeling in me. As might be expected, I got no good from this reading, but the reverse. The poet's state of mind was too like my own.

To the Arnoldian this might well be expected: a cautionary tale against going to literature with anything other than 'disinterestedness'. I don't agree. However understandable it is, it also seems to me both extraordinary and symptomatic that Mill should have turned away from Byron *because* 'the poet's state of mind was too like my own'. If it isn't too much of a presumptuously unkind, ahistorical fiction to say so, I think that Mill should rather have carried on with himself, carried on with Byron, carried on reading about those in Byron who risked carrying on with themselves as their own problems. 'I felt', said Mill, 'that the flaw in my life, must be a flaw in life itself' (p. 88). For it seemed to Mill that if the achievement of his life's aim of social reform would not offer him happiness, that must be because social reform itself, though removing misery, left happiness still to be pursued—but pursued as an illusion which, clearly, no amount of well-being could ever satisfy. At a second stage Mill found the flaw to be in himself—but only in so far as that self was philosophically representative of the want of the immaterially personal which his utilitarian education and analysis had initially left out of account. It is a brave but also mentally tidy solution.

But Byron's men—his Manfred and his Cain—are to varying degrees *unsure* whether the flaw is in themselves or in life and it is more frightening that the two alternatives are not seen as first identical and then separable, in two stages, but confused and confusing at once. In an emphatically unArnoldian experimental chaos of boundaries, Manfred and Cain hurl themselves against the Life Source through its apparent representatives, with one question implicit in their very being: is my life Life and how It has to be?

If it *is*, then let my life dare to show even in itself, like a microcosm, Life's flaws to Life itself and make It admit them:

> Cain.   . . . but now I feel
> My littleness again. Well said the spirit
> That I was nothing!
> Adah.   Wherefore said he so?
> Jehovah said not that.
> Cain.   No: *he* contents him
> With making us the *nothing* which we are;
>   (III.i.68–71)

Let words at least spell out what my life seems left silently to imply. Cain screams at his Creator: is man no more than this, a thing screaming at its creator? But the screams can't get out of themselves; the impersonal protest at the example of his pain and the personal pain itself are trapped, indistinguishably, within the same language. 'And the power which thou dost feel / Shall be what thou must conceal' is the curse thus laid upon Manfred (I.i.220–21). Both *Manfred* and *Cain* are composed out of such hellish circles: What knowledge have we been allowed? The miserable knowledge that knowledge itself does not give happiness. And that miserable knowledge cannot sustain itself as higher meta-knowledge *about* knowledge but, conscious of its own lack of content, collapses into misery. Arnold refers to Goethe's famous remark that Byron could not really think but thought like a child. But in Byron's cosmology feeling is often the fallen condition of thought; a mark that both reveals and conceals the confusion that we live in. And that is a big *idea*.

'To me', says Byron in *Childe Harold's Pilgrimage*, 'High mountains are a feeling': I become them, they become me (III.72, 75). Blind feeling—itself barely distinguishing the inner feel of things outside and the feeling given from outside to things within—is the body's confused thought-process: 'my first impressions are always strong and confused . . . there must be a sense or two more than we have as mortals'. In a world of creatures who are all soul, blind feeling will find other senses:

> When elements to elements conform,
> And dust is as it should be, shall I not
> Feel all I see, less dazzling, but more warm?
> The bodiless thought?
>
> (*CHP*, III.74)

The speculations in *Don Juan* are the nearest Byron gets to bodiless thought. But in the present world's human 'conflict of its elements', feeling is a shorthand, a sketch, a self-baffled clue. The feeling with which Manfred and Cain hurl themselves against Life is a volatile compound of what Life has done to them and they to Life—they can no longer tell the difference. That is Cain's confusion—helplessness disguised as defiance; helplessness whose only help was half to will itself into further helplessness in order at least to provoke an unequivocal answer from the Creator. To Cain it would seem too tricksy, too merely implicit for Manfred to be left 'Thyself to be thy proper Hell!' (*Manfred*, I.i.251): let him be damned outwardly too, explicitly, in the minimal relief of confirmation. *Cain* is Byron's extreme version of the rebellious, awkward attitude of the children of Israel throughout the Old Testament. Byron's Hebrew stands before God and in secondary assertiveness calls

himself a passive 'he' rather than a primarily powerful 'I': 'He
is—such as thou mad'st him'—'if he's evil, / Strike him!'; 'if he
be good, / Strike him, or spare him, as thou wilt!'. For—

> . . . Good and Evil seem
> To have no power themselves, save in thy will—
> And whether that be good or ill I know not . . .
>
> *(Cain,* III.i.274–76)

This is like Marino Faliero: if I haven't the power to punish,
what does it matter whether I feel forgiveness or not? What
such men primarily feel is pre-empted, just as Job himself felt
pre-empted: 'If I justify myself, mine own mouth shall con-
demn me' (9.20). Their subsequent emotions feel secondary
even to themselves, as sullenness does. Hence the floating
lameness of 'And whether *that* be good or ill I know not': there
is no human level from which to judge whether good *is* good;
thought collapses. This isn't simply childish, in the vulgar
sense that Arnold and Arnold's Goethe deplored in Byron; it
goes more deeply back to the origins of adult childishness in the
children of fallen Adam and their loss of a true understanding
of their relation to God the Father. Byron deeply admired 'The
Book of Job' and perhaps it is only Job in the Old Testament
who is able to find a syntax in which not to seem childishly
rebellious: 'Though he slay me, yet will I trust in him: but I
will maintain mine own ways before him' (13.15). Cain will not
hedge his speech around with the mediation of 'though/yet/but'
and therefore risks seeming only to say 'I will maintain mine
own ways'.

When Cain finds that the power which initially got him 'his
own way' has finally got him into a powerless mess, the Fall has
happened again. That fall is the second phase of life—the phase
of self-consciousness—which can come, as with Mill, when
adolescence has to give way to adulthood or when adulthood
finds itself, in modern parlance, within mid-life crisis: 'the
state, I should think, in which converts to Methodism usually
are, when smitten by their first "conviction of sin" '.[37] An
amalgam of psychology and metaphysics, *Cain* is the story of
the rise of fallen individualism and all that Goethe points to in
his 'is one man alive when others are alive?'. For Cain is both
second and first. That is to say, he is the first second man—

of the human second generation, the first man *born* fallen, without experiencing the Fall, still within sight of the Eden from which Adam was cast out: 'What had *I* done in this?—I was unborn' (I.i.67). The original of Sardanapalus in this respect, he is the man who wants to make the start for himself, individually, and only believes in the Fall when his own acts have repeated it. To himself he is the first man—'with / Thoughts which arise within me, as if they / Could master all things'—yet *within* that self he also has what seems to him a secondary sense of being, as though just another creature in the world—'where I seem nothing' (I.i.176–78); primary to himself, that very primariness is secondary in the world's eyes: 'the mystery of my being' (1.320).

It is Byron's merit to go right through that fall, where an internal sense of individual importance has itself increasingly to interiorize the sense of its own external unimportance too. Byron goes right through with it, rather than half round it like Mill, and with all the risk of further pride even in so doing. He does it in a confusion of mixed motives, held up as mixed, for the sake of what, felt as right, is trapped within something gone wrong. For it is extraordinary (and, indeed, what makes Byron a metaphysical voyager rather than a static moralist) to find that that is what evil is: not the opposite of good so much as right things gone wrong, yet retained within wrong by force of memory. Cain's 'as thou wilt' is compounded of the same elements as 'thy will be done', but in the wrong relation. Cain is the extreme of the Old Testament attitude of protest, protest, and protest again—but finally obedience. So finally at the end of the play, he is the guilty father of all that in us responds even now to the right-wrongness within him:

> And *he* who lieth there was childless. I
> Have dried the fountain of a gentle race,
> Which might have graced his recent marriage couch,
> And might have tempered this stern blood of mine,
> Uniting with our children Abel's off-spring!
> (III.i.556–60)

The murder of Abel leaves the mark of Cain within the genetic code of our very imaginations. And when Byron angrily said to his wife, 'A woman cannot love a man for himself who does not love him in his crimes. No other love is worthy the name',[38] or when his confession of terrible feelings towards her was itself a savagely ambivalent desire *not* to feel them, then truly he was one of the children of Cain—Cain who, before his Creator, wanted only that help and love which was not to be won by asking for it. 'Strike him, or spare him' looks like it is primarily looking for trouble when in fact it needs to look for help. It invites being read as assertive first-person monologue, but that in itself is really its own fallen and secondary disguise for being half of an unconsummated dialogue which, hearing nothing in reply, shouts louder. Those louder shouts are a confused plea that the shouts themselves should be reinterpreted more quietly; but of course they muff and muffle their own unconscious wish to be heard not as defiance but as prayer. 'You say I never attempt to "justify" myself. You are right—at times I can't & occasionally I wont defend by explanations' (*LJ*, III, 119): take it or leave it say the sons of Cain.

Cain's descendants then are committed to living life from the fallen starting-point of a primary individualism which they themselves, from within its terms, can hardly admit to be a disguise of their basic secondariness after all. But the difference between Byron and Cain is that Byron knows that what seem to be instinctively natural reactions in us are really a code for something more thoughtful trying to work itself out within embodied feelings—and Cain only sees this after he finds he didn't really want to kill Abel and yet had invented murder by taking his first impulses literally. 'But he can not be dead!—Is silence death?' (III.i.349). Cain never wanted to admit a code or disguise even in his natural reactions; Byron sometimes did want to admit it and then could not. For, even if you want to, you cannot leave behind your embodied meaning for interpretation and yourself mentally interpret it at the same time. It is the same double-bind as we saw at the end of Section Two when Marino Faliero, embodying within himself the meaning of his life not only inside but also out, disdained a metalanguage by which to get above himself, but left it all to silence: 'What shall I say to ye? / Since my defence must be your condemnation'. The tiger in Byron chose to leap once only, leaving behind in his language an almost physically raw code which we either 'get' or don't. When we do get it, it comes more rapidly direct and yet also more invisibly through the air than the meanings of almost any other poet. He leaves sheer mentality behind him rather than explain with it. For he knows about the secret communication that fallen individualism has to resort to.

William Harness reports on Byron's secret communication thus:

> While washing his hands, and singing a gay Neapolitan air, he stopped, looked round at me, and said, 'There always was a madness in the family.' Then after continuing his washing and his song, as if speaking of a matter of the slightest indifference, 'My father cut his throat.' The contrast between the tenor of the subject and the levity of the expression, was fearfully painful: it was like a stanza of *Don Juan*.[39]

Leaving it thus, Byron set himself adrift from a world of stably palpable meaning and almost accidentally became what in *Childe Harold's Pilgrimage* he calls a wanderer o'er eternity and in *Don Juan* an orphan of the heart. For once he set himself adrift, even the protectively aesthetic distance that could express itself through currents of wit and cynicism and nihilism is not final or stable. Because he could not contain his own meaning, or containing it could not express or explain it, he had to leave it behind his own back, as it were:

> For me, I know nought; Nothing I deny,
>   Admit, reject, contemn; and what know *you*,
> Except perhaps that you were born to die?
>   And both may after all turn out untrue.
>
>   (*DJ*, XIV.3)

'Time must decide; and eternity won't be the less agreeable or more horrible because one did not expect it.' Taking things lightly was only a belated preliminary—till lightness itself carried Byron into strange high seriousness: 'I doubt if doubt itself be doubting' (IX.17).

> Initially, therefore, laughter is the province of the Devil. It has a certain malice to it (things have turned out differently from the way they tried to seem), but a certain beneficent relief as well (things are looser than they seemed, we have greater latitude in living with them, their gravity does not oppress us).
>
> The first time an angel heard the Devil's laughter, he was

horrified . . . The angel was all too aware the laughter was aimed against God and the wonder of His works. He knew he had to act fast, but felt weak and defenceless. And unable to fabricate anything of his own, he simply turned his enemy's tactics against him. He opened his mouth and let out a wobbly breathy sound in the upper reaches of his vocal register . . .

. . . People nowadays do not even realize that one and the same external phenomenon embraces two completely contradictory internal attitudes. There are two kinds of laughter, and we lack the words to distinguish them.[40]

No one more shows us this lack, or gives us, almost from nowhere, more feeling for states of being virtually beyond words, than does Byron. For this we should read him more than perhaps we do.

NOTES

1. See David Wigoder, *Images of Destruction* (London, 1987), pp. 154–55. In thinking about Byron I am grateful for conversations with Bernard Beatty, Kevin Jones and Brian Nellist. In what follows *Don Juan* is cited as *DJ*.

2. *The Essays of Michel de Montaigne*, translated by Charles Cotton, 3 vols (London, 1913), II, 337 ('Of glory'); also quoted in Wigoder, p. 260. For James Hamilton Brown's testimony that in 1823 Byron said it was his constant rule to read an essay of Montaigne a day, see *His Very Self and Voice: Collected Conversations of Lord Byron*, ed. E. J. Lovell (New York, 1980), p. 387.

3. Montaigne, III, 31 ('Of Repentance').

4. *Childe Harold's Pilgrimage*, IV.130 (hereafter cited as *CHP*).

5. *Byron's Letters and Journals*, ed. L. A. Marchand, 12 vols (London, 1973–82), IX, 42. Hereafter cited as *LJ*.

6. *His Very Self and Voice*, p. 269.

7. Milan Kundera, *The Book of Laughter and Forgetting* (Harmondsworth, Middlesex, 1986), pp. 105–06.

8. Søren Kierkegaard, *Either/Or*, trans. D. F. and L. M. Swenson and W. Lowrie, 2 vols (London, 1944), II, 191, 193.

9. Bernard Malamud, *The Natural* (Harmondsworth, Middlesex, 1984), p. 148.

10. See *LJ*, III, 96; also II, 14.

11. *Works of William Cowper*, ed. R. Southey, 15 vols (London, 1836), I, 280–81.

12. John Stuart Mill, *Autobiography*, ed. J. Stillinger (Oxford, 1971), p. 87.

13. *Autobiography*, p. 81. On the suicidal logic behind the cultivation of happiness, see Leslie Stephen, *Hours in a Library*, vol. III (London, 1899), pp. 260–62.

14. *Autobiography*, p. 88. In his essay of 1833, 'The Two Kinds of Poetry', it is Shelley that Mill contrasts with Wordsworth.

15. Montaigne, III, 329 ('Of Experience').

16. Ibid., p. 288 ('Of Physiognomy').

17. *LJ*, V, 203; VIII, 133; V, 192; VII, 225.

18. *His Very Self and Voice*, p. 52.

19. *Autobiography*, p. 90; Mill also makes reference to Coleridge's 'Dejection Ode' on p. 81.

20. John Ruskin, *Modern Painters*, vol. III, part iv, ch. 17, paras 23, 35. Ruskin is also preaching against his own manic-depressive tendencies.

21. Ruskin, *Works*, The Library Edition, ed. E. T. Cook and A. D. O. Wedderburn, 39 vols (London, 1903), XXXIV, 361 (footnote 2).

22. *LJ*, VIII, 144, 187, 210, 223, 152, 57.

23. Ruskin, *Praeterita* (London, 1949), p. 337 (vol. II, ch. 7, para. 136).

24. Ruskin, *Works*, XXV, 405.

25. *Modern Painters*, vol. II, part iii, sect. i, ch. 10, para. 4 (footnote).

26. See *Modern Painters*, vol. V, part ix, ch. 7, para. 21 (footnote); *Don Juan* itself of course is never finished but Byron dies: cf. Montaigne, III, 20, on the coincidence of work and workman ('Of Repentance').

27. *Modern Painters*, vol. V, part viii, ch. 4, para. 14.

28. *Praeterita*, pp. 134–36 (vol. I, ch. 8, paras 168–69).

29. Montaigne, I, 40 ('Of Quick or Slow Speech').

30. *Praeterita*, p. 70 (vol. I, ch. 4, para. 88).

31. Milan Kundera, *The Unbearable Lightness of Being* (London, 1987), p. 8. The very title of the book is significant to readers of Byron.

32. See Ruskin's bitterness in *Praeterita*, pp. 204–06 (vol. I, ch. 12, paras 244–46).

33. *Complete Prose Works of Matthew Arnold*, ed. R. H. Super, 11 vols (Ann Arbor, Michigan, 1960–77), IX, 227, 233.

34. Ibid., III, 132; IX, 224.

35. Ibid., III, 364, 370 (also see p. 347).

36. *His Very Self and Voice*, p. 106.

37. For a case-history see Wigoder, p. 169 for what Byron calls barbarous middle age (*DJ*, XII.1). Wigoder complains about tidy solutions on pp. 94, 220; his chaos is emphatically Byronic (for example pp. 100 and 153 on the shifting boundaries of the self and pp. 164–65, 198, 211 on manic-depressive incongruities).

38. *His Very Self and Voice*, p. 106.

39. Ibid., p. 45.

40. Milan Kundera, *The Book of Laughter and Forgetting*, pp. 61–62. Kundera makes interesting remarks on the borders between meaningfulness and a sense of the absurd on pp. 216–17 and 232–33.

For an account that places less emphasis on the differences between Wordsworth and Byron see my 'On the Strength of Limitation', *Stand Magazine*, 24, no. 4 (Autumn, 1983), 34–45.

Index of Proper Names
and Works